T0397161

The Politics of the Past in Early China

Why did the past matter so greatly in ancient China? How did it matter and to whom? This is an innovative study of how the past was implicated in the long transition of power in early China, as embodied by the decline of the late Bronze Age aristocracy and the rise of empire across the first millennium BCE. Engaging with a wide array of historical materials, including oral traditions, excavated manuscripts, and transmitted texts, Vincent S. Leung moves beyond the historiographical canon as it explores how the past was mobilized as a powerful rhetorical agent in diverse political, literary, and philosophical argument. Appeals to the past in early China were not simply a cultural attitude, but were rather deliberate acts of articulating political thought, and challenges to critical distance during periods of crisis. Significant for power politics in the crafting of the past.

VINCENT S. LEUNG is Associate Professor of Chinese History at Lingnan University, Hong Kong.

The Politics of the Past in Early China

VINCENT S. LEUNG
Lingnan University, Hong Kong

CAMBRIDGE
UNIVERSITY PRESS

University Printing House, Cambridge CB2 8BS, United Kingdom

One Liberty Plaza, 20th Floor, New York, NY 10006, USA

477 Williamstown Road, Port Melbourne, VIC 3207, Australia

314–321, 3rd Floor, Plot 3, Splendor Forum, Jasola District Centre,
New Delhi – 110025, India

79 Anson Road, #06–04/06, Singapore 079906

Cambridge University Press is part of the University of Cambridge.

It furthers the University's mission by disseminating knowledge in the pursuit of
education, learning, and research at the highest international levels of excellence.

www.cambridge.org
Information on this title: www.cambridge.org/9781108425728
DOI: 10.1017/9781108348843

© Vincent S. Leung 2019

This publication is in copyright. Subject to statutory exception
and to the provisions of relevant collective licensing agreements,
no reproduction of any part may take place without the written
permission of Cambridge University Press.

First published 2019

Printed and bound in Great Britain by Clays Ltd, Elcograf S.p.A.

A catalogue record for this publication is available from the British Library.

Library of Congress Cataloging-in-Publication Data
Names: Leung, Vincent S., 1976– author.
Title: The politics of the past in early China / Vincent S. Leung.
Description: Cambridge, United Kingdom ; New York, NY : Cambridge
University Press, 2019. | Revision of author's thesis (doctoral) – Harvard
University 2011. | Includes bibliographical references.
Identifiers: LCCN 2019001275 | ISBN 9781108425728
Subjects: LCSH: Historiography – China – History.
Classification: LCC DS734.7 .L4228 2019 | DDC 931–dc23
LC record available at https://lccn.loc.gov/2019001275

ISBN 978-1-108-42572-8 Hardback

Cambridge University Press has no responsibility for the persistence or accuracy of
URLs for external or third-party internet websites referred to in this publication
and does not guarantee that any content on such websites is, or will remain,
accurate or appropriate.

To
W. K. Leung, S. Y. Sin, and W. H. Leung

Contents

Acknowledgments	*page* ix

Introduction	1
Beyond Didacticism: Methods and Perspectives	3
Organization and Terminology	17

1 Time out of Joint: Uses of the Past from the Western Zhou to the Early Warring States — 20

Western Zhou: Moments of Origins, Exemplary Acts, and the Genealogical Past	24
The *Analects*: Past Cultural Practices, Moral Interiority, and the Deliberative Self	40
The *Mozi*: The Origin of Disorder and the Problem with the Deliberative Self	53
Conclusion	71

2 A Parenthetical Past: Deep History and Anti-history in the Late Warring States — 75

Guodian *Laozi*: Cosmogony, Deep History, and a Feminine Genealogical History	79
The *Mengzi*: Bioethics, Moral Potentiality, and the Antihistorical Imagination	92
Conclusion	100

3 Specter of the Past: Bureaucratic Amnesia under the Rise of the Qin Empire — 102

Preamble: Bibliocaust, or Empire and Time	104
The Legalist Premise of a Discontinuous Past	109
Legalists and Their Trouble with History	113
The Qin Resolution: Bureaucratic Amnesia and the End of History	121
Conclusion	128

vii

viii — Contents

4 **The Rehabilitation of Antiquity in the Early Han Empire** — 130
  Jia Yi's *Xinshu*: Historicizing the End of History — 132
  Lu Jia's *Xinyu*: A Classical Encapsulation of the Past — 139
  Conclusion — 150

5 **Sima Qian's Critical Past** — 153
  "Huozhi Liezhuan": Natural Economy and the Futility
    of Governance — 155
  "Pingzhun Shu": Imperial Expansion, Magical Currencies,
    and Original Disorder — 164
  Violence, Civilization, and Critical History — 174

  Epilogue — 177

Bibliography — 181
  Primary Sources — 181
  Secondary Scholarship — 182
Index — 198

Acknowledgments

It is a pleasure to finally write this ledger of many debts. It is about time. The creation of this book has been a long, exhilarating journey, and it would not have been possible without the generosity of many institutions, teachers, colleagues, and friends. First and foremost, I would like to express my gratitude to my teachers at Harvard. It was under their exemplary intellectual guidance that this project first took shape as my dissertation. I am indebted, most of all, to the tremendous mentorship of Michael Puett. Between the many seminars and countless conversations, he illuminated for me the exciting world of early China. His critically adventurous scholarship was a great source of inspiration for me as I embarked on my own journey in the bygone world of early China. Peter Bol's questions were always incisive and probing, and the book would have been much poorer if not for his sharp critique. I am also greatly indebted to Li Wai-yee's inspiring instruction over the years; it was in her seminars that I learned how to read once again, this time not as a mere spectator of words but as an interlocutor of texts.

Harvard had been a most hospitable intellectual home for me for more than a decade, and as a graduate student, one can hardly hope for a more supportive research environment than the one at the East Asian Languages and Civilizations Department. I am grateful for the years of intellectual nourishment as well as the predoctoral financial support that allowed me to carve out a viable existence as a reader of old texts. I would also like to thank the Fairbank Center for the Graduate Student Associate Fellowships in my last two years at the university; they provided much-needed financial support that allowed me to complete the dissertation which formed the basis of this book.

In the years since I left Cambridge, I have been very fortunate to have received research support from the University of Pittsburgh, New York University, and Lingnan University. The History Department at the University of Pittsburgh provided a convivial space for continuing this project in those heady first years out of graduate school. I am also grateful to the university's Asian Studies Center and Humanities Center for their research support and funds that allowed me to advance the manuscript significantly. My year-long stay as a visiting scholar at New York University's Institute for the Study of the Ancient World (ISAW) was simply fantastic; I am grateful for the opportunity to work out key issues of the manuscript there in dialogues with its pre-eminent cohort of scholars of antiquity. In the home stretch of this very long process, I am grateful for the research support of the History Department of Lingnan University; the teaching relief, in particular, gave me a chance to finally whip this unruly morass of words into a somewhat legible thing.

One summer back in the late 1990s, I came across Burton Watson's *Ssu-Ma Ch'ien: Grand Historian of China* in a library in Boston. Intrigued by what I had read, I then picked up – and devoured – the Grand Archivist's *The Letter to Ren An*. In my own autobiographical musings, that is the moment when I decided that I must learn everything about the world in which such a remarkable thing – *The Letter to Ren An* – could have been made. What I did not anticipate at the time was that this one chance encounter would lead to many more in the years ahead; it set me on a path filled with many marvelous friends and colleagues. All of you have not only shaped my thinking in relation to this book, directly or indirectly; your cheerful smiles and good humors have also sustained me in this quixotic quest of a career in academia. From the beginning, on and around Divinity Avenue, I learned a great deal from the brilliant cohort at Harvard; there are simply too many to name here, but I must specifically thank Michael Ing, Maria Sibau, Jeffrey Moser, Rod Campbell, and Hong Yue for their terrific friendship all these years. Allison Miller, Chris Foster, Du Heng, and Billy French, too – you were a most magnificent, delightful early China cohort. During my brief but immensely rewarding time in New York City, I thank Lillian Tseng and Guo Jue for their generous feedback and support for my work. Conversations with friends and colleagues at ISAW, over a great many meals and pints, have much broadened my understanding of the ancient world; I thank Elizabeth Murphy, Perrine Pilette, Ethan Harkness, Adam Schwartz, Jan Bemmann, Nicholas Reid, Jonathan Skaff, and David Ratzan for their friendship. I also appreciate the opportunities to have collaborated on various early China projects with Paul R. Goldin, Charles Sanft, Garret

Acknowledgments xi

P. S. Olberding, and Leslie Wallace; I am grateful for your fellowship in the field, and your scholarship has inspired me in a great many ways.

During my time at Pittsburgh, I had the incredible good fortune to be able to call Evelyn Rawski and Katheryn Linduff my colleagues. I also thank the Asian studies cohort there – Katherine Cartliz, Nicole Constable, Tom Rawski, James Cook, and the late Linda Penkower – for their tremendous collegiality and support. I am also grateful to Hsu Cho-yun for his valuable feedback on the manuscript at an early stage of the process. The junior cohort at Pittsburgh were simply marvelous; I thank these wonderful human beings for creating such a joyous, supportive environment: Molly Warsh, Pernille Røge, Mari Webel, Benno Weiner, David Luesink, Mina Rajagopalan, John Stoner, Dan Asen, Katja Wezel, Jamie Miller, Raja Adal, James Pickett, Patryk Reid, Loukas Barton, Bruce Venarde, and Gregor Thum. I am also grateful to William G. Liu for his support this past year at Lingnan as this project nears completion.

I must also express my gratitude to my teachers at the University of Massachusetts, Amherst, who set me on a path that ultimately led to the publication of this book. Shen Zhongwei was an exemplary teacher and adviser, and without his inspiring model I would never have had the courage to embark on this academic pursuit. In Doris Bargen's marvelous classes on Japanese literature, I learned how to revel in literary splendor for the first time. I am also grateful to Alvin Cohen; his classes on classical Chinese instilled in me a rigor and meticulousness in parsing the language of early Chinese texts that allowed me to confidently confront, for the first time, the richness and elegance of this dead language.

Different parts of this book were presented at various universities, workshops, and conferences over the years, including the University of Virginia's East Asia Center, Columbia University's Early China Seminar, the University of Oregon's East Asian Languages and Literatures Department, Yale University's East Asian Languages and Literatures Department, Bucknell University's China Institute, Academia Sinica's Institute of Chinese Literature and Philosophy, the University of Hong Kong's Institute for the Humanities and Social Sciences, Hong Kong Baptist University's Jao Tsung-I Academy of Sinology, the Association of Asian Studies Annual Conference (San Diego, 2013), the Inaugural Association of Asian Studies in Asia Annual Conference (National University of Singapore, 2015), and of

xii *Acknowledgments*

course, the Institute for the Study of the Ancient World and the University of Pittsburgh's Asian Studies Center, Humanities Center, and History Department. I am grateful for the audiences' engagement and lively responses at these various venues; your comments and criticisms have shaped the arguments of the book in many different, important ways.

Librarians at the Harvard-Yenching Library, the Hillman Library at the University of Pittsburgh, the Institute for the Study of the Ancient World, and the Fong Sum Wood Library at Lingnan University were indispensable to the research for this book. I thank them for their extraordinarily able assistance over the years. I would like to express my gratitude in particular to Zhang Haihui, Head of the East Asian Library at the University of Pittsburgh, for her tireless efforts in getting all the materials I needed during my years at Pittsburgh.

I would also like to thank my editor Lucy Rhymer for shepherding this project so expertly, with such enthusiastic support, from the very beginning. I am also grateful to the anonymous readers at both Cambridge University Press and Harvard University Press for going through the manuscript with such care and patience. I am much obliged to them for their thoughtful and sharp criticisms, which helped me vastly improve the arguments in this book. The faults and shortcomings that remain, needless to say, are entirely my own.

Finally, I would like to express my deep gratitude to my family. Without the steadfast support and good cheer of my parents and my sister, none of this would have been possible or even mattered at all. It is to them that this book is dedicated.

Introduction

In early China, the past was ubiquitous. It is no exaggeration to say that almost every text in the extant corpus refers to the past in one manner or another. Some of them merely gesture towards it, say, by invoking the commonplace but densely loaded term for "antiquity" (*gu* 古), while others would gaze upon the bygone world and interrogate it relentlessly for their own edification. Over the long first millennium BCE, in a profusion of bronze and stone inscriptions, silk manuscripts, and bamboo and wooden slips, a very expansive landscape of the past unfolded. In the oldest extant writings from early China, namely the oracle-bone inscriptions, we see a crowded "ancestral landscape" that was integral to the royal divinatory practices of the late Shang dynasty (*c.*1300–1045).[1] In some of the oldest transmitted texts, such as parts of the *Classic of Documents* (*Shu* 書) and *Classic of Poetry* (*Shi* 詩), as well as bronze inscriptions of the Western Zhou dynasty (*c.*1045–771 BCE), we find regular and frequent references to the history of the Zhou state. In subsequent centuries, amongst the plethora of political and ethical essays that would come to be categorized as the "masters texts" (*zishu* 子書), one would be hard pressed to find a single text, from the Confucian *Analects* (*Lunyu* 論語) to the *Han Feizi* 韓非子, that does not refer to the historical exploits of one sage-king or another in antiquity.[2] Even texts on technical arts were no exception; amongst the entombed texts at the Qin site Shuihudi 睡虎地 from the late third century BCE, for instance, legal statutes were buried alongside a state chronicle, an almanac, and a transcript of a speech about the barbaric

---

[1] I borrow this evocative term from the title of David Keightley, *The Ancestral Landscape: Time, Space, and Community in Late Shang China, ca. 1200–1045 B.C.* (Berkeley: University of California, Berkeley, 2000),

[2] I follow the use of the term "masters texts" as the translation of the Han dynasty term *zishu* 子書 in Wiebke Denecke, *The Dynamics of Masters Literature: Early Chinese Thought from Confucius to Han Feizi* (Cambridge, MA: Harvard University Asia Center, 2010).

past.[3] By the early imperial period, towards the end of the first millennium BCE, besides the ubiquitous citations of antiquity across almost all texts, a stock of historical anecdotes also served as a popular rhetorical currency in the writings of the political elite.[4] The past had a sustained, looming presence in the early Chinese corpus.

Readers working through these different texts from early China, however, will soon find that this vast landscape of the past is a convoluted one. Each text conjures up a particular vision of the past or seizes upon a certain historical moment that is meaningful to what it wishes to say in the present; if one were to put together all these different narrative pieces about the past, what emerges is a rather perplexing whole that is replete with alternative, competing, or even contradictory accounts of the same events, past figures, or historical eras. For instance, while the masters texts commonly refer to an idealized "antiquity" (*gu*) and the historical accomplishments of the "sages" (*shengren* 聖人), we soon discover that they have radically different understandings of what constituted "antiquity" and the proper qualifications of a "sage." Some texts, such as the *Laozi* 老子, found it necessary to evoke the primordial past, a time before the creation of all things, while others would narrow their attention to just the anthropological age, such as the *Shiji* 史記 by Sima Qian 司馬遷 (d. *c.*86 BCE), which begins its history of the world with stories of the Five Thearchs (*wu di* 五帝). Devolutionary views of the past predominate in a variety of texts, such as the *Han Feizi* from the late third century BCE, while others would put forward evolutionary narratives, such as, to name just one example, Lu Jia's 陸賈 essay the "Foundation of the Way" ("Daoji" 道基) from the early decades of the Han dynasty (206 BCE–220 CE).

Such markedly divergent delineations of the past abound. Their common attentiveness to the past belies their radically distinct understanding of the bygone world and their diverse investment in the idea of history. Canonical, popular figures and events that appear across multiple texts did not aggregate to a unified historical field, but rather they

---

[3] Here, "state chronicle" refers to the *Biannian ji* 編年記, "almanacs" refers to the *Ri shu* 日書, and historical speech refers to the *Yushu* 語書 discovered at the site. See *Shuihudi Qin mu zhujian* 睡虎地秦墓竹簡, ed. Shuihudi Qin mu zhujian zhengli xiaozu 睡虎地秦墓竹簡整理小組 (Beijing: Wenwu chubanshe, 1990).

[4] Sarah A. Queen and Paul van Els, eds., *Between History and Philosophy: Anecdotes in Early China* (Albany: State University of New York Press, 2017).

Beyond Didacticism: Methods and Perspectives

embodied countless variations of the supposed shape of the past. Reading across the early Chinese corpus, therefore, one encounters the past, or more precisely their past, broken up into a thousand little pieces. The vast landscape of the past that emerges from this multitude of historical narratives is a contorted and contentious space.

This book studies this landscape of the past in early China. It asks not only *what* the shape of this landscape was, but also *why* there was such a landscape to begin with. Beyond just describing key sites of this landscape of the past, it will also study its formation and transformation as a function of the changing political condition over the course of the first millennium BCE. As the late Bronze Age aristocratic order collapsed and new bureaucratic empires gradually emerged in this period, what might have compelled the political elite to turn their gaze backwards and invest in the construction of elaborate historical terrains? If the past mattered to some of them a great deal, *why* and *how* did it matter to them? This study approaches these invocations and elaborations of the past in the early Chinese corpus not as artifacts of a cultural convention or intellectual habit, but as signs of a deliberate mobilization of the past as ideological capital for the construction or destruction of political arguments or ethical ideals. The past was implicated in a variety of ways as a powerful resource in the contentious imagination of relations of power. This book is a study of the history of this politics of the past in early China.

Beyond Didacticism: Methods and Perspectives

I am hardly the first reader to have noticed this pervasiveness of the past in early Chinese texts. It is almost a cliché at this point, after more than a century of modern scholarship on the subject, to say that writings from early China tend to be historically minded, or that veneration of the past is one of the civilizational traits of ancient China. There has been, accordingly, a massive amount of scholarship on this topic. The arguments in this book are built on this foundation that past generations of scholars have assiduously cultivated. At the same time, they are also crafted in relation to what I consider to be some of the paradigmatic problems and blind spots in these earlier studies. Let me elaborate.

This long tradition of scholarship on the history of the past in early China is very rich – with a staggering number of works published in the

4 *Introduction*

last century – but also surprisingly narrow. This is due, to a large extent, in my estimation, to the overwhelming and undue emphasis placed on just a few historiographical works as their key sources. To study the "attitude to the past" held by the ancient Chinese, scholars had almost always opted to look first or only at their historiographical works as the most relevant sources.[5] Conversely, it is largely within the scholarship on early Chinese historiography that one finds extended discussion of how the early Chinese imagined the past and how that evolved over time. In other words, there has been a conflation, witting or unwitting, between the study of historiography and the study of the idea of the past in early China. There is an implicit identification between ideas about the past supposedly beheld by those who lived in early China and the content of the historiographical works that they compiled and consumed.

Now, there is nothing wrong about this assumption per se, of course, but in my view it is severely and unnecessarily limiting. Why confine oneself to just the historiographical works, if the question is why and how the past mattered to the early Chinese political elite? To write a historiographical work is one way of engaging with the past but it is hardly the only way; the idea of the past was mobilized in so many different manners in all kinds of texts for a great variety of argumentative ends in early China. To write a history of the past in early China, I would argue that one must attend to the wider spectrum of political and ethical writings beyond just those that are ostensibly, self-reflexively, historiographical.

To elaborate on this methodological point, let me first discuss this body of scholarship on the Chinese historiographical tradition and the sort of history of the past that they have typically proffered. In this

---

[5] I use the phrase "attitude to the past" from the title of Herbert Butterfield, *History and Man's Attitude to the Past: Their Role in the Story of Civilisation* (London: School of Oriental and African Studies, 1960), a work that I will refer to later as a typical example of the type of comparative civilizational scholarship that argues for a predominant didacticism in traditional Chinese historiography. And these few "historiographical works" are the usual suspects: the *Shu* 書; *Guoyu* 國語; *Zhanguoce* 戰國策; *Chunqiu* 春秋 and its various commentaries, especially the *Zuozhuan* 左傳; and of course the *Shiji* by Sima Qian and *Hanshu* 漢書 by Ban Gu 班固, namely mostly works that one can find under the traditional "histories" (*shi* 史) bibliographical category. For a history of this bibliographical category, see Stephen Durrant, "Histories (*Shi* 史)," in *The Oxford Handbook of Classical Chinese Literature (1000 BCE–900 CE)*, ed. by Wiebke Denecke, Wai-yee Li, and Xiaofei Tian (New York: Oxford University Press, 2017), 184–200.

varied body of work, spanning more than a century, a few paradigmatic ideas have predominated from the beginning to today. Most prevalent and important of all is the argument that Chinese historiographical writings are fundamentally didactic in nature, or that the ancient Chinese, as a matter of cultural attitude and intellectual habit, assigned great importance to a proper knowledge of the past for the many lessons that it had to offer for those in the present. Histories are a "brilliant mirror" (*mingjing* 明鏡) for the people of a country, as Liang Qichao 梁啟超 put it more than a century ago, reusing a very old metaphor perhaps most famously used in the title of the *Comprehensive Mirror to Aid Governance* (*Zizhi tongjian* 資治通鑑) by Sima Guang 司馬光 (1019–1086), in his withering critique of traditional historiographical practices.[6] Looking at this historiographical mirror, we learn who we are, and also what we ought or ought not to do in the present. Relatedly, history is also the retrospective arena in which correct moral judgment of past figures and events can and should be dispensed. This presumption of a fundamental didacticism in Chinese historiographical writings has been widely shared across different scholarly traditions, not only in China but also globally in the United States, Europe, and Japan. In one of the earliest works in the English language on the subject, namely Charles Gardner's *Chinese Traditional Historiography*, published in 1938, we are told that Confucius edited the *Spring and Autumn Annals* (*Chunqiu* 春秋) in order to draw on "lessons of the past" to demonstrate that moral justice always prevails in the world.[7] The purpose in drawing on the past and in writing history is to instruct those in the present on the principles of our moralistic cosmos. By the postwar decades, a time when we saw an elevated output of scholarship on the subject, this supposed didacticism in the Chinese historiographical tradition had become a truly commonplace assumption. In the collection of essays on the subject, *Historians of China and Japan* published in 1961, for instance, the editors suggested that due to the influence of Confucius, Chinese historiography "came to be fraught with a solemn ethical function, the duty of expressing 'praise and blame,' that was to hang

---

[6] Liang Qichao 梁啟超, "Zhongguo zhi jiushi" 中國之舊史, in *Zhongguo lishi wenxuan* 中國歷史文選, 2 vols. (Beijing: Zhonghua shuju, 1962), Volume 2, 352–365.

[7] Charles Gardner, *Chinese Traditional Historiography* (Cambridge, MA: Harvard University Press, 1938), 13.

6 *Introduction*

over it, often to its detriment, throughout its subsequent development."[8] Around the same period, Burton Watson, in his important introduction to the works and thought of Sima Qian, Grand Archivist of the Former Han empire (206 BCE – 9 CE), *Ssu-Ma Ch'ien: Grand Historian of China*, argued for the first awakening of the "historical consciousness" sometime in the Zhou period, with the development of a rationalistic and humanistic view of history that culminated in the composition of various didactic works of history that were meant to instruct those in the present with meticulous, accurate records of the past.[9] Across the Atlantic, in the United Kingdom, the great Joseph Needham also declared that for the "Chinese mind," history "serves an essential moral purpose," not only as a guide to governance but also in "encouraging virtue and deterring vice."[10] These are all but a few typical articulations of this scholarly consensus that traditional Chinese historiography, starting with the major works from early China, was informed by a deep-seated didactic purpose; that it had always been a moralistic and moralizing endeavor.[11]

[8] William G. Beasley and Edwin G. Pulleyblank, *Historians of China and Japan* (London: Oxford University Press, 1961), 2. See also the contribution of one of the coeditors, Edwin G. Pulleyblank, titled "Chinese Historical Criticism: Liu Chih-chi and Ssu-ma Kuang," where he argues that in imperial China, historical records "served an essential moral purpose by holding up good and bad examples through which virtues could be encouraged and vice deterred" (143).

[9] Burton Watson, *Ssu-ma Ch'ien: Grand Historian of China* (New York: Columbia University Press, 1958), 135–137. I follow Michael Nylan in using the word "archivist" to translate *shi* 史 as part of the Han official title *taishi ling* 太史令. See Michael Nylan, "Sima Qian: A True Historian?", *Early China*, 23–24 (1998), 203–246.

[10] Joseph Needham was speaking specifically about the *Zizhi tongjian*, but he extrapolated from it to the whole of the historiographical tradition of premodern China. Joseph Needham, *Time and the Eastern Man* (London: Royal Anthropological Institute of Great Britain & Ireland, 1965), 14.

[11] One may also note the examples, from around the globe in the various major Sinological traditions, of Homer H. Dubs, "The Reliability of Chinese Histories," *Far Eastern Quarterly* 6.1 (1946), 23–43; Yu-Shan Han, *Elements of Chinese Historiography* (Hollywood: W. M. Hawley, 1955); Charles O. Hucker, *China's Imperial Past: An Introduction to Chinese History and Culture* (Stanford: Stanford University Press, 1975), 23–28; Xu Fuguan 徐復觀, *Liang Han sixiang shi* 兩漢思想史 (Hong Kong: Chinese University of Hong Kong Press, 1975), Volume 3, esp. 157–159; Nemoto, Makoto 根本誠, *Chûgoku reikishi rinen no kongen* 中国歴史理念の根源 (Tokyo: Seikatsusha, 1943); Naitō Torajirō 内藤湖南, *Shina shigakushi* 支那史學史 (Tokyo: Kobundo, 1949); and Etienne Balazs, *Chinese Civilzation and Bureaucracy: Variations on a Theme* (New Haven: Yale University Press, 1964), 129–141.

Beyond Didacticism: Methods and Perspectives 7

This scholarly consensus on the didactic nature of Chinese historiography has had a remarkably stable career. It has remained quite widely accepted to this day, and is still often reiterated as an uncontroversial claim about the Chinese historiographical tradition. From just a decade ago, for instance, one still finds a confident declaration that "the revelation of the *dao* [the Way] at work and the related correct moral judgment of historical events ... are the main aims of traditional Chinese historiography."[12] What may account for the success and longevity of this particular interpretation? To be certain, one reason is that it does contain an element of truth. There is indeed plenty of evidence to support this claim that the past was utilized for the ethical education that it affords its readers (and, by extension, the critical function that historical narratives can have in the remonstrance of those who were

    The latter two are distinctive in their emphasis on the political rather than ethical lessons in the writing and reading of histories, a consequence of the bureaucratization of the writing of history in premodern China; the lessons may be different, but histories are didactic all the same.

[12] Joachim Gentz, "Historiography," in *Keywords Re-oriented* (Göttingen: Universitätsverlag Göttingen, 2009), 59. For other recent examples in the last few decades, one could mention On-Cho Ng and Q. Edward Wang, *Mirroring the Past: The Writing and Use of History in Imperial China* (Honolulu: University Hawaii Press, 2005); Grant Hardy, *Worlds of Bronze and Bamboo* (New York: Columbia University Press, 1999); Anthony E. Clark, "Praise and Blame: Ruist Historiography in Ban Gu's *Hanshu*," *Chinese Historical Review* 18 (2011), 1–24; Wang Shumin 王樹民, *Zhongguo shixue shi gangyao* 中國史學史綱要 (Beijing: Zhonghua shuju, 1997); Du Weiyun 杜維運, *Zhongguo shixue shi* 中國史學史 (Taipei: Sanmin shuju, 1993). In the past decade or so, there have also been a number of new works focusing on "truth claims" in early Chinese historiography; there are a great number of new insights in these works on the nature and goals of early Chinese historiographical culture, but the presumption of primacy of a moralistic, didactic agenda largely prevails: see the essays in Helwig Schmidt-Glintzer and Achim Mittag, eds., *Historical Truth, Historical Criticism, and Ideology: Chinese Historiography and Historical Culture from a New Comparative Perspective* (Leiden and Boston: Brill, 2005); Paul Goldin, "Appeals to History in Early Chinese Philosophy and Rhetoric," *Journal of Chinese Philosophy* 35.1 (2008), 79–69, which in turn draws on the insightful discussion in Anthony S. Cua, "Ethical Uses of the Past in Early Confucianism: The Case of Hsün Tzu," *Philosophy East and West* 35.2 (1985), 133–156. In this context, I should also note the recent work by Garret P. S. Olberding, *Dubious Facts: The Evidence of Early Chinese Historiography* (Albany: State University of New York Press, 2012), which addresses the question of what constituted factual evidence in early Chinese political speeches, as preserved in various historiographical works, and has subtly shifted the focus from normative moral didacticism to strategic political persuasiveness.

8   *Introduction*

politically powerful).[13] That can be found not only in the historical
writings themselves, but also in the long tradition of historical
criticisms in imperial China; these scholars would often refer to
the authoritative pronouncements in early and medieval works of
literary criticism, such as Liu Xie's 劉勰 *Wenxin diaolong* 文心雕龍
and Liu Zhiji's 劉知幾 *Shitong* 史通 (from the late fifth and the
eighth centuries respectively) as additional support for the veracity
of this view that, as a matter of cultural attitude, the past served
a didactic purpose in traditional China. Another reason for the
successful career of this idea, besides this semblance of truthfulness,
is perhaps its resonance and consistency with the area-studies paradigm constitutive of the study of traditional China throughout
much of the twentieth century. It is a framework that is designed
to abstract from a reading of the historical materials structural
patterns and essential attributes specific to the supposed culture of
China for the purpose of comparative civilizational studies.[14] It is
indeed quite striking that in so much of this earlier discussion of the
Chinese historiographical tradition, there has been such a strong
desire and willingness to seek unitary cultural explanations, most

---

[13] This understanding of the role of didacticism in early Chinese historiography
often extends into the topic of remonstrance (*jian* 諫). Histories, properly
written, contain the correct moral lessons, and can therefore be used to
remonstrate against the moral failings of the rulers in the present. As Mark
Edward Lewis noted, "Literary accounts of the past, as opposed to court
chronicles, had been a tool of criticism and opposition," in his *Writing and
Authority in Early China* (Albany: State University of New York Press, 1999),
316. David Schaberg, in his article "Remonstrance in Eastern Zhou
Historiography," *Early China* 22 (1997), 133–179, dealt with this relationship
between remonstrance and the writing of history in a very interesting way; he
suggested that it was the need to remonstrate that may have implicated and
necessitated a desire to preserve the words and deeds of the past.

[14] On this point, I am indebted to the insightful critique of the field by
Michael Dutton, "The Trick of Words: Asian Studies, Translation, and the
Problem of Knowledge," in *The Politics of Method in the Human Sciences:
Positivism and Its Epistemological Others*, ed. George Steinmetz (Durham, NC:
Duke University Press, 2005). I also appreciated the critique of the genealogy of
comparative Sinological studies by Haun Saussy, "Outside the Parenthesis
(Those People Were a Kind of Solution)," *MLN* 115.5 (2000), 849–891. I very
much agree with his assessment that "Reflections on Asian culture too often
present us with an antithesis [between East and West] . . . where what we need is
a transition" (884). See also Masao Miyoshi and Harry Harootunian, eds.,
Learning Places: The Afterlives of Area Studies (Durham, NC: Duke University
Press, 2002), esp. 1–18.

Beyond Didacticism: Methods and Perspectives 9

popularly this presumption of a fundamental didacticism as a motivating factor in their engagement with the past. The diversity of voices, the many competing uses of history, which were quite plain to see in the sources themselves, were systemically elided in favor of the phantasm of cultural attributes, a supposedly master inventory of essential traits that would faithfully describe and explain the culture of traditional China for those outside it. It is not surprising at all that this well-worn cliché about the moralizing, didactic tendency of the Chinese historiographical tradition is so widely accepted and so often reiterated in works on global comparative studies of historiographical writings. It is a culturalist framework designed to render the unfamiliar familiar by conjuring up a unitary other with essential traits.[15]

A number of recent works in the field have begun to point out, wittingly or unwittingly, the limitation of this approach in reading early Chinese writings about the past. They fall into two broad categories, asymmetrical in respect to the types of texts that they focus on. In one category, the scholars survey a wide array of texts, beyond the typical historiographical canon, to study a broad constellation of ideas about the past. With their consideration of a variety of texts, they quite readily move beyond the confines of this didactic reading; the old framework is simply not sufficient to account for the rich, diverse historical imagination that was at work behind this plethora of texts. The discussion of the "philosophy of history" in early China by Roger Ames in his *The Art of Rulership* is an early example of this effort. In this study of the *Huainanzi*

---

[15] For recent examples, see Jeremy Popkin, *From Herodotus to H-Net: The Story of Historiography* (New York and Oxford: Oxford University Press, 2015); and Daniel Woolf, *A Global History of History* (Cambridge and New York: Cambridge University Press, 2011). See also Georg G. Iggers and Edward Q. Wang, *Turning Points in Historiography: A Cross-cultural Perspective* (Rochester, NY: University of Rochester Press, 2001); Du Weiyun 杜維運, *Zhongguo shi xue yu shi jie shi xue* 中國史學與世界史學 (Taipei: Sanmin shuju, 2008); Needham, *Time and the Eastern Man*; and Butterfield, *History and Man's Attitude to the Past*. This point is also current in broader comparative studies between early China and the ancient Mediterranean world, such as G. E. R. Lloyd, *Adversaries and Authorities: Investigations into Ancient Greek and Chinese Science* (Cambridge: Cambridge University Press, 1996), 26: "Chinese thinkers of many different philosophical persuasions were repeatedly harking back to the teachings of the Sage-kings. Sometimes, to be sure, that is just for form's sake . . . Nevertheless the idea that there is past wisdom, that there were, once, Sage-kings, is a commonplace."

淮南子, he gave a brief but valuable account of the "philosophy of history" of the major intellectual traditions, namely Confucianism, Daoism, and Legalism.[16] More recently, Mark Edward Lewis in his monumental *Writing and Authority in Early China* presented one of the richest and most detailed accounts of the different ideas of history in early China; similarly, Scott Cook in his article "The Use and Abuse of History in Early China from *Xun Zi* to *Lüshi Chunqiu*" looked beyond just the historiographical canon and discovered, in the process, the important role that history played in the political and ethical debates of the Warring States period, (453–221 BCE).[17] A few years later, we also saw the publication of Mu-Chou Poo's "The Formation of the Concept of Antiquity in Early China." While the start of the essay described "reverence toward the past (*zungu* 尊古)" as another "prominent phenomenon" in Chinese culture, Poo quickly proceeded to explain that his project was to *historicize* this phenomenon; it was not simply a cultural given but a historical, evolving phenomenon susceptible to explanations based on changing sociopolitical factors. Poo did not accept that the past was simply revered, as a matter of fact, but set out to investigate "*why* the past was revered" at all.[18] Then he proceeded to discuss a broad range of texts, from the Western Zhou corpus to writings from the end of the Han dynasty, to see how various individuals or texts tried to "uphold the authority that antiquity could bring."[19] In a similar vein, and around the same time, Heiner Roetz speculated that there was a growing opposition to "an unreflected traditionalistic appeal to the past" from earlier times, paving the way for a process of "dehistoricization" in the late Warring States period; in this reading, the frequent appeal to the past was more a historical than a cultural phenomenon in early China.[20]

[16] Roger Ames, *The Art of Rulership: A Study in Ancient Chinese Political Thought* (Honolulu: University of Hawaii Press, 1983), 1–27.

[17] Lewis, *Writing and Authority in Early China*, 99–146; Scott Cook, "The Use and Abuse of History in Early China from *Xun Zi* to *Lüshi Chunqiu*," *Asia Major* 18.1 (2005), 45–78.

[18] Mu-Chou Poo, "The Formation of the Concept of Antiquity in Early China," in *Perceptions of Antiquity in Chinese Civilization*, ed. Dieter Kuhn and Helga Stahl (Heidelberg: Edition Forum, 2008), 85–102, esp. 85, emphasis added.

[19] Ibid., 100.

[20] Heiner Roetz, "Normativity and History in Warring States Thought: The Shift Towards the Anthropological Paradigm," in Schmidt-Glintzer, Mittag, and Rüsen, *Historical Truth, Historical Criticism, and Ideology*, 85, 88. For further

Beyond Didacticism: Methods and Perspectives

In the same decade, we also saw the publication of a great body of work on early historiographies by Kai Vogelsang; it may appear that he hews relatively close to earlier scholarship in its predominant focus on the historiographical canon, but his discerning reading of the same canon in the end amounts not to a summary description of a cultural tradition of historical writings, but to an account of a diversity of voices that wrestled with the proper relationship between men and their past. In his article "The Scribe's Genealogy," he warns us against the danger and potential fallacy of presuming the existence of a tradition (of scribes and scribal practices in early China), with its implication of "continuity, immutability, and eternal presence." In its place, he recommends the genealogical method, of the Foucauldian mold, that aims to discover "discontinuity, for contingency and singularity, the attempt to prove that *there was no tradition.*"[21] This is a truly radical break from much of the earlier work which rests on the very idea of a "tradition" of historical writings.[22]

In the other category of these new, innovative works, the focus is not on a wide variety of texts but on a very small set, sometime even just a single text. Both David Schaberg's and Li Wai-yee's monographs on the *Zuozhuan* 左傳 are great examples of this type of recent work that has moved far away from the old preoccupation with didacticism. In their intensely close reading of a single corpus, they saw no prevailing moralistic impulse behind the text, or at least not just one, but rather an "intersection of varying conceptions of interpretation and rhetoric brought to bear on the past" for the two and a half centuries of history that the *Zuozhuan* covers. Vogelsang's insightful review article of the latter monograph, titled "The Shape of History," performs a similar feat in restoring the historicity and multiplicity of the uses of history in

discussion of Roetz's important insight, see the discussion of the *Mengzi* in Chapter Two of this book.

[21] Kai Vogelsang, "The Scribes' Genealogy," *Oriens Extremus* 44 (2003), 3–10, esp. 3, emphasis in the original. I have benefited greatly from a reading of Vogelsang's body of work, including this aforementioned article and *Geschichte als Problem: Entstehung, Formen und Funktionen von Geschichtsschreibung im Alten China* (Wiesbaden: Harrassowitz, 2007).

[22] I would also include Olberding, *Dubious Facts* (see note 12) as an example of this recent wave of new scholarship, with its subtle shift of focus from normative moral didacticism to strategic political persuasiveness in the early historiographical works. The presumption of moral didacticism looms large in the study of early historiographical works, but many new studies are coming out of its long shadow.

early China.[23] One may also cite some of the recent works on the *Shiji* which produced a similar interpretive effect; Michael Nylan discerned a pious religiosity in Sima Qian's historical endeavor, while Michael Puett sees his narratives as embodying a "tragedy of creation" in the history of mankind, for instance.[24] Rens Krijgsman, in his reading of the "Baoxun" 保訓, an excavated manuscript of the Qinghua collection, discerns not one but two ways of speaking about the past, namely the anecdotal and documentary genres, each with its own political uses.[25] These innovative new works, with their intense focus on particular works, oftentimes a single title, did not appeal to any essentialist cultural presumptions, but instead recovered from these texts highly strategic, imaginative uses of the past beyond mere moralistic didacticism.[26]

In this book, I hope to build on these recent works of scholarship in their quietly radical departure from the more established paradigm. Like many of them, I also contend that it is necessary to engage with texts beyond just the few canonical historiographical works, such as the

[23] Kai Vogelsang, "The Shape of History: On Reading Li Wai-yee," *Early China* 37 (2014), 579–599.

[24] Nylan, "Sima Qian: A True Historian?"; and Michael Puett, *The Ambivalence of Creation: Debates Concerning Innovation and Artifice in Early China* (Stanford: Stanford University Press, 2001), 177–212. In a similar vein, one should also note the recent book by Tamara Chin, *Savage Exchange: Han Imperialism, Chinese Literary Style, and the Economic Imagination* (Cambridge, MA: Harvard University Press, 2014), which contextualized the writing of the *Shiji*, and the historiographical innovation in form and content that it embodied, as a critical response to – not simply an intellectual reflection of – the new imperialism of the early Han empire.

[25] Rens Krijgsman, "Cultural Memory and Excavated Anecdotes in 'Documentary' Narrative: Mediating Generic Tensions in the Baoxun Manuscript," in Queen and Van Els, *Between History and Philosophy: Anecdotes in Early China*, 347–379. This reading is built, in part, on Dirk Meyer, *Philosophy on Bamboo: Text and the Production of Meaning in Early China* (Leiden: Brill, 2012).

[26] Wai-yee Li, *The Readability of the Past in Early Chinese Historiography* (Cambridge, MA: Harvard University Press, 2008), 27; and David Schaberg, *A Patterned Past: Form and Thought in Early Chinese Historiography* (Cambridge, MA: Harvard University Asia Center, 2001). The "Introduction" to the new, complete translation of the *Zuozhuan*, by Stephen Durrant, Wai-yee Li, and David Schaberg, *Zuo Tradition = Zuozhuan: Commentary on the "Spring and Autumn Annals"* (Seattle: University of Washington Press, 2016), Volume 1, xvii–xcv, has also quietly shed much of the old essentialist cliché but attends to the multiplicity of voices and competing understandings of history in the *Zuozhuan*.

Beyond Didacticism: Methods and Perspectives 13

Zuozhuan and the *Shiji*. They are simply not coextensive with the entire cultivation of the field of the past in early China; the past was mobilized in so many ways across the entire spectrum of political and ethical debates, and the composition of historiographical works was but one particularly self-reflexive way of engaging with the bygone world. Moreover, also following these recent works, I also hope to set aside the old presumption that writings about the past were fundamentally guided by didactic impulses, and move beyond the culturalist approach that searches for civilizational attributes in these scattered historical narratives from early China. There was never a cultural master key that could fully explain this tradition of writings about the past, despite the desire amongst many comparativists wishing there to be so. Rather, I see it as a tradition that was always in the process of becoming. The argument here is not an ontological one; it is beyond my capability to deny absolutely, as a matter of existence, the possibility of such a deep structure of beliefs that inform this entire body of texts from early China. I simply wish to suggest that much would remain hidden in our reading of these texts if we presumed the existence of such an essentialist master key, which may or may not be there to begin with. Rather than piecing together scattered articulations about the past into a supposed cultural whole with a didactic bent, this book will attend to the many disparate, irreconcilable voices from one period to the next. The analysis will aim to discover less a symphony of cultural predilections than a cacophony of fierce debates and bitter disagreements.

Moving away from the assumption that attention to the past was fundamentally a culturally determined gesture, this book will approach the various articulations about the past in early China as deliberate mobilization of the field of the past as ideological capital towards the construction or destruction of various political arguments and ethical ideals. Different figures in early China engaged with the historical field, constituted by a protean repertoire of past events and figures, transformed pieces of it into ideological capital in narrative forms, and then deployed them towards the production of arguments in the debates with their interlocutors.[27] In this framework, it is also necessary to

---

[27] The use of the term "capital" here follows Pierre Bourdieu, in his discussion of "symbolic capital," and, by extension, the classical usage of the term by Marx in the *Capital*. Narratives about the past accumulated and functioned as "capital," as a means of production of arguments towards disputative gains.
Pierre Bourdieu, "Forms of Capital," *Journal of Economic Sociology* 3.5

14   *Introduction*

approach these scattered texts that relate themselves to the past as dialogic artifacts. They are remnants of past dialogues that took place in early China. It follows that every text must have, or presume the existence of, an addressee, contemporary or historical, imagined or otherwise, and therefore be fundamentally argumentative.[28] In any conversation, what is simply presumed to be true would never require articulation, only new ideas would necessitate persuasion of others, and therefore all texts are intrinsically argumentative. In the chapters that follow, I will attempt to describe these various dialogues and debates, founded in part on competing visions and uses of the past, over a whole host of political and ethical issues in this transition from the Zhou aristocratic order to the first rise of the Qin and Han empires in early China. It is out of these fierce debates, from one period to the next, that this vast landscape of the past emerged and evolved in the first millennium BCE.

Another, perhaps simpler, way to describe this approach is to say that any discussion of the past was always informed and animated by concerns of the present. The past is a usable thing, and it can be called upon to serve the needs of the present. In many ways, the approach of this study overlaps with this utilitarian view; it is for the debates of the present that the past was appropriated and used as argumentative capital. Much scholarship on various historiographical traditions was done based on this model, and even in the field of early China this has gained a fair amount of currency, in conjunction with the focus on the didactic nature of historical writings.[29] Eric J. Hobsbawm, in his

(2002), 60–74; and Karl Marx, *Capital: A Critique of Political Economy* (London: Penguin Books, 1981), Volume 3, 953.

[28] The use of the term "dialogic" follows the works of Mikhail M. Bakhtin, in his *The Dialogic Imagination: Four Essays*, trans. Michael Holquist (Austin: University of Texas Press, 2004). Heteroglossia, rather than monoglossia, is assumed within the evolving language of the early Chinese texts under consideration in this monograph. In addition, I also found useful the methodological reflections in Rita Felski, "Context Stinks!", *New Literary History* 42.4 (2011), 573–591; following Bruno Latour's actor-network theory, Felski argues that we should see texts as "nonhuman actors," not to be arrested by presupposed historical contexts. Bruno Latour, *Reassembling the Social: An Introduction to Actor-Network Theory* (Oxford and New York: Oxford University Press, 2005).

[29] Joachim Gentz recently suggested that in fact this is one of two key intents behind the composition and compilation of Chinese historiographical works: "Or, in other words, is it not a well-known fact, and therefore redundant to stress, that historiography in China was constructed in literary tropes? Either for

Beyond Didacticism: Methods and Perspectives

seminal article "The Social Function of the Past: Some Questions" from almost half a century ago, defined many of the assumptions and goals of this approach. In it, Hobsbawm argued that social formations and relations of production of each historical period demand and necessitate that period's own version of the past, useful for its self-understanding, legitimation, and perpetuation over time. "To be a member of any human community is to situate oneself with regard to one's (its) past, if only by rejecting it." And therefore it is a task for historians to "analyse the nature of this 'sense of the past' in society and to trace its changes and transformations."[30]

In the field of early China, this interpretive move is particularly popular in the scholarship on the early imperial period, namely the time of the Qin and the early Han empires. The broad political, economic, and social transformation (i.e. base structure) brought about by the imperial unification was presumably reflected in the historiographical works of this period (i.e. superstructure). Mark Edward Lewis, in his recent contribution to *The Oxford History of Historical Writing*, argues that the creation of a "unified empire" under the Qin "entailed rethinking China's past in terms of the emergence of such a unified realm," and writings from centuries past were "synthesized and transformed to articulate the fact of unification."[31] Similarly, in his monograph on the Qin's stele inscriptions, Martin Kern argues that the

> educative purposes: to teach through praise and blame of historical precedents, or *to serve particular interests of political and social legitimation of those who held power?*" Gentz, "Historiography," 57–58, emphasis added.

[30] Eric J. Hobsbawm, "The Social Function of the Past: Some Questions," *Past and Present* 55 (1972), 3–17, esp. 3. This seminal article represents a culmination of earlier works rather than a pioneering effort in exploring the idea of different uses of the past. See, for example, the collection of essays in William John Bosenbrook and Hayden White, eds., *The Uses of History: Essays in intellectual and Social History, Presented to William J. Bossenbrook* (Detroit: Wayne State University Press, 1968). It may also be fruitful to compare this class-based view of Hobsbawm with the more anthropologically oriented view of the usefulness of history, as articulated by Michael Herzfeld: "understanding history, not as a set of referential data, but as something that people use to buttress their identity against the corrosive flow of time." Michael Herzfeld, *Anthropology: Theoretical Practice in Culture and Society* (Malden, MA: Blackwell Publishers, 2001), 59. The idea that the past is animated by the concerns of the present has been a widely accepted notion in the social sciences in the past decades.

[31] Mark Edward Lewis, "Historiography and Empire," in *The Oxford History of Historical Writing, Volume 1: Beginnings to AD 600*, ed. Andrew Feldherr and Grant Hardy (Oxford: Oxford University Press, 2011), 440–462, esp. 440.

16   *Introduction*

Former Han political elite had subtly shaped the accounts of Qin history for their own ideological ends.[32] In yet another example, Grant Hardy's *Worlds of Bronze and Bamboo*, the argument is that the composition of *Shiji* was in part motivated by Sima Qian's desire to "contribute to the era's [i.e. Han dynasty's] great quest for restoration, unity, and synthesis."[33] These and many other similar works in the field have contributed a great deal in drawing attention to how historical narratives were written and crafted according to the concerns of the present. Each period seeks its own usable past, and all historical narratives are necessarily artifacts of the sociopolitical conditions of their own time. While Hobsbawm is the most concerned with how this works in the world of nation-states and their creation of "invented traditions," these works have shown us that similar developments also took place in early imperial China despite the vastly different historical conditions.[34]

This study is very much informed by these works in their probing studies of the idea of a usable past, both within the field of early China and more broadly across other traditions of historical writing in world history. I follow their keen observation that the writing of historical narratives was always animated by present concerns. In my view, however, they do tend to ascribe a relatively narrow range of utility to the field of the past; it is either a direct reflection of a certain sociopolitical order or an instrument for the legitimation or naturalization of a new world order. In this study, I would like to expand the analysis beyond just issues of ideological reflection or political legitimation to capture a much wider range of the usefulness of the past, the many different relationships to power that the past was made to serve, whether ideological or critical, legitimizing or delegitimizing.

---

[32] Martin Kern, *The Stele Inscriptions of Ch'in Shih-Huang: Text and Ritual in Early Chinese Imperial Representation* (New Haven: American Oriental Society, 2000), esp. 154–196.

[33] Hardy, *Worlds of Bronze and Bamboo*, 23.

[34] "'Invented tradition' is taken to mean a set of practices, normally governed by overtly or tacitly accepted rules and of a ritual or symbolic nature, which seek to inculcate certain values and norms of behavior by repetition, which automatically implies continuity with the past. In fact, where possible, they normally attempt to establish continuity with a suitable historic past." Eric J. Hobsbawm, "Introduction: Inventing Traditions," in *The Invention of Tradition*, ed. Eric J. Hobsbawm and Terence O. Ranger (Cambridge: Cambridge University Press, 1983), 1.

Organization and Terminology 17

Relatedly, this study aims to look at writings about the past not simply as an epiphenomenon of social, economic, or political changes, a Marxist structure of analysis implicit in Hobsbawm's formulation of the "social function of the past." Instead, these utterances about the past in early China are treated, in this study, not as an epiphenomenon but as the phenomenon in itself.

The grounds that I will explore in this book are, therefore, at once old and new. This expansive landscape of the past, stretched across the early Chinese corpus, has long been attested. Parts of it are already thoroughly surveyed in earlier scholarship, but yet so much of it is still terra incognita. The emphasis on just the canon of historiographical works, and within them the presupposition of didacticism in both their production and reception, have delimited our ability to see this history in the process of becoming. Moving beyond the boundary of the historiographical canon, and setting aside this culturalist assumption of didacticism, this study hopes to uncover new vistas on this landscape of the past.

Organization and Terminology

This work engages with a long period in early Chinese history. It is divided into five chapters, with the topics of each following a roughly chronological order, from the start to almost the end of the first millennium BCE. In dynastic terms, this is from the beginning of the Western Zhou to the middle of the Former Han. Despite this very broad chronological context, this is not intended to be an exhaustive work. The goal is not to describe the *entire* landscape of the past in this one work, but to focus on what I consider to be some of the key moments in the history of the politics of the past in early China.

The first chapter, "Time out of Joint," studies the transformation in the uses of the past from the late Bronze Age regime of the Western Zhou to the time after its collapse in the sixth to fifth centuries BCE. It traces the predominance of genealogical histories at the start of the first millennium BCE, and then the new uses of the past that emerged in the wake of its disappearance in parts of the Confucian *Analects* and the *Mozi* 墨子. The second chapter, "A Parenthetical Past: Deep History and Anti-history in the Late Warring States," focuses on the ambivalence towards the utility of historical knowledge in the fourth and early

18 *Introduction*

third centuries BCE, as seen in the cosmogonic narratives and ethical theories of this period. Specifically, I will present a detailed analysis of the Guodian *Laozi* 郭店老子 as well as the *Mengzi* 孟子 as key examples of texts that seriously questioned the increasingly hegemonic importance of the historical field in political and ethical debates. The third chapter, "Specter of the Past: Bureaucratic Amnesia under the Rise of the Qin Empire," studies how Legalist texts from the mid- to late Warring States reorganized the field of the past in relation to its idea of the laws (*fa* 法), and concludes with a discussion of how the Qin radicalized this Legalist historical vision at the end of the third century BCE. Chapter Four, "The Rehabilitation of Antiquity in the Early Han Empire," studies the works of Jia Yi 賈誼 and Lu Jia 陸賈 as two responses, articulated through different ideas about the meaning of the past, to the problematic legacy of the Qin in the early Han. The last chapter, Chapter Five, "Sima Qian's Critical Past," studies the Grand Archivist's commitment to historiography, materialized in the *Shiji*, as a mode of critique against what he considered the perils of early Han imperialism. The Epilogue, in the end, offers a summary of the findings of this study.

Finally, I should explain the key terminologies that I will be using. By *the past*, I simply refer to the temporal domain anterior to the present. *History*, on the other hand, may refer to one of two things: things and their development in the past themselves, or narratives about the past.[35] In this study, I will rely on various historical narratives, preserved in a variety of media (e.g. bronze inscriptions, stone inscriptions, excavated bamboo slips, transmitted texts) from early China, to tease out the different ways in which the past was capitalized for a whole range of dialogues and debates among political elites. As such, the two terms *the past* and *history* are at times used interchangeably, depending on the context. The past is the entire temporal field anterior to the present; it can be transformed into ideological and argumentative capital once it is fashioned into a historical narrative, variable in length from a single word *gu* ("antiquity") to an anecdote or a complex tale, intended for dialogues with an implicit or explicit interlocutor. *Politics*

---

[35] This is largely due to the contemporary usage of the word "history" in English. As Michel de Certeau describes, "The word 'history' vacillates between two poles: the story which is recounted (*Historie*) and what is produced (*Geschichte*)," in his *The Writing of History*, trans. Tom Conley (New York: Columbia University Press, 1988), 288.

Organization and Terminology 19

refers to relations of power, defined broadly as the structure and mechanism of submission between two or more individuals. The *politics of the past*, therefore, refers to how the field of the past was implicated, as ideological capital in narrative forms, in the imagination and construction of relations of power.[36]

[36] I should note that this study does not engage with the question of *memory* in early China. *Memory* is what one remembers from the past, and *history* is those pieces of the past that fall outside collective memory and therefore need to be put into narratives. As Collingwood put it, "the past only requires historical investigation so far as it is not and cannot be remembered," in his *The Idea of History* (Oxford: Clarendon Press, 1962), 58. Pierre Nora put it even more strongly; he suggested that memory and history are now in "fundamental opposition." "History ... is the reconstruction, always problematic and incomplete, of what is no longer. Memory is a perpetually actual phenomenon, a bond tying us to the eternal present; history is a representation of the past." Pierre Nora, "Between Memory and History: *Les lieux de mémoire*," *Representations* 26 (1989), 7–24, esp. 7–8. In this sense, this study is definitely not a study of collective memory in early China, but rather a history of these "representations of the past" that are always "problematic and incomplete." For studies of memory in early China, one may refer to the excellent works by K. E. Brashier, i.e. *Ancestral Memory in Early China* (Cambridge, MA: Harvard University Asia Center, 2011) and *Public Memory in Early China* (Cambridge, MA: Harvard University Asia Center, 2014); see also the broader discussion on the distinction between "historical culture" and "memory" in Peter Lambert and Björn K. U. Weiler, eds., *How the Past Was Used: Historical Cultures, c.750–2000* (Oxford: The British Academy and Oxford University Press, 2017), 1–48, esp. 11–13.

1 | *Time out of Joint*
Uses of the Past from the Western Zhou to the Early Warring States

Boyi 伯夷 and Shuqi 叔齊, allegedly historical figures from the last decades of the second millennium BCE, made their first appearances in the received corpus at least some 500 years after their time in a few scattered references in the *Analects* (*Lunyu* 論語).[1] There, in the sayings attributed to Confucius (Kongzi 孔子, *c.* 551–479 BCE), they were celebrated as morally exalted figures, who demonstrated their "humaneness" (*ren* 仁) for – or despite – their overt defiance against the newly founded Western Zhou dynasty (*c.*1045–772 BCE). For their adamant refusal to serve the Western Zhou court, they starved themselves to death on a mountain. For that, Confucius referred to them as "worthy men of antiquity" (*gu zhi xianren* 古之賢人), who must have been without rancor because they "sought humanness and achieved it" (*qiu ren de ren* 求仁得仁).[2] These enigmatic words of praise, which count as some of the first commentary on these figures, are not the last that we will hear about them. Their names and stories will continue to be invoked in the following centuries across texts of diverse persuasions.[3] The familiarity of the legend of Boyi and Shuqi, cultivated by more than two millennia of commentaries, can make us forget

---

[1] There are four mentions of Boyi and/or Shuqi in the *Analects*: 5.23, 7.15, 16.12, 18.8. Yang Bojun 楊伯峻, *Lunyu yizhu* 論語譯注 (Beijing: Zhonghua shuju, 1980).

[2] Yang Bojun, *Lunyu yizhu*, 7.15. Translations from the *Lunyu* throughout this book are often adaptations from the excellent rendition by Burton Watson, *The Analects of Confucius* (New York: Columbia University Press, 2007); I also use my own translation when I depart from Watson's reading.

[3] For a comprehensive survey of early references to the story of Boyi and Shuqi in pre-Qin and early Han texts, see Aat Vervoorn, "Boyi and Shuqi: Worthy Men of Old?", *Papers on Far Eastern History* 28 (September 1983), 1–22. See also the more elaborate discusion of the same materials, also by Aat Vervoorn, in the "The Origins of Eremitism and Its Development in the Warring States Period," in his *Men of the Cliffs and Caves: The Development of the Chinese Eremitic Tradition to the End of the Han Dynasty* (Hong Kong: Chinese University Press, 1990), 19–74.

Time out of Joint   21

the peculiar fact that they made their first appearances in the extant corpus more than half a millennium after their supposed time. How is it possible that they were not mentioned once in the entire extant corpus of the Western Zhou dynasty? They did not appear at all in the sections of the *Classic of Documents*, the *Lost Documents of the Zhou* (*Yizhoushu* 逸周書), the *Classic of Poetry*, and the *Classic of Changes* (*Yijing* 易經) that may contain old material from the Western Zhou.[4] What may have prompted this new and abiding interest in them after so much time, more than five centuries, had passed since they railed against the Zhou kings and suffered their horrible fate?

The case of Boyi and Shuqi, with their curious absence and subsequent appearances in the extant corpus, is not an isolated one. There are many more such legendary figures of antiquity who made their first appearances in the textual remains starting around the middle of the first millennium BCE. In fact, as scholars in the past century have noted, it is in the historical period subsequent to the fall of the Western Zhou that most of the canon of historical and cultural heroes of ancient China came to be fashioned. For instance, almost a century ago, in a celebrated argument in his *Gushibian* 古史辨, Gu Jiegang 顧頡剛, using the examples of the legendary sage-kings Yao 堯, Shun 舜, and Yu 禹, discovered that the earlier the supposed time of a historical figure, the later he made his first appearances in the received corpus.[5] More recently, David Schaberg, in his article "Song and the Historical Imagination in Early China," also noted the primacy of individuals and their actions in the narratives and songs from the Warring States and

---

[4] The words "Boyi" 伯夷 are in the *Shangshu* 尚書 but they are not to be confused with the "Boyi" from the end of the Shang dynasty that we are discussing here. It is an earlier figure that bears the same name who, according to legend, served the sage-king Shun 舜. Qu Wanli 屈萬里, *Shangshu jishi* 尚書集釋 (Taipei: Lianjing chuban shiye gongsi, 1983), 254.

[5] Gu Jiegang 顧頡剛, "Yu Qian Xuantong Xiangsheng Lun Gu Shi Shu" 與錢玄同先生論古史書, in *Gushibian* 古史辨, 7 vols. (Shanghai: Guji chubanshe, 1982), Volume 1, 63–64. While Gu Jiegang uses the example of Yu 禹, Yao 堯, and Shun 舜, he clearly intends this to be a general argument for the early Chinese corpus at large. On the figures Boyi and Shuqi, Gu Jiegang even suspected that they may be fictional altogether, or, if they had actually existed, that the dramatic details of their story such as their suicides must have been fictional inventions from later periods. See Gu Jiegang, "Lun Yao Shun Boyi shu" 論堯舜伯夷書, *Gushibian*, Volume 1, 43–44. This argument is also reiterated more recently in Poo, "The Formation of the Concept of Antiquity in Early China."

22   *Time out of Joint*

early Han times.[6] It is also worth noting that in the case of the
scholar Yuan Ke 袁珂, in his attempt to reconstruct the canon of
ancient Chinese mythological heores and historical figures in antiquity, he had to rely on the *Shanhaijing* 山海經, a late Warring States
or Han dynasty compilation (*c.* third to first centuries BCE), for
accounts of these individual figures – despite their alleged antiquity,
they appeared in the extant corpus many centuries after their supposed time.[7] All in all, beginning around the middle of the first
millennium BCE, we begin to see a proliferation of accounts of
historical individuals in the extant corpus. The figures of the individuals – specific men, women, and their actions – increasingly became
a focal point in how the political elite imagined and wrote about the
past. Figures of relative antiquity such as Boyi and Shuqi were
dragged back to the discursive scene almost half a millennium
after their death, and their actions became a point of interest across
a range of political and ethical debates. The landscape of the past
became increasingly dotted with such individuals and elaborate
accounts of their ambitions and deeds.

What, one might ask, prompted this attention to the figures of the
individuals and their historical actions in the centuries after the fall of
the Western Zhou? What fundamental transformation took place with
the decline of the late Bronze Age aristocracy of the Western Zhou that
made accounts of individuals and their actions attract the sort of
intellectual attention and rhetorical investment that we see in the extant
literature beginning no later than the early Warring States in the late
fifth century? What lay in the wake of the fall of the Western Zhou that
translated itself into this persistent and consistent fascination with
historical individuals such as Boyi and Shuqi? One answer, one that
I will pursue at length in this chapter, is that this was an effect of the
transformation in how the past was capitalized in the imagination of
relations of power from the Western Zhou dynasty in the first few
centuries of the first millennium BCE to the time after its collapse.
More specifically, I will argue that the fall of the Western Zhou

---

[6] David Schaberg, "Song and the Historical Imagination in Early China," *Harvard
    Journal of Asiatic Studies* 59.2 (December 1999), 305–361.
[7] Yuan Ke 袁珂, *Zhongguo gudai shenhua* 中國古代神話, rev. edn (Beijing:
    Zhonghua shuju, 1960). See also Richard Strassberg, *A Chinese Bestiary: Strange
    Creatures from the Guideways through Mountains and Seas* (Berkeley:
    University of California Press, 2002), 3–30.

Time out of Joint

precipitated a paradigmatic shift in the political utility of historical knowledge, which was marked by a decline in the importance of the genealogical past and the introduction of a new type of historical imagination, one that is founded on a new understanding of the role and capacity of individuals as historical actors capable of effecting material changes. It was a momentous transformation that also implicated a whole host of other issues and debates, including an individual's relation to his family and state, as well as notions of historical continuity and rupture. I will elaborate upon all these over the course of this chapter.

To chart this transformation from the Western Zhou to the early Warring States period, I will discuss three set of primary materials: Western Zhou texts, the *Analects*, and the *Mozi*.[8] The first category, Western Zhou texts, refers primarily to the bronze inscriptions (*jinwen* 金文) ranging from the tenth to the eighth centuries BCE. I will also draw on portions of the *Classic of Documents* and *Classic of Poetry* as supplementary materials.[9] Then, I will turn to a reading of the *Analects*, where we will see not a simple departure from, but a metamorphosis and inversion of, the genealogical past that predominated in the Western Zhou. It is also in the *Analects* that we will encounter a new figure of the deliberative individual central to the historical imagination of the early Warring States period. Then, in the last part of this chapter, I will turn to the *Mozi*, the portions of this large text that possibly date to the early Warring States period. There, we will see a vision of the past that is radically different to the one in the *Analects*. Yet, interestingly, we will encounter the same figure of the deliberative individual that appeared in the *Analects*. After the collapse of the Western Zhou, by the time of the early Warring States, we can observe a common departure from the type of genealogical past that once dominated the historical imagination of the political elite under the late Bronze Age aristocratic order. There was not a single new paradigm, however, that emerged to take its place. What we would see, between the *Analects* and the *Mozi*, is competing models of how the past should once again be understood, capitalized, and

---

[8] The thorny issues of the dating of these texts be dealt with in each of the three respective sections below in this chapter. In the context of each body of materials, I will explain how they map onto this period, from the Western Zhou to the early Warring States.

[9] In one instance, I also draw on the *Yizhoushu* 逸周書. See note 26 below.

24   *Time out of Joint*

appropriated to imagine proper relations of power. While they both subscribe to this new figure of deliberative individuals, a key historical agent at the basis of their new visions of the past, they differ vastly on his roles and capacity. This divergence would constitute a major contour of the landscape of the past in early China.

Western Zhou: Moments of Origins, Exemplary Acts, and the Genealogical Past

Let us begin with a document from the first decades of the Western Zhou from around the turn of the first millennium BCE. It is the bronze inscription on the Da Yu *ding* 大盂鼎.[10] Discovered in the 1820s, and now housed at the National Museum of China in Beijing, this bronze cauldron is dated by most scholars to the reign of either King Cheng 成王 (r. *c.*1024–1005 BCE) or King Kang 康王 (r. *c.*1004–967 BCE).[11] With 291 characters, it is one of the longest bronze inscriptions we have from the Western Zhou.[12] Despite its unusual length, the formal structure of the Da Yu *ding* inscription is fairly typical among the bronze inscriptions of the Western Zhou. It begins with a speech by the king charging a subordinate, in this case a certain man named Yu 盂, with a specific

---

[10] For this and all other bronze inscriptions cited in this book, I refer to the reproductions and transcriptions in *Yin Zhou jinwen jicheng: xiuding zengbu ben* 殷周金文集成：修訂增補本, 8 vols. (Beijing: Zhonghua shuju, 2007). For philological details of the various bronze inscriptions, I refer to the summary discussion by the various contributors in Constance A. Cook and Paul R. Goldin, eds., *A Source Book of Ancient Chinese Bronze Inscriptions*, Early China Special Monograph Series no. 7 (Berkeley, CA: The Society for the Study of Early China, 2016); as well as the older discussion in Shirakawa Shizuka 白川靜, *Kinbun Tsūshaku* 金文通釋, 7 vols. (Kōbe-shi: Hakutsuru Bijutsukan, 1964–1984), and Chen Mengjia 陳夢家, *Xi Zhou tongqi duandai* 西周銅器斷代, 2 vols. (Beijing: Zhonghua shuju, 2004). For the transcriptions in this chapter, I render archaic graphs in their modern forms for greater readability, largely following the recommendations in Cook and Goldin, *A Source Book of Ancient Chinese Bronze Inscriptions*.

[11] Shirakawa, *Kinbun Tsūshaku*, Volume 1, 2, 647. In this chapter, I follow the Western Zhou reign dates in Chen Mengjia 陳夢家, *Xi Zhou niandai kao* 西周年代考 (Taipei: Shangwu yinshuguan, 1945). I also refer to David S. Nivison, "The Dates of Western Chou," *Harvard Journal of Asiatic Studies* 43.2 (1983), 481–580.

[12] Specifically, it is the second-longest bronze inscription, after the Mao Gong *ding* 毛公鼎 (Duke of Mao cauldron) inscription of 491 characters, from the late Western Zhou period.

Western Zhou: Moments of Origins

set of duties, and it concludes with a list of gifts that the subordinate received as a result.[13]

Following is the first half of the inscription, the king's speech to his subordinate Yu; it involves a specific command, one that is articulated by way of a narrative of the past:

It was the ninth month. The king was in the Ancestral Zhou, where he gave his command to Yu. The king spoke thus: "Yu, the immensely brilliant King Wen received the great Mandate from Heaven. King Wu succeeded King Wen, and he established the state, ridding it of evils, spreading the Mandate to the four quarters, and rectifying the people [therein]. Amongst the government officials, none dared to get intoxicated when using alcohol; when presenting their burnt and grain offerings in sacrifice [to Kings Wen and Wu], no one dared to offer toasts. For this reason, Heaven watched over its son [i.e. King Wu] and offered protection for this Former King, for him to spread the Mandate to the four quarters. I heard that the Yin lost its Mandate, because their border officials and administrators, numbering exactly a hundred, all overindulged in alcohol! That was the reason why they lost their military command. Oh, from a young age, you were entrusted with great responsibilities, and I have been giving you rudimentary instructions. Do not undercut me, the One Man. Now, I have modeled myself after and possessed the correct virtue of King Wen. Just as King Wen commanded two or three government officials, I now command you, Yu, in leading the luminous [Zhou order], respectfully harmonizing the norms of virtue. Without any delay, day or night, submit your admonitions to the court; dashing back and forth, fearful of the awesomeness of Heaven." The king said, "I charge you, Yu, to model yourself after your ancestor the Duke of Nan whom you have succeeded."

隹（唯）九月，王在宗周令盂。王若曰：盂，丕顯文王，受天有大令，
在珷（武）王嗣玟（文）作邦，闢厥匿（慝），匍（敷）有四方，畯正
厥民。在于御事，䠶，酉（酒）無敢酖，有祡（柴）蒸祀無敢酖。
古（故）天異（翼）臨子，灋保先王，【敷】有四方。我聞殷述（墜）令，
唯殷邊侯田（甸）雩（越）殷正百辟，率肆（肆）于酉（酒），古（故）
喪師。已，汝妹（昧）辰又（有）大服。余唯即朕小學，汝勿逸余乃辟
一人。今我唯即井（型）廩（稟）于玟王正德，若玟王令二，三正

---

[13] For a detailed description of the structure of Western Zhou bronze inscriptions, see Edward L. Shaughnessy, *Sources of Western Zhou History: Inscribed Bronze Vessels* (Berkeley: University of California Press, 1991), 73–84; also see Edward Shaughnessy, "Western Zhou Bronze Inscriptions," in *New Sources of Early Chinese History*, ed. Edward L. Shaughnessy (Berkeley, CA: Society for the Study of Early China and the Institute of East Asian Studies, 1997), 57–84.

（征）。今余隹（唯）令女（汝）盂召（詔）榮敬雝德巠（經）。敏朝夕
入讕（諫），享奔走，畏天畏（威）。王曰：而。令女汝盂井（型）乃嗣
祖南公。[14]

The first thing to note here is that the past plays an integral role in this piece of political rhetoric deployed by the king towards his subject. The apparent political authority that the king had over his subject was wholly constructed on the ground of history. Specifically, the speech begins with a reference to a historical event, namely the Zhou conquest of the Shang, with a series of laudatory citations of the accomplishments of founding rulers King Wen (*Wen wang* 文王) and King Wu (*Wu wang* 武王). Touting the accomplishments of one's forebears is commonplace in all political rhetoric, especially under an aristocratic order, but in the case of the Da Yu *ding* inscription the attention to this particular piece of the past holds a special significance. The founding moment of the Zhou, and particularly the deeds of King Wen and King Wu, are not just idle, albeit inspiring, historical references, but they constitute the very model of political actions that the Zhou king in the present must emulate faithfully.[15]

To elaborate on this point, let us return to the king's speech. After recounting the accomplishments of the founding rulers of the Zhou, the king specifically declared the following: "Now, I have modeled myself after and possessed the correct virtue of King Wen. Just as King Wen commanded two or three government officials, I now command you, Yu, in leading the luminous [Zhou order], respectfully harmonizing the norms of virtue." The historical knowledge of the work of King Wen and King Wu constitutes a usable past in an eminently practical sense. What they did at the founding moment of the Zhou dynasty provided an exemplary model of actions for later kings, who only needed to emulate

---

[14] *Yin Zhou jinwen jicheng: xiuding zengbu ben*, 2837. The translation is my own, with some adaptions from the excellent version by Gilbert Mattos, "Shang and Zhou Ritual Bronze Inscriptions," in *Hawaii Reader in Traditional Chinese Culture*, ed. Victor H. Mair, Nancy S. Steinhardt, and Paul Goldin (Honolulu: University of Hawaii Press, 2005), 14–15; and Cook and Goldin, *A Source Book of Ancient Chinese Bronze Inscriptions*, 32–34.

[15] William E. Savage, in his great analysis of Western Zhou "political theology," similarly observed that, "Like other traditional societies, the Western Chou looked upon the past as a time of origins, a time of beginnings that had a paradigmatic value for the present. The most significant event in history was the founding of the dynasty." William E. Savage, "Archetypes, Model Emulation, and the Confucian Gentleman," *Early China* 17 (1992), 6.

Western Zhou: Moments of Origins

(*xing* 井) and approximate them as closely as possible to ensure that the order they created would perpetuate and continue to prevail.[16] Now, if it is the duty of the present-day Zhou king to follow the precedent set by the founding figures King Wen and King Wu, then what is the responsibility of the subject? The answer is, quite straightforwardly, that he too follows the example set by his own forefathers: "The king said, 'I charge you, Yu, to model yourself after your ancestor the Duke of Nan whom you have succeeded'" (王曰：盂。令女汝盂井（型）乃嗣祖南公).

The exact identity of this "Duke of Nan" (*Nan gong* 南公) is unknown, but given the exclusive use of the term *si* (嗣) within the Western Zhou corpus in referring to familial heritance or inheritor, it must be referring to an ancestor of Yu. He is typically identified as Yu's deceased grandfather in most studies of the Da Yu *ding*, but Tang Lan 唐蘭 went as far as identifying him as the youngest maternal half-brother of King Wu.[17] In any case, the point remains the same: while the Zhou king declares that he is following the precedent of his ancestors, his subordinate Yu is charged with following the precedent of his own forefather, who presumably also served the Zhou court during its founding years. In both cases, they are said to *xing*, or "model after," their respective ancestors. The argument here is that the proper way to act in the present is to emulate the examples of our respective forefathers.

The Da Yu *ding* inscription concludes as follows:

The king said, "Yu, in following [your ancestor's work], assist me, your ruler, in military matters. Be diligent and expedient in matters of punishment and litigations. Day and night, assist me, the One Man, to govern over the four quarters. For me, you will inspect the territories and peoples that the Former Kings had received. I now bestow upon you a jar of aromatic sacrificial spirits ... [list of gifts omitted in translation]. I bestow upon you the flag of your ancestor the Duke of Nan for use in hunting." [Further list of gifts omitted.] The king said, "Yu, act respectfully and properly, do not disregard my command." In response to the exaltation by the king, Yu

---

[16] The character 井 is a graphical cognate of the character 型 in Western Zhou inscriptions. See definition (c) for the entry *xing* 刑/型 in Axel Schüssler, *A Dictionary of Early Zhou Chinese* (Honolulu: University of Hawaii Press, 1987), 688.

[17] Tang Lan's argument as cited in Wang Hui 王輝., *Shang Zhou jinwen* 商周金文 (Beijing: Wenwu chubanshe, 2006), 69–70n23.

herewith made this treasured cauldron of the ancestor Duke of Nan. It was in the twenty-third year of the king's reign.

王曰：「盂，迺召（紹）夾死（尸）司戎，敏敕（諫）罰訟，夙夕召我一人烝四方，雩（越）我其遹省先王受民受疆土。賜女汝鬯一卣 ... 賜乃祖南公旂，用狩。... 王曰：盂，若敬乃正，勿灋（廢）朕令。盂用對王休，用作祖南公寶鼎。唯王廿又三祀。

The subordinate Yu, acting under the banner of his grandfather the Duke of Nan, both literally and figuratively, will help the Zhou king maintain the order among the people and land inherited from former kings of the Zhou. Through their respective emulation of the work of their ancestors, they will be able to maintain the order that their ancestors created in the first place. Imitations of the founding political actions by one's ancestors ensure a continuous extension of the original order to the present.

This pattern of political rhetoric seen on the Da Yu *ding* is typical among Western Zhou bronze inscriptions. A majority of the inscriptions describe similar official exchanges between a Zhou king and his subject. They almost always begin with the present-day Zhou king recounting the virtues of King Wen, and sometimes those of King Wu, and the founding order that they created through their actions. Then, after declaring that he will model himself after King Wen, he exhorts his subject to similarly model himself after his own ancestors, in order to maintain the Zhou order. Li Feng, in his recent monograph on the state and bureaucracy of the Western Zhou, also noted the ubiquity of this invocation of the founding rulers in the bronze inscriptions throughout this late Bronze Age dynasty. He also made an important observation that in Western Zhou bronze inscriptions, only King Wen and King Wu were ever said to have directly received the so-called "Mandate of Heaven" (*tianming* 天命). This led Li to posit that the figure of King Wen, and to a lesser extent King Wu, constitute the very source of political authority for the Zhou court.[18]

---

[18] Feng Li, *Bureaucracy and the State in Early China: Governing the Western Zhou* (Cambridge: Cambridge University Press, 2008), 294–299. See also the article by Wang Ming-Ke, "Western Zhou Remembering and Forgetting," *Journal of East Asian Archaeology* 1 (1999), 231–250; the author argues that the Western Zhou elite inscribed their histories in a selective and strategic way informed by their social organization.

Western Zhou: Moments of Origins

There is a purposeful conflation of originary and exemplary actions in these Western Zhou bronze inscriptions. The founding acts of the first rulers were immediately considered exemplary, and emulation or repetition of them could maintain or even expand the very same new order that they had created generations ago. In other words, the particular dynamics at the founding moment of the Zhou are presumed to be paradigmatic and foundational to its rule over time. That is not to say that one must repeat the founding reign of the Zhou dynasty in each generation, down to every act and word, but that the later generation should and can only perpetuate the great order of the Zhou, as initiated by the founding rulers, by emulating their exemplary acts.[19]

This fascination with moments of origins, and the emulation of past exemplary actions, is not limited only to the bronze inscriptions, but can also be seen in the transmitted corpus from the early first millennium BCE. In the *Classic of Poetry*, for instance, there is the famous example of the poem "Shengmin" 生民. It recounts not only the legendary birth of Hou Ji 后稷, the mythological progenitor of the Zhou clan, but also the origin of the agricultural practices and sacrificial rituals of the clan. At the very end of the poem, it says that "Hou Ji founded the sacrifices, and without blemish or flaw, they have gone on until now" (后稷肇祀，庶無罪悔，以迄于今).[20] Here, we see a direct

---

[19] "These characteristics of Western Chou political theology show that politico-religious relations of dominance often were translated into relations of heritage. An important part of Western Chou legitimacy rested on the possession of family history, ancestral glory, and inherited status. In other words, access to the past, to history, represented a basic assumption about relations of dominance and subordination between men," as Savage notes in his article "Archetypes, Model Emulation, and the Confucian Gentleman," 6.

[20] Qu Wanli 屈萬里, *Shijing quanshi* 詩經詮釋 (Taipei: Lianjing chuban shiye gongsi, 1983). There has been a great amount of debate on the dates and the composition of the poems in the *Classic of Poetry*, which in all likelihood did not reach its current transmitted form, as a collection of poems, until the early imperial period, many centuries after the Western Zhou. I found particularly persuasive the overview and arguments by Edward L. Shaughnessy in his article "Unearthed Documents and the Question of the Oral versus Written Nature of the *Classic of Poetry*," *Harvard Journal of Asiatic Studies* 75.2 (December 2015), 331–375. I continue to find useful the summary given by Michael Loewe in his edited volume *Early Chinese Texts: A Bibliographical Guide* (Berkeley, CA: The Society for the Study of Early China, 1993), 415–424. There is likely a Zhou core, or remnant of Zhou materials, in the *Classic of Poetry*. In the end, I can neither prove nor disprove that this and other poems that I will be citing are in fact from the Western Zhou period, but nevertheless I still find my references to them defensible, for two reasons. First, the argument I am making here does

30

linkage between origin and efficacy. One understands the efficacy of a set of rituals by understanding its origin. Or, the efficacy of the rituals is a result of their originary nature. Moreover, the poem emphasized in its very last line that these rituals, as they were from their moment of origin, had continued to the present day. As in the bronze inscriptions, order can be extended to the present by a repetition of actions constitutive of that very order at its moment of origin.[21]

Similar ideas can be seen in other poems in the *Poetry*. For instance, in the poem "Liangsi" 良耜, after an elaborate description of certain agricultural work which, when done properly, would ensure that "the barns and brim are full, and wife and children at peace" (百室盈止，婦子寧止), the poem exclaims in its conclusion that "we shall succeed, we shall continue, continue the men of old" (以似以續，續古之人).[22] The poem "Zaishan" 載芟, after an idealized description of how the fields are cleared and seeds are planted in order to produce the harvests for the ancestral sacrifices, concludes with this fact that: "Not only here is it like this, not only now is it so. From long ago it has been thus" (匪且有且，匪今斯今，振古如茲).[23] Though less explicitly concerned with identifying the moment of origin for these agricultural and ritual practices, these poems nevertheless do emphasize the importance of faithfully repeating past practices in the present, since what was once

not hinge on the fact that this or any particularly poem must date from the Western Zhou period, whatever that may even mean; it is more about a pattern of rheotric across a body of texts – bronze inscriptions, poems, and political speeches – and losing the support of any one particular text, due to its inauthenticity, is not entirely detrimental to the argument. Second, even if turns out to be the case that one or more of these poems do postdate the Western Zhou period, it would not invalidate the argument about this pattern of rhetoric about the past entirely. This is a *chronologically elastic* argument. It would simply mean that this particular way of capitalizing the past persisted beyond the Western Zhou period. Therefore, in this chapter, I will be referring to these poems, confident in the scholarly consensus that they could in fact be Western Zhou materials, but at the same time I am also mindful that they could be later compositions, in which case the essential argument will nevertheless stand with additional chronological revisions.

[21] Cf. Willard Peterson, "Reading *Sheng Min*," in *Ways with Words: Writing about Reading Texts from Early China*, ed. Pauline Yu, Peter Bol, Stephen Owen, and Willard Peterson (Berkeley, Los Angeles, and London: University of California Press, 2000), 31–33.

[22] Unless otherwise noted, all translations from the *Classic of Poetry* are adapted from Arthur Waley, *The Book of Songs: The Ancient Chinese Classic of Poetry*, ed. Joseph R. Allen (New York: Grove Press, 1996), 304.

[23] Ibid., 304.

Western Zhou: Moments of Origins

efficacious in the past will continue to be efficacious in the present.[24] Order is maintained by establishing a continuity of practices through their faithful repetition over time.

Representations of similar ideas can also be found in the early stratum of the *Classic of Documents*.[25] In the chapter "Li zheng" 立政, for instance, the Duke of Zhou (*Zhou gong*周公) explained the downfall of Jie 桀, the last ruler of the Xia 夏 dynasty, by his inability to continue the traditional, inherited way of making official appointments: "Jie's character was such that he did not follow precedents in making appointments, and therefore his character was violent and ruined the future [of his kingdom]" (桀德惟乃弗作往任，是惟暴德，罔後).[26] In the chapter "Jiu gao" 酒誥, King Cheng argued that the injunction against alcoholic indulgence by King Wen was one of the reasons why the Zhou was able to conquer the Shang, and provides the model for how the Zhou court can continue to maintain the mandate:

[24] Stephen Owen made a similar argument in "Reproduction in the *Shijing* (*Classic of Poetry*)," *Harvard Journal of Asiatic Studies* 61.2 (December 2001), 287–315. Similar observations can be made of many other poems in the *Poetry*, such as "Chuci" 楚茨, "Xin nanshan" 信南山, "Da tian" 大田, and "Jia le" 假樂. See Qu Wanli, *Shijing quanshi*, 403–408, 12–13, 94–50.

[25] As on the *Classic of Poetry*, the scholarship on the *Classic of Documents* recently focused on the contexts of its composition and transmission, and by extension the dates of its materials. See the recent lively discussion in Martin Kern and Dirk Meyer, eds., *Origins of Chinese Political Philosophy: Studies in the Composition and Thought of the Shangshu (Classic of Documents)* (Leiden: Brill, 2017). See also a great summary of the earlier consensus in Loewe, *Early Chinese Texts*, 376–389. On the use of materials from the *Classic of Documents* in this chapter, my position is similar to the one I articulated in relation to the *Classic of Poetry* (see note 20 above). I refer to parts of the text that are likely to contain Zhou materials, and in the case that they are proven to be later materials, the essential argument about this pattern of rhetoric still stands with additional chronological consideration. The overall argument of the book, as the reader will see, does not depend on a strict, entirely certain chronology of the texts.

[26] Unless otherwise noted, translations from the *Shangshu* are my own, based on the edition in Qu Wanli, *Shangshu jishi*. I have also consulted the translation by Bernhard Karlgren, *The Book of Documents* (Gothenburg: Elanders Boktryckeri Aktiebolag, 1950). Also, a very similar point was made about the last ruler of the Shang dynasty, namely Zhou 紂, in the "Shang shi" 商誓 chapter of the *Yizhoushu*逸周書. In it, he failed because he did not follow the canonical precedent (*dian* 典) set by the founder of Shang, namely Tang 湯. This chapter is tentatively dated to around the mid-Western Zhou by Huang Peirong 黃沛榮, "Zhoushu yanjiu" 周書研究, PhD dissertation, Guoli Taiwan daxue zhongwen yanjiusuo, 1976.

King [Cheng] said: "Feng, the princes of states and managers of affairs from our Western lands and you, the young one, have been able to follow King Wen's instructions and are not excessive in wine. Therefore, up to the present time, we have been able to receive Yin's mandate."

王曰，封，我西土棐祖邦君、御事、小子，尚克用文王教，不腆于酒。故我至于今，克受殷之命。[27]

Now, after this brief detour into the *Poetry* and the *Documents*, let us return to the bronze inscriptions. The Da Yu *ding*, as we have noted, is from the first decades of the Western Zhou, so to what extent is this argument applicable to later periods in the Western Zhou? Quite remarkably, the type of literary pattern and political rhetoric that we saw in that one early inscription remained quite consistent throughout the Western Zhou. Take, for example, the Ban *gui* 班簋 from the mid-Western Zhou, roughly a century after the Da Yu *ding*, in the second half of tenth century BCE during the reign of King Mu (r. 956–918). It records an exchange between King Mu and one of his relatives, Mao Ban 毛班, a descendant of King Wen. Mao Ban had just successfully finished a three-year-long military conquest in the east for the Zhou court, and the inscription commemorates his successful campaign upon his return. The first half of the inscription is a detailed description of the conquest, related as a charge by King Mu to Mao Ban; the second half is a speech by Mao Ban on his understanding of the success of the campaign and his request for a posthumous title for his deceased father, Mao Gong 毛公:

Mao Ban bowed and said, "Alas! My illustrious deceased father once received favor from the Zhou court. As a great grandchild of King Wen and his royal consort, he rose to a prominent position and had great accomplishments. The descendants of King Wen all studied his example and emulated him, and no one dared to compare himself to him. I, Mao Ban, do not hope to ask for anything, except for a posthumous title 'Great Order' for my deceased father, which my future descendants will forever be able to treasure."

班拜稽首曰：烏虖，丕丕孔（揚）皇公受京宗懿釐，毓文王，王姒聖孫，登于大服，廣成厥工，文王孫亡弗懷井（型），亡克競厥烈，班非敢覓，唯作卲考爽，益（諡）曰大政。子子孫孫多世其永寶。[28]

[27] Qu Wanli, *Shangshu jishi*, 162. This particular translation is based on Karlgren, *The Book of Documents*, 45.
[28] *Yin Zhou jinwen jicheng: xiuding zengbu ben*, 4341.

Western Zhou: Moments of Origins   33

Here, we see once again the language of "modeling" or "emulation" (*xing*) regarding the work of a past exemplary figure, in this case the speaker's father, Mao Gong. Moreover, there appears to be this desire to relate, however tenuously, the accomplishment of Mao Gong and his genealogical tie to King Wen, so that this past model for emulation would be clearly linked back to the founding rulers of the Zhou. The idea of emulation, and the concern for continuity with the founding moment of the dynasty, especially the figure of King Wen, still very much inform the political rhetoric in this mid-Western Zhou bronze inscription.

In English-language scholarship on the Western Zhou of the past couple of decades, it has been suggested that there was an expansive ritual reform first underway in the mid-tenth century that then culminated in the early ninth century which radically redefined elite privileges.[29] The evidence for the historicity of this ritual reform is almost entirely drawn from the bronze inscriptions and stylistic features of the vessels themselves, since it was not mentioned in the transmitted texts, and one of the key pieces of evidence is the Shi Qiang *pan* 史墙盤 inscription. It is one of the longest inscriptions from the late Western Zhou (at 284 characters), with brief descriptions for the first seven generations of the Zhou kings and five generations of a certain Wei 微 clan, whose present-day head archivist, Qiang, commissioned its casting.[30] Notwithstanding the historicity of this late Western Zhou ritual reform, I would suggest that the Shi Qiang *pan* inscription is largely consistent with what we have seen so far in these different Western Zhou texts in terms of how they capitalized the past. It begins, not surprisingly at all, with a description of the founding achievement of King Wen: "It is said that in antiquity, when King Wen first took control

---

[29] The most recent, and most substantial, case made for it is by Lothar von Falkenhausen, *Chinese Society in the Age of Confucius: The Archaeological Evidence* (Los Angeles: Costen Institute of Archaeology, University of California – Los Angeles, 2006), 29–73. See also the discussion in Feng Li, *Landscape and Power in Early China: The Crisis and Fall of the Western Zhou 1045–771 BCE* (Cambridge: Cambridge University Press, 2006).

[30] Cook and Goldin, *A Source Book of Ancient Chinese Bronze Inscriptions*, 93–100. My understanding of the Shi Qiang *pan* benefited greatly from the discussion in Falkenhausen, *Chinese Society in the Age of Confucius*, 56–73; David M. Sena, "Arraying the Ancestors in Ancient China: Narratives of Lineage History in the 'Scribe Qiang' and 'Qiu' Bronzes," *Asia Major* 25.1 (2012), 63–81; and Yin Shengping 尹盛平, *Xi Zhou Wei shi jiazu qingtongqi qun yanjiu* 西周微氏家族青銅器群研究 (Beijing: Wenwu chubanshe, 1992).

34 *Time out of Joint*

and brought harmony to governing the people, the Deity Above sent down refined virtue and grand protection, which King Wen spread out to all the spirits above and below, and thus united and received tribute from the ten thousand states" (曰古文王，初盭龢于政，上帝降懿德大屏，匍（敷）有上下，合受受萬邦).[31] Then, it proceeds to give a similar description of the Zhou king of each subsequent generation: King Wu, King Cheng, King Kang 康, King Zhao 昭, King Mu 穆, and finally King Gong 共, the latter being the reigning ruler when the inscription was cast. For the first five generations of kings, brief descriptions of their work and accomplishments such as the one cited above for King Wen were given in the inscription. For King Mu and the present-day King Gong, it gives the following laudatory description:

Prayerful and illuminated, King Mu modeled (*xing*) himself [after the former kings] and followed the great plan. Continuing the pacification, the Son of Heaven respectfully maintains the long-standing glory of Kings Wen and Wu. The Son of Heaven, extending their glory without harm, loyally prays to those spirits above and below; broadening the far-reaching strategy, he shines bright like the sky without tiring. The Deity Above and Hou Ji provided special protection, giving the Son of Heaven extended long life, large fortunes, and abundant harvests. The southern (*Man*) peoples of the outer regions have all hastened to visit.

祗景穆王，井（型）帥宇（訏）誨（謀）。申恉天子，天子貂（紹）黂（纘）文武長烈，天子眉無匄（害），眔祁（祇）上下，亟（極）熙慕（謨），昊照亡斁，上帝司（后）稷尤保受（授）天子綰令，厚福豐年。方蠻亡不迅見。

Here, once again, the task for the Zhou kings is to follow precedents; for King Gong, it is very specifically the "long-standing glory" (*changci* 長剌) of the founding rulers King Wen and King Wu. Despite the much longer genealogical span, it is essentially the same relation between past and present that we first saw in the Da Yu *ding* inscription.

After the descriptions of the Zhou kings, the inscription turned to the parallel generations in the Wei clan. It begins with the "High Ancestor" (*gaozu* 高祖), who volunteered his service to King Wu in the first years of the Zhou dynasty:

---

[31] Translation of the Shi Qiang *pan* follows the excellent rendition by Constance A. Cook in Cook and Goldin, *A Source Book of Ancient Chinese Bronze Inscriptions*, 93–100, with minor modifications, especially in the concluding section of the inscription.

Western Zhou: Moments of Origins

Tranquil and somber, the High Ancestor located Wei in a numinous place and, once King Wu had cut up the Yin, my glorious ancestor Archivist Wei went to visit King Wu, who then commanded the Duke of Zhou to lodge hin in Zhou and give him a place to stay. All-encompassing and kind, Ancestor Yi assisted and acted as a counterpart for his ruler and took on the ruler's distant plans as if they were as close as his own abdomen and heart.

青（靜）幽高祖，在微霝靈處，雩（越）武王既哉（哉）殷，微史烈祖乃來見武王，武王則令周公舍寓（于）周俾處。甬（通）更（惠）乙祖，迻（差）匹厥辟，遠猷腹心。

Then, the inscription detailed the work of successive generations of the heads of the Wei clan, concluding with Shi Qiang ("Archivist Qiang") himself, the current head of the clan, who commissioned the casting of this bronze vessel and the inscription. It ends as follows: "I make a precious sacrificial vessel, an adorned treasure, for expressing reverence to my florious ancestor, my Accomplished Deceased Father, who in turn gives to me, Qiang, blessings and good fortune; and I embrace his spirit, exorcise evil, and gain prosperity to live a long life to a hoary old age, in service to his highness" (用作寶尊彝, 烈祖文考弋（式）寶，受（授）牆爾哉（祉）福，懷髮（祓）彔（祿），黃耇彌生，龕(堪)事厥辟）. Just as Qiang's ancestors once served the Zhou court, Qiang himself wishes to be able to do the same in the present, extending the relationship that the two families had enjoyed, from the first years of the Zhou, when the first ancestors volunteered their services to King Wu, to the present. The relationship between King Wu and the Wei ancestor had acquired a paradigmatic significance. Historical continuity to this original moment, at the founding of the dynasty, legitimates the possibility of the continuing relationship between the Wei family and the Zhou court centuries later in the present day.

For the last part of our discussion of the Western Zhou period, I will turn to a negative narrative. Beginning in the mid- to late Western Zhou, we begin to see inscriptions that articulate the opposite of what we have just observed. That is, they bemoan the loss of historical continuity and proper inheritance from the founding rulers of the Zhou. One prominent example is the Shi Xun *gui* 師旬簋 from sometime in the ninth century BCE.[32] The inscription begins in a typical

---

[32] Various dates have been given for the Shi Xun *gui*. Guo Moruo 郭沫若 suggested that it is contemporary with the *Mao gong ding* from the reign of King Xuan (r. 827–782 BCE), as cited in Wang Hui, *Shang Zhou jinwen*, 185.

36   *Time out of Joint*

fashion; it proclaims the founding achievement of King Wen and King Wu, including the fact that they had received the Mandate from Heaven. It also mentions the great assistance that the ancestors of Shi Xun had provided for them:

The king reportedly said: "Shi Xun! The illustrious Kings Wen and Wu, having received the Mandate from Heaven, defeated King Zhou of Shang to rescue its people. Your wise ancestors provided able assistance to the former kings. They became his close associates, and they assisted him in every way. There were great accomplishments, and a harmonious order was achieved. Therefore, the Deity Above did not abandon us, and protected our Zhou kingdom. The people within the four quarters were all prosperous and at peace."

王若曰：師訇，丕顯文武，膺受天令，亦則於（唯）汝乃聖祖考克尃（傅）右先王，作厥肱股用夾召厥辟奠大令，盩（庱）穌雩（越）政，肆皇帝亡吳（斁），臨保我又（有）周，雩（越）四方民亡不康靜。[33]

After this fairly typical opening, the inscription took an unusual turn: "The king said: 'Shi Xun! It is sad that today Heaven sends down destruction. Our virtue did not follow the model [of our ancestors], and therefore we did not inherit and continue [the work of] the former kings'" (王曰：師訇，哀才（哉）。今日天疾畏威降喪，首（慎）德不克畫，古（故）亡丞于先王). The king continues to say that because of this dire situation, he will promote Shi Xun and hope that he will be able to provide proper assistance for restoring order to the Zhou world once again. The inscription then concludes, as is customary, with a list of gifts that the king conferred upon Shi Xun and a dedication to Shi Xun's ancestors.

In the Shi Xun *gui* inscription, we see a capitalization of the past that is the same as the type that we saw in the other Western Zhou materials, except that it did so in negative terms. Instead of a simple enjoinder to emulate the successful relations that their respective ancestors had with each other, the Zhou king urged Shi Xun to provide services to the court because of the opposite, because there was a rupture in the emulation and continuation of the exemplary work of the founders. Understanding this discontinuity as the cause of disorder in the present

---

More recently, Constance Cook noted that it likely dates to the first year of King Yi 懿 (r. 899–893 BCE); see Cook and Goldin, *A Source Book of Ancient Chinese Bronze Inscriptions*, 112.

[33] *Yin Zhou jinwen jicheng: xiuding buzeng ben*, 4342. The translation is my own.

Western Zhou: Moments of Origins

underscores the predominance of this particular paradigm in the capitalization of the past during the Western Zhou. It is a model where actions by the Zhou founders were considered exemplary and inherently efficacious, and their emulation by later generations would ensure the continuation of that founding order into the present.[34]

* * *

Now, let us summarize this reading of the Western Zhou materials. First and foremost, we see that the field of the past played an absolutely integral role. Narratives about the past were regularly mobilized as a key resource for legitimizing the political authority and actions of the ruling elite in the present. More specifically, we also saw a particular investment in the founding moment of the dynasty, the work of the founding rulers King Wen, King Wu, and their associates, as exemplary models the emulation and repetition of whom from one generation to the next would ensure the continuance of this founding order. The past, in this context, became relevant as a series of originary, exemplary moments, and a knowledge of them is essential if we wish to emulate them to perpetuate the same political order in the present.

This way of capitalizing the past by the Western Zhou political elite has a number of significant implications. First, it is fair to say that in the Western Zhou, all history must be family history. Given that the historical moments of interest are only those originary actions and the points of continuity within one's genealogical past or that of the ruling family, the past was essentially delimited to the genealogical field. Second, more implicitly, this use of the past also suggests a relatively circumscribed role for individuals as historical actors. Since the ideal is for one to identify and imitate the exemplary actions of one's ancestors and those of the ruling family, the realm of meaningful and effective political action was essentially delimited to just the contexts of the family and the state. Proper political actions were necessarily seen as genealogical inheritance, and an individual becomes politically relevant and effective only as a descendant of a family that can establish a history with the ruling family. It is a tightly closed genealogical past that we see in these different narratives that circulated

---

[34] Besides the bronze inscriptions, we can also find similar expressions of anxiety over one's failure to continue the work of the ancestors in the received texts from this period. See, for instance, the *Shijing* poems "Wen wang" 文王 and "Yun han" 雲漢. Qu Wanli, *Shijing quanshi*, 444–451, 527–530.

38 *Time out of Joint*

amongst the Western Zhou political elite. The political state was coextensive with this elite network of families, and their collective past was deemed the only meaningful history. Pieces of the past that fall outside the realm of the family or the state had little or no meaning or relevance to this political elite invested in preserving the status quo.

This, moreover, implies a radically conservative political vision amongst the Western Zhou political elite. Political ideals were always attributed to the past actions of one's ancestors, and therefore the most that an individual could achieve was to repeat past successes. The goal was to conserve what had already been achieved at the moments of origin of the dynasty. With imitation and emulation as the primary mode of political action, there was no theoretical space for any sort of innovation. Innovation would have necessitated deviation from the originary exemplary models, and any such deviation must ultimately lead to disorder, as we saw in the Shi Xun *gui* inscription. Except for the founding figures, historical individuals who appeared in these Western Zhou materials acquired their significance only as eager imitators of the past actions of their ancestors, and in the end, since they were only allowed to participate in the making of the political order because of their pre-existing membership of their families, they emerged as little more than secondary effects of their genealogical past.

In late Bronze Age China, under the Western Zhou, the genealogical past predominated the historical imagination of the political elite. In a state that was constituted by a complex network of clans, like the Western Zhou, this is hardly surprisingly. Out of the vastness of the past, it was this one piece that mattered to them. The past was invoked as the ground for a demonstration of genealogical continuity, and, by extension, proper membership in the political network of the Western Zhou. But this was not a genealogical past that was supposed to extend indefinitely into distant antiquity; rather it was limited to the founding moments of the Zhou order (including, of course, the triumphant conquest of the Shang). The virtuous and valorous acts of the founders of the dynasty, including King Wen, King Wu, and their associates, provided the authoritative template for political actions; it was an originary political order that is susceptible to corruption through deviation, and therefore it must be continually maintained through faithful emulation. This was another function of the genealogical past, besides demonstrating one's

Western Zhou: Moments of Origins 39

political membership. It was also the only legitimate and authoritative repository of political action.

The Western Zhou ended in the year 771 BCE. Its disintegration, formally in that year and then gradually in effect in the decades afterwards, also marked the beginning of the end of this singular predominance of the genealogical past. This genealogical mapping of the past would not completely disappear, of course; family histories, in a variety of forms, will continue to be written and serve diverse interests in the centuries afterward.[35] However, we will also begin to see, in this long period after the collapse of the Western Zhou order, new and alternative ways of making sense of the past. In a way, the rest of this book is about the many new and different ways of remaking the past after the collapse of this late Bronze Age aristocratic order, and with it a dissipation of this singular focus on the genealogical past, originary moments, and exemplary actions. In the rest of this first chapter of the book, I will begin this account with the examples of two key texts from the early Warring States (*c.* fifth and early fourth centuries BCE), namely the *Analects* and the *Mozi*. Why these two texts, one might ask, among all the texts that came along after the fall of the Zhou order? As I hope to demonstrate in the rest of this chapter, there are special interpretive gains to be made by reading across these three sets of materials, namely the Western Zhou texts, the *Analects*, and the *Mozi*. They are vastly different texts in many respects, to be certain, yet, if we start looking at how they each relate to the idea of the past, a significant contrast emerges. The materials in the *Analects* and the *Mozi* represent two starkly different visions of the past, with two distinct political and ethical agendas; at the same time, they are both subtle, critical responses to the Western Zhou genealogical imagination of the past. Between these three sets of texts, an expansive, contentious landscape of the past emerged.

---

[35] See, for example, Guolong Lai, "Genealogical Statements on Ritual Bronzes of the Spring and Autumn Period," in *Imprints of Kinship: Studies of Recently Discovered Bronze Inscriptions from Ancient China*, ed. Edward L. Shaughnessy (Hong Kong: The Chinese University Press, 2017), 235–260, for how genealogies continued to be written and inscribed on ritual bronzes in the period immediately following the end of the Western Zhou.

40

The *Analects*: Past Cultural Practices, Moral Interiority, and the Deliberative Self

On first reading, one may very well mistake passages in the *Analects* as a continuation, however tenuous and imperfect they may be, of the Western Zhou paradigm of capitalizing the past towards the construction of political relations, especially with respect to its conservative stance.[36] The past, often denoted by the term *gu* 古 ("antiquity") in the *Analects*, is consistently an authoritative standard, a marker for

[36] It is well established, at this point, that the received version of the Confucian *Analects* is a composite text, with various historical layers by multiple hands, that reached its present form only during the Han dynasty. Michael Hunter, in his monograph *Confucius beyond the Analects* (Leiden: Brill, 2017), 317, further suggested that the very idea of an *Analects* was wholly an "artifact of the Western Han period." It remains plausible, according to Hunter (314), that the text does contain materials that date back to the early Warring States (and were then collected and fashioned into the different editions of the *Analects* in later periods). Edward Slingerland, in his review of Hunter's book, *Early China* 41 (2018), 474, further elaborated on this point, concluding that we are "completely justified in continuing to see the *Lun yu* as the most accurate record of the historical Kongzi's teachings, and therefore as a natural starting point for any account of pre-imperial Chinese thought." In this study, basing myself on the philological discussion of the text in the decades past, I use the term "Analects" to refer to a set of ideas that very likely had some currency and circulation in the early Warring States period among the political elite. They may have gained their authoritative voice through their attribution to their putative speaker, namely Confucius, but I do not presume that they had anything to do with the historical Confucius. At the same time, I do presume the possibility of coherence across these seemingly scattered texts from this collection of putative sayings of Confucius. In this respect, my approach is akin to that of Amy Olberding in her series of work on the *Analects*: "I wish, in short, to treat the text as a received text, a text historically presented to readers as containing if not a wholly unified vision, a generally intelligible and coherent vision." Amy Olberding, *Moral Exemplars in the* Analects: *The Good Person Is That* (New York: Routledge, 2012), 2. Moreover, I should note that the arguments that I will be making here are, relatively speaking, chronologically elastic. They are constructed to be robust against a degree of chronological uncertainty of the sources. See the discussion of the compositional history of the text in Tae Hyun Kim and Mark Csikszentmihalyi, "History and Formation of the *Analects*," in *Dao Companion to the* Analects, ed. Amy Olberding (Dordrecht: Springer Netherlands, 2014), 21–36; Bryan W. van Norden's introduction to *Confucius and the* Analects: *New Essays*, ed. Bryan W. van Norden (New York: Oxford University Press, 2002), 13–18; E. Bruce Brooks and A. Taeko Brooks, *The Original Analects: Sayings of Confucius and His Successors* (New York: Columbia University Press, 1998); and D. C. Lau, trans., *Analects* (New York: Penguin Books, 1979), 220–233. For the Han history of the *Analects*, besides the aforementioned monography by Hunter, see Mark Csikszentmihalyi,

The Analects: *Past Cultural Practices*

various self-evident political and ethical ideals. Take, for example, the following passage from Book Four of the *Analects*: "The Master said, 'People of antiquity were sparing in their words. This was because they were afraid their actions may fall short'" (子曰：古者言之不出，恥躬之不逮也).[37] Here, an implicit connection, a positive correlation, is established between exemplary behaviors and the field of antiquity. Antiquity is taken as the temporal location for exemplary actions, and just as we are far removed from antiquity, we have also fallen from behaving in exemplary ways. Similarly, in Book Fourteen, the Master said, "In antiquity, people studied for their own sake; nowadays, they do so for the sake of others" (古之學者為己，今之學者為人).[38] There is a clear division between antiquity and the present, and they are self-evidently correlated with what is considered ideal and what is not.

This positive valorization of antiquity is evident in many passages of the *Analects*. The Master himself, Confucius, declared his fondness for it time and again. For instance, in Book Seven, he says, "I was not born understanding anything. I love antiquity. I work diligently to comprehend it" (我非生而知之者，好古，敏以求之者也).[39] Here, there is not even a specification of what exactly was good in antiquity, but the entire field of antiquity was simply considered an enlightening thing. And, of course, the idea of antiquity also figures in one of the most celebrated lines from the *Analects*: "The Master said, 'I transmit and do not innovate. I trust and am fond of antiquity. I humbly dare to compare myself to Old Peng'" (子曰：述而不作，信而好古，竊比於我老彭).[40] Not only did Confucius profess his fondness for studying antiquity as a means for self-cultivation, but here he went one step further to claim that he does not innovate at all but only "transmit" (*shu* 述) what had already been done in the past.

One may argue for a clear resemblance here between the *Analects* and the Western Zhou materials with respect to their apparent cultural and political conservatism. They both attribute their ideals to a time before the present, for instance, and the notion of "transmission" (*shu* 述) in the *Analects* would seem to be quite comparable to the ideal of emulative and imitative actions (*xing*) espoused in the Western Zhou

"Confucius and the *Analects* in the Hàn," in Van Norden, *Confucius and His Successors*, 134–162.
[37] Yang Bojun, *Lunyu yizhu*, 4.22. [38] Ibid., 14.24. [39] Ibid., 7.20.
[40] Ibid., 7.1.

42   *Time out of Joint*

bronze inscriptions. However, upon closer reading of the *Analects*, it would become clear that in fact these superficial resemblances are no more than structural remains of a subtle but radical deconstruction of the Western Zhou paradigm for capitalizing the past as a genealogical field. These *Analects* passages, as I will now argue, represent a deliberate departure from the Western Zhou paradigm, by transposing the source of political authority from the genealogical past to the moral center of individuals through a reversal of the relationship between men and history.

To begin with, let us return to this idea of *gu*, or antiquity, in the *Analects*. It is clear that Confucius speaks very approvingly of *gu*, that "antiquity" is something that we should learn from somehow. Suppose one agrees with Confucius; then what and how is this person supposed to learn exactly? What is the actual content of this "antiquity"? If we were to follow Confucius in "trusting" and "loving" antiquity, what exactly are we trusting and loving here? In the world of the Western Zhou, the answer would have been the exemplary actions of one's ancestors, typically from the founding moments of the dynasty, but nothing of the kind can be identified in the *Analects*. First of all, unlike the Western Zhou texts, there appears to be virtually no interest in the significance of moments of origins, or originary actions, the type that we see in the poem "Shengmin," with its emphasis on the first creation of agriculture, or numerous bronze inscriptions in their frequent reiterations of the founding of the Zhou. In the *Analects*, there is no interest in the founding accomplishments of King Wen and King Wu (or any other dynastic founders) as a point of positive reference. The only mention of King Wen in the *Analects* is a rumination on his passing.[41]

Second, despite the importance of familial relations in the *Analects* for its ethical program, there is not a single mention of an ancestor in it. There are only nuclear families in the *Analects*, while the families in Western Zhou materials were always the extended (patriarchal) lineages. A Western Zhou official may proclaim that he was emulating his distant ancestor from the first years of the dynasty, while in the *Analects*, one's virtue is cultivated through immediate familial (or

---

[41] Ibid., 9.5.

The Analects: *Past Cultural Practices*   43

official) relations.[42] There are no distant ancestors populating the landscape of the past; the family is a much smaller unit in the *Analects*.

The past – or "antiquity" – matters a great deal in the *Analects* but it is not at all the same past that we saw in Western Zhou materials. Then what is it exactly? Let us now turn to a few *Analects* passages that refer specifically to the contents of antiquity:

The Master said, "In archery hitting the target is not the point – people are not all of equal strength. That was the way of antiquity."

子曰。射不主皮。為力不同。科古之道也。[43]

Duke Ai asked Zai Wo about the altar to the god of the soil. Zai Wo replied, "The Xia rulers planted it with pines, the men of Yin [i.e. Shang] planted it with cedars, and the men of Zhou plant it with chestnuts. This, they say, made the common people tremble." When the Master heard of this, he said, "Completed affairs one does not comment on; things done one does not carp over; what is past one does not criticize."

哀公問社於宰我。宰我對曰。夏后氏以松。殷人以柏。周人以栗。曰使民戰栗。子聞之曰。成事不說。遂事不諫。既往不咎。[44]

Yan Yuan asked about how to order the state. The Master said, "Use the Xia calendar, ride in the chariots of the Yin, wear the caps of the Zhou, and for music, the Shao and Wu. Do away with the Zheng tunes and stay away from artful talkers. The Zheng tunes are excessive, and artful talkers are dangerous."

顏淵問為邦。子曰。行夏之時。乘殷之輅。服周之冕。樂則韶舞。放鄭聲。遠佞人。鄭聲淫。佞人殆。[45]

This is far from an exhaustive inventory of passages from the *Analects* that refer to the past; more relevant passages will be brought up later. However, even with this limited set, we can already discern a distinct pattern in the articulation of the past in the *Analects*. Instead of moments of origins or exemplary actions of ancestors, the past is

---

[42] There are numerous passages in the *Analects* devoted to this point. For a most concise statement, see passage 1.7, which says that learning is achieved through perfecting one's relationship with one's parents (*fumu* 父母), rulers (*jun* 君), and friends (*pengyou* 朋友).

[43] Yang Bojun, *Lunyu yizhu*, 3.16.   [44] Ibid., 3.21.   [45] Ibid., 15.11.

painted as *a repertoire of cultural practices*.[46] It is interesting to note that although the text does ascribe specific cultural practices to different periods in history, there is no suggestion of a progressive narrative at all. It is not the case that one practice evolved into another one, or that there is a logic at all behind the replacement of one practice by another from one period to the next. It is simply that people did different things at different times (and places), and we, in the present day, have some knowledge of what was done in the past.

The enumeration of these different cultural practices, as in the passages cited above, serves more than just antiquarian curiosity. Rather, they are almost always shot through with an evaluative dimension. For instance, in the second passage cited above (3.21), Zai Wo criticized the Zhou practice, and Confucius criticized him in turn for being unduly critical. In the last passage (15.11), the different past practices mentioned were meant to address the question of how to govern a state, and so the endorsement of the Xia calendar, Yin chariots, and Zhou caps was effectively Confucius' positive evaluation of them. His warning against "Zheng tunes," on the other hand, implies a negative evaluation. These are inventories of cultural practices where each item is critically graded. See, for another example: "The Master said, 'Zhou studied the two [earlier] dynasties. Elegant and refined were its ways. I follow Zhou'" (子曰。周監於二代。郁郁乎文哉。吾從周).[47] The Master studied and assessed past practices in search of efficacious instruments for his own edification in the present.

A knowledge of past cultural practices *demands* one's evaluation, in order that one decides which practice to follow in the present. At a very general level, this agrees with the Western Zhou idea that one must always follow precedents. But it also introduces a new intermediary element, namely this evaluative moment. In the Western Zhou paradigm, one identifies and imitates exemplary actions within one's genealogical past; evaluation is therefore unnecessary and irrelevant. In the *Analects*, however, one is not bound to just the genealogical past;

---

[46] Another term that I could use here is "rituals" (*li* 禮), a term of central importance in the *Analects* itself, to describe these various cultural practices from the past. I opted to use the term "cultural practices" instead for it is even more all-encompassing, and therefore a more accurate rendition. For the idea of *li* in the *Analects*, see Kwong-loi Shun, "*Ren* and *Li* in the Analects," in Bryan W. van Norden, *Confucius and the* Analects: *New Essays* (New York: Oxford University Press, 2002), 53–72.

[47] Yang Bojun, *Lunyu yizhu*, 3.14.

The Analects: *Past Cultural Practices*   45

exemplary actions from any period, by whomever, are all possible models for emulation in the present. Then, after identifying them, one evaluates them against one another in order to decide which one to follow. There is a structural similarity here between the Western Zhou materials and the *Analects*: wary of harmful innovations and deviations from past practices, one should identify and follow exemplary actions in the past. But the *Analects* has abandoned the genealogical dimension integral to the Western Zhou paradigm. Moving beyond the confines of the genealogical past, the *Analects* conceives of an open, much more expansive, historical field with a diverse repository of exemplary cultural practices, all of which are potential candidates as useful models for the present.

This new model in seeing and using the past in the *Analects* depends on the feasibility of this evaluative component. How does one actually evaluate? What are the criteria for this evaluation? What is the site on which this evaluation takes place? The *Analects* passages never gesture towards the existence or even the possibility of an objective set of standards for deliberation (unlike the *Mozi*, as we shall discuss in the next section). Rather, it seems to suggest the exact opposite – the evaluations are always subjective. It is always a personal decision, one that emanates from the moral interiority of an individual. In the end, there is no impersonal, external standard that we can rely on, but the decision ultimately rests with the individual himself. Confucius chose to "follow Zhou," and not the other two earlier dynasties; the text gave no reason for it except for his own moral certitude.

To posit the possibility of and necessity for these personal evaluations is to attribute a deliberative capacity to the figure of the individual.[48] Individuals had to deliberate too in the Western Zhou, between whether to follow or not to follow their ancestors' actions. But in the *Analects*, the individual is no longer confronted with just an either–or decision. He has to weigh alternatives against one another and decide on the one for emulation in the present. In the Western

---

[48] I should add that by "individuals," I refer to all human beings. I agree with
    Heiner Roetz's assessment that "Confucian anthropology ... denies any
    relevant natural distinction between men." See his discussion of "The Concept
    of 'Man'" in the monograph *Confucian Ethics of the Axial Age:
    A Reconstruction under the Aspect of the Breakthrough toward
    Postconventional Thinking* (Albany: State University of New York Press, 1993),
    123–126.

46   *Time out of Joint*

Zhou materials, exemplary actions are simply what one's ancestors did successfully, particularly the originary actions within one's genealogical past, but in the *Analects*, it is an open question on what is indeed exemplary and efficacious in the present; ultimately, each person decides according to moral biases interior to himself. Liberated from the confines and dictates of the genealogical past, one now faces uncertain choices.[49]

"The Good Person is *That*," as Amy Olberding eloquently encapsulates, in the subtitle of her monograph, her reading of the "exemplarist virtue ethics" in the *Analects*.[50] It is a moral vision that, according to Olberding, begins not with "precise definition" or "elaborate conceptual schemata" but with our admiration and emulation of one or another moral exemplar. "The virtuous person is *that* and the theoretical charge rests in devising a satisfying account of what our various instances of *that* share."[51] This is resonant with my own reading of the

---

[49] On the "deliberative capacity" of individuals in the *Analects* and classical Confucianism, there is a staggering amount of scholarship that focuses on the definition of the Confucian human subject and his nature. I am particularly inspired by the discussion of the distressed moral subjects in Michael D. K. Ing, *The Vulnerability of Integrity in Early Confucian Thought* (New York: Oxford University Press, 2017), as well as the importance of exemplarism and emulation in Olberding, *Moral Exemplars in the* Analects. On the specific question of individualism and conformity, I found particularly helpful the discussions in Stephen A. Wilson, "Conformity, Individuality, and the Nature of Virtue: A Classical Confucian Contribution to Contemporary Ethical Reflection," in Van Norden, *Confucius and the* Analects, 94–118; and Erica Brindley, "Moral Autonomy and Individual Sources of Authority in the *Analects*," *Journal of Chinese Philosophy* 38.2 (2011), 257–273. More distantly, I was also inspired by the discussion of the "self" in classical Confucianism by Kwong-loi Shun, "Early Confucian Moral Psychology," in *The Dao Companion to Classical Confucian Philosophy* (Dordrecht: Springer Netherlands, 2014), 263–289; as well as his book chapter "Conception of the Person in Early Confucian Thought," in *Confucian Ethics: A Comparative Study of Self, Autonomy, and Community*, ed. Kwong-Loi Shun and David B. Wong (New York: Cambridge University Press, 2004), 183–202. This view of the role and capacity of the individuals has departed significantly from the older paradigm, most influentially set by Herbert Fingarette in his *Confucius: The Secular as Sacred* (New York: Harper and Row, 1972), where he argued against the very notion of an "inner psychic life" in the *Analects*. See also the related reflections and arguments in David Hall and Roger Ames, in their *Thinking through Confucius* (Albany: State University of New York Press, 1987).

[50] Olberding, *Moral Exemplars in the* Analects, 76–99. Also see her article, "Dreaming of the Duke of Zhou: Exemplarism and the *Analects*," *Journal of Chinese Philosophy* 35.4 (2008), 626.

[51] Olberding, "Dreaming of the Duke of Zhou," 627, emphasis in the original.

The Analects: *Past Cultural Practices* 47

Analects, but I would add to it that these exemplars that we choose to emulate – such as the Duke of Zhou – are often figures from the past (or "historical notables," in Olberding's formulation).[52] In my reading, there are also disembodied cultural practices from the past that one may emulate. There is a strong historical dimension to this "exemplarist" ethics in the *Analects*; the search for morally exemplary individuals and practices often prompts one to rummage through the field of the past.

It was in the early Warring States period that we can observe the emergence of this figure of the deliberative individual, across different texts that have survived from this period. It is a new figure whose exercise of his deliberative capacity would have great political consequences. In the case of the *Analects* passages, we see a great faith in the capability of individuals in effecting changes and establishing order. The self-cultivation program outlined in the text – pivoted around key terms such as "humaneness" (*ren* 仁) and "rituals" (*li* 禮) – can be seen as an attempt to cultivate this moral interior of individuals. Once properly cultivated, they would be able to choose and follow the right course of actions based on an educated assessment of the relative efficacy of past cultural practices.

There are many facets and expressions of this deliberative individual in the *Analects*. For instance, there is this attention to our reflective interiority as an object of cultivation:

The Master said, "When you see a worthy person, think about how you can equal him. When you see an unworthy person, reflect on your own conduct."

子曰。見賢思齊焉。見不賢而內自省也。[53]

The Master said, "It's hopeless! I have yet to see anyone who can recognize his faults, look inside himself, and put the blame there."

子曰。已矣乎。吾未見能見其過。而內自訟者也。[54]

This focus on the utility of introspection, the very idea of a reflective "interior" (*nei* 內) within an individual, has a radical quality that becomes apparent when juxtaposed with materials from the Western Zhou. Once entirely irrelevant in the political imagination of the late Bronze Age under the Western Zhou, the moral interiority of men is now

---

[52] Ibid., 631. [53] Yang Bojun, *Lunyu yizhu*, 4.17. [54] Ibid., 5.27.

48   *Time out of Joint*

a central concern of ethics and fully integrated into the political discourse in the *Analects*.

This deliberative capacity of individuals, situated within their moral interiority, is a primary object of cultivation in the *Analects*. Cultivation practices denoted by terms such as *xue* 學 ("learning"), *sheng* 省 ("reflection"), and perhaps most importantly *li* 禮 ("rituals"), elaborated throughout the text, all ultimately aimed at refining this responsive moral center that resides within each of us. The goal is to achieve *ren*, or "humaneness," a proper ethical anchor within a person that enables consistently proper decision making from one context to another. To be cultivated, or to be *ren*, is not simply to be "ethical" or "good," whatever those terms may mean in the context of the *Analects*, but more precisely, it is to have the ability to decide what is good or bad, or what is "likable" or not: "The Master said, 'Only the humane person is able to like others and is able to hate others'" (子曰：唯仁者能好人能惡人).[55] To be *ren* is be able to exercise one's deliberative capacity.[56]

In Western Zhou bronze inscriptions, one is said to *xing* or "emulate" past exemplary actions. That word has all but disappeared in the *Analects*. Instead, Confucius *cong* 從 or "follows" past cultural practices (e.g. the aforementioned "I follow Zhou," 3.14). While the term *xing* suggests a mechanical imitation of something outside oneself, the term *cong* connotes choices and deliberation. To follow one thing is to not follow another. The passage from *xing* to *cong*, from rote imitation to evaluative adaptation, marked the emergence of the deliberative individual as a legitimate political subject after the fall of the Zhou order.[57]

In this new world articulated through these passages of the *Analects*, individuals and their decisions are now what essentially guarantee

---

[55] Ibid., 4.3.

[56] This point can be considered in conjunction with Michael Puett's argument that, in the *Analects*, individuals are born with "raw substance" that we must work on in order to give it proper patterns. Puett, *The Ambivalence of Creation*, 43–51. I am, of course, isolating one meaning of the term that I found particularly prominent in the context of the discussion here. For a broader, insightful overview, see Karyn Lai, "*Ren*: An Exemplary Life," in Olberding, *Dao Companion to the* Analects, 83–94.

[57] Contrary to my reading, Savage sees much a much greater degree of similarity and continuity between the Western Zhou model and the *Analects*, in terms of the idea of emulation. See "Archetypes, Model Emulation, and the Confucian Gentleman," 18–25.

The Analects: *Past Cultural Practices*   49

continuing order, in contrast to the idea that a most ideal political order always pre-exists an individual in the Western Zhou materials. It is therefore not surprising to see that the *Analects* attributes tremendous power to individual historical figures. For instance, in one of the best-known passages, Confucius ruminates on the passing of King Wen:

The Master's life was endangered in Kuang. He said, "King Wen is deceased, but his culture remains here with me. If Heaven had intended to destroy that culture, then those who come after him could not have inherited that culture. But if Heaven is not ready to destroy culture, what can the people of Kuang do to me?"

子畏於匡。曰。文王既沒文不在茲乎。天之將喪斯文也。後死者不得與於斯文也。天之未喪斯文也。匡人其如予何。[58]

Here, the survival of a particular order, a whole culture, hinges on just one person. Elsewhere, Confucius lavished praise on the character and accomplishments of past sage-kings such as Yao 堯 and Yu 禹 (e.g. 8.18, 8.19, 8.21). More subtly, this is also true in his praise for Boyi and Shuqi, the two figures with whom I started this chapter. They were failed dissidents, but nevertheless, they did forcefully exercise their deliberative capacity to the point of their own death. In the *Analects*, individuals and their decisions have tremendous historical agency. In turn, past figures and their work all become part of the historical repository of cultural practices that one should study, evaluate, and follow (or not follow).

This sharp turn to individuals as a potential source of order also signals a transposition of the locus of political authority. In the Western Zhou, the recipe for establishing order lies in a set of exemplary actions in the distant genealogical past external to oneself, while in the *Analects*, the source for political order is ultimately located in the moral center of individuals and the decisions that they make. In this sense, the locus of political authority has shifted from an external set of past actions to the internal deliberative capacity of men in the present. And with this, there is also a reversal in the relation between history and individuals in the *Analects*. In the Western Zhou materials, history as a series of originary exemplary actions defines and delimits the possible realm of actions, the basic script that one must follow. One is measured by the degree of conformity with or of deviance from them.

---

[58] Yang Bojun, *Lunyu yizhu*, 9.5.

50   *Time out of Joint*

In the *Analects*, however, the past is now a function of one's individual deliberation; one cultivates his ethical center in order to formulate judgments about the past, and decides which particular practice is worthy to be continued in the present. The authority that the past once had over individuals is now transposed to the individuals themselves over the past.

To conclude this discussion of the *Analects*, let me briefly note the social location of this new figure of the deliberative individual. Earlier, we observed that the *Analects* has largely forsaken the genealogical dimension that was trenchant in the Western Zhou materials, where one is authorized to act only as a descendant of a certain clan or otherwise bears some genealogical ties to the royal clan. As we also noted in the conclusion to the section on the Western Zhou, the realm of meaningful and effective political actions was essentially reduced to just the contexts of the family and the state. In the *Analects*, the family and the state are still a very significant context for actions, as is evident in the famous dictum by Confucius: "The ruler should act as a ruler; the subject, a subject; the father, a father, the son, a son" (君君。臣臣。父父。子子).[59] However, while family and state are clearly still viable and important contexts for the cultivation of the self and the establishment of order, they are no longer the only contexts for effective action in the *Analects*. The decoupling of exemplary precedents and the (absent) genealogical past (in relation to the royal genealogies) in the *Analects* effectively means that it is no longer a prerequisite to be an heir or an official in order to act in a politically meaningful way. Instead of having to claim membership of a certain family or the state for any political legitimacy, individuals are now authorized to act simply based on their innate deliberative capacity, this ethical potential that we all presumably possess. Authority comes *not* from our genealogical membership but from the demonstrated refinement of our moral interiority as individuals.

One of the clearest expressions of this opening up of the contexts for politically meaningful action is the idea of friendship in the *Analects*. Of the different cardinal human relationships that are the means for and expression of one's ethical cultivation in the *Analects*, only friendship represents a horizontal association. The others, i.e. parents, rulers,

[59] Ibid., 12.13.

The Analects: *Past Cultural Practices* 51

brothers, spouses, are socially hierarchical by definition.[60] The possibility of this voluntary horizontal association, which lies outside one's family and state, implies that there is a remainder of the self that falls outside the family and the state, that a person can and does have an identity beyond just being his father's son or his ruler's subject. Moreover, in the *Analects*, friendship is considered to be at least as powerful as any of the other cardinal relationships for self-cultivation. Being a good friend is as important as being a filial son or a loyal subject:

Zixia said, "If he treats worthy persons as worthy and is respectful to them, does all in his power to serve his father and mother, gives his best in the service of the ruler, and in dealings with friends is faithful to his word, though some may say he lacks learning, I would surely call him learned!"

子夏曰。賢賢易色。事父母能竭其力。事君能致其身。與朋友交。言而有信。雖曰未學。吾必謂之學矣。[61]

This passage clearly indicates that there are three social sites for self-cultivation: family, state, and friendship. The following passage gives a more elaborate description of the ethical utility of friendship. It is a pathway towards achieving the ethical ideal of *ren*: "Master Zeng said, 'The gentleman uses the arts in acquiring friends and uses friends in helping him to achieve humaneness' (曾子曰。君子以文會友。以友輔仁)."[62] This elevation of the significance of friendship to the same level as that of familial and political associations is a new development in the early Warring States period.[63] There were people who were friends too

---

[60] I should also mention the presence of the master–disciple relationship as the fifth kind of hierarchical human relation in addition to the four that are mentioned here. Curiously, unlike the other four, this hierarchical relationship is never theorized but only performed in the text of the *Analects* itself. See David Elstein, "Beyond the Five Relationships: Teachers and Worthies in Early Chinese Thought," *Philosophy East and West* 62.3 (2012), 375–391; and Denecke, *The Dynamics of Masters Literature*, 90–127.

[61] Yang Bojun, *Lunyu yizhu*, 1.17.   [62] Ibid., 12.24.

[63] There is very little scholarship on the subject of friendship in early China. See Aat Vervoorn, "Friendship in Ancient China," *East Asian history* 27 (2004), 1–32; Michael Nylan, "On the Antique Rhetoric of Friendship," *Asiatische Studien–Études asiatiques* 68.4 (2014), 1225–1265; Yuanguo He, "Confucius and Aristotle on Friendship: A Comparative Study," *Frontiers of Philosophy in China* 2.2 (2007), 291–307; and Norman Kutcher, "The Fifth Relationship: Dangerous Friendships in the Confucian Context," *American Historical Review* 105.5 (2000), 1615–1629.

52 *Time out of Joint*

in the Western Zhou, of course, but with effective political action limited to just the family or the state, as we have discussed, friendship simply did not figure in the Western Zhou political imagination. This positive valorization of friendship in the *Analects,* however, points back to the primacy of this new figure of the deliberative individual that emerged in this period. It is possible now to conceive of an individual as possessing a singular identity, based upon his deliberative interiority, who can relate horizontally to other individuals, compared with being defined through vertical relations as the descendant of a certain family or the subject of a state. Individuals are now imagined as independent ethical entities who can roam around in a space outside, or between, the family and state, establishing associations with one another without risking political irrelevance or oblivion. Moreover, it is now in this new tertiary space that one can cultivate his moral interiority in order to partake in the making of political orders.[64]

In this reading, the seemingly innocuous opening line of the *Analects,* on the pleasure of seeing a friend from afar, is no longer just an expression of a quotidian sentiment but an eloquent pronouncement for the arrival of a new episteme:

The Master said, "Studying, and from time to time going over what you've learned—that's enjoyable, isn't it? To have a friend come from a long way off—that's a pleasure, isn't it? Others don't understand him, but he doesn't resent it—that's the true gentleman, isn't it?"

子曰：「學而時習之，不亦說乎？有朋自遠方來，不亦樂乎？人不知而不慍，不亦君子乎？」[65]

The use of rhetorical questions (i.e. "that's a pleasure, isn't it?") invites and presumes spontaneous agreement from the audience, thus establishing the self-evident quality of this new worldview. In this new

---

[64] It is worth noting that this introduction of a new space outside the family and the state recalls another philosophical scheme that arose after the collapse of an aristocratic class. I have in mind G. W. F. Hegel's *Philosophy of Right,* first published in 1821. There, Hegel divided the cultivation of an "ethical life" of an individual into three spheres: family, civil society, and the state. The idea of a "civil society" where individuals fraternize with one another, as an "object of his particular aims," in the *Philosophy of Right* resonates with this sphere of friendship that we see in texts of the early Warring States period, including the *Analects.* Georg Wilhelm Friedrich Hegel, *Hegel's Philosophy of Right,* trans. T. M. Knox (London and New York: Oxford University Press, 1967), 122.

[65] Yang Bojun, *Lunyu yizhu,* 1.1.

The Mozi: *The Origin of Disorder* 53

world according to the *Analects*, the past is now imagined as a repertoire of cultural practices that demand evaluation and interpretation for adaptation in the present by deliberative individuals presumed to possess a moral interiority that can and must be cultivated within the family, state, or circle of friends. This deconstruction of the Western Zhou model for the capitalization of the past led to the corrosion of political authority in the originary actions in the genealogical past; the *Analects* sees in this new figure of the deliberative individual, liberated from the confines of the family and state, a new source of historical agency and political authority for imagining a new order for the future.[66]

The *Mozi*: The Origin of Disorder and the Problem with the Deliberative Self

In this section we turn to the *Mozi*, not engaging with the entire received text but only with the "Core Chapters" that contain materials that likely date to the first half of the Warring States period (or, more narrowly speaking, the long fourth century BCE).[67] Similar to the

[66] I use the term "deconstruction" specifically here, in the sense that components of the original structure, namely the Western Zhou model, were retained in the *Analects* while their relationship to each other was reconfigured. The idea of exemplarism persisted, for instance, but the exemplary models were no longer situated within the genealogical past but transposed to the open historical field.

[67] For a recent state-of-the-field summary of the textual history and dating of the *Mozi*, see the "Introduction: Different Voices in the *Mozi*: Studies of an Evolving Text," by Carine Defoort and Nicolas Standaert, in *The Mozi as an Evolving Text: Different Voices in Early Chinese Thought*, ed. Carine Defoort and Nicolas Standaert (Leiden: Brill, 2013), 1–34, esp. 1–19. The use of the term "Core Chapters" follows A. C. Graham in his series of important works on the *Mozi*. It refers to Chapters 8 to 39 of the text. See A. C. Graham, *Divisions in Early Mohism Reflected in the Core Chapters of Mo-tzu* (Singapore: Institute of East Asian Philosophies, 1985). Watanabe Takashi's study of the evolution of the Mohist tradition remains the most detailed in modern scholarship to date; his suggestion is that the Core Chapters were produced from the late fifth century, soon after Mozi's death, to the end of the Warring States period; see his *Kodai Chūgoku shisō no kenkyū: Kōshi den no keisei to Ju Boku shūdan no shisō to kōdō* 古代中國思想の研究: 孔子傳の形成と儒墨集團の思想と行動 (Tokyo: Sōbunsha, 1973). My approach to using the *Mozi* for the arguments of this study is similar to those with regard to the use of the *Analects* (see note 36 above). I take it that these were ideas, now preserved in this part of the *Mozi*, possibly circulated in the early Warring States. It is not a unitary work from a single pair of hands, but that does not necessarily pre-empt the possibility of

54   *Time out of Joint*

preceding discussion of the *Analects*, we will observe a set of departures
from the paradigm embodied in the Western Zhou materials. But more
than that, we will also observe a complex set of differences and overlaps
between the *Mozi* and the *Analects* on how they each imagine the past
for their respective political visions. While the *Analects* never explicitly
refers to the *Mozi*, neither the text nor the eponymous figure, the *Mozi*
formulates many of its arguments as polemics against the ideas and
practices of the Confucians (*ru* 儒) or even the figure of Confucius
himself. There are two chapters not so subtly entitled "Against the
Confucians" ("Fei Ru" 非儒) (only one of which is still extant as
Chapter 39), and there are also two triads of chapters (i.e. the "Fei
le" 非樂 and "Fei ming" 非命 triads) that vehemently inveighed against
practices of musical performance and the idea of fate, both of which the
Mozi attributes to the Confucian tradition of its time.[68] Given its
dramatic opposition to the ideas and practices of the Confucians, one
might expect to find in the *Mozi* a very different, if not entirely antithetical, use of the past. This may appear to be the case on a first reading
of the *Mozi*, but in fact, as we delve into the text, we shall discover no
such simple diametrical opposition between the two texts at all.
Instead, what we will discover first is an ideological common ground,
founded on the figure of the deliberative individual that we discussed
earlier. Their well-known disagreements on a range of political and
ethical issues, as I hope to demonstrate, are not the result of two
distinct, rival sets of philosophical beliefs or cultural commitments.[69]
Instead, they stemmed from two different interpretations of this common figure of the deliberative individual as a historically and politically
significant subject. It is the same basic stuff with which the *Mozi* and

> coherence at a certain level behind the ideas of these various chapters. In fact, the
> very idea of it being an "evolving" text already implies the recognition that it is
> a single entity or at least a coherent ecosystem of ideas.
>
> [68] I refer to the edition of the *Mozi* by Sun Yirang孫詒讓, *Mozi jian gu* 墨子閒詁
> (Beijing: Zhonghua shuju, 2001). Citations will include chapter number
> followed by page numbers.
>
> [69] The theatre of philosophical rivalry between the "Confucians" and the
> "Mohists" is a staple of many accounts of early Chinese thought. See, for just
> a few of literally hundreds of examples, Ian Johnston's concise account of it in
> his *The Mozi: A Complete Translation* (New York: Columbia University Press,
> 2010), lxvii; Benjamin I. Schwartz, *The World of Thought in Ancient China*
> (Cambridge, MA: The Belknap Press of Harvard University Press, 1985),
> 135–172; and Yu-lan Fung, *A Short History of Chinese Philosophy* (New York:
> The Macmillan Company, 1948), 49–59.

The Mozi: The Origin of Disorder

the *Analects* constructed their own landscape of the past, but the edifices that they each erected in the end would be vastly different and very much at odds with each other.

Please allow me to begin at a somewhat far-fetched place, not immediately the treatment of antiquity in the Core Chapters but the method of its analysis. That, to me, is in fact one of the most striking features of the *Mozi*.[70] The Core Chapters are a sprawling whole that engages with a very diverse set of topics. They appear to cohere, in the eyes of at least this reader, not over the similarity or relatedness of these different subject matters, but for their consistent method of analysis. To put this even more strongly, the specific arguments about various subjects seem, at times, to be incidental to a demonstration of a certain supposedly universal hermeneutic that is applicable for a proper analysis of any object. One may say, for example, that the chapter "Condemning Music I" ("Fei yue shang" 非樂上) is as much a declaration of the Mohist's distaste for lavish musical performances as it is more fundamentally a demonstration of the power of the Mohist mode of argumentation that allowed its author(s) to arrive at such an iconoclastic position. In this sense, the *Mozi* is a text about its own methodology; its teachings in the end lie not in the collective whole of its pronouncements on the various subjects, be it music, ghosts, or fatalism, but in this idea of a systematic methodology, an objective structure of reasoning, that can and should be applied to all things towards an aggregate understanding of the world.

What, then, is this methodology of the *Mozi*? For such a hermeneutically interested text, it is not surprising to find in it a declaration of its own method of analysis. It is in the chapter "Against Fate III" ("Fei ming xia" 非命下). It begins with an argument for the necessity of a pre-established "standard" (*yi* 儀) when making statements:

Master Mozi spoke, saying: "In general, it is not permissible, when making a statement, to fail to establish a standard (*yi*) first and [then] speak. If you do not establish a standard first and [then] speak, it is like using the upper part of a potter's revolving wheel and trying to establish the direction of the sunrise and sunset with it. I think that, although there is a distinction between the sunrise and the sunset, you will, in the end, certainly never be able to find it and establish it."

---

[70] To avoid being repetitious, "Mozi" refers to the Core Chapters of the *Mozi* heretofore.

子墨子言曰：凡出言談，則必可而不先立儀而言。若不先立儀而言，
譬之猶運鈞之上而立朝夕焉也。我以為雖有朝夕之辯，必將終未可得而
從定也。[71]

Then, it continues to state the three specific "criteria" (*fa* 法), constitutive of this common standard (*yi*), that must be met by any statement:

This is why, for a statement, there are three criteria (*fa*). What are the three criteria? I say there is examining it, there is determining its origin, and there is putting it to use. How do you examine it? You examine the affairs of the first sages and great kings. How do you determine its origin? You look at the evidence from the ears and eyes of the multitude. How do you put it to use? You set it out and use it in governing the state, considering its effect on the ten thousand people. These are called the "three criteria."

是故言有三法。何謂三法？曰：有考之者，有原之者，有用之者。惡乎考
之？考先聖大王之事。惡乎原之？察眾之耳目之請？惡乎用之？發而為政
乎國，察萬民而觀之。此謂三法也。[72]

The three criteria for any argument are therefore based, respectively, on historical exemplars, collective senses, and a calculus of effectiveness. Of course, one should be wary of such an overt declaration of methods; there is always the possibility of a gap between what the text says it is doing and what it actually does. Nevertheless, putting this question aside for the moment, in the context of this study, it is important to note the essential, integral role that history is given in this text the *Mozi*. It clearly declares that historical knowledge, specifically the deeds of exemplars from the past, is essential for the formulation of any truthful and meaningful statement in the present-day world.

True to its own words, we do find numerous invocations of the past as argumentative means throughout the *Mozi*. Historical figures and their deeds, often prefaced by temporal markers such as *gu* 古 ("antiquity") and *xi* 昔 ("formerly"), are cited as compelling evidence for

---

[71] Sun Yirang, *Mozi xiangu*, 37.278. Unless otherwise noted, translations from the *Mozi* are adaptations from Johnston, *The Mozi: A Complete Translation*. I have also benefited from consultation of the translation by John Knoblock and Jeffrey Riegel, *Mozi: A Study and Translation of the Ethical and Political Writings* (Berkeley: Institute of East Asian Studies, University of California, Berkeley, 2013).

[72] Sun Yirang, *Mozi xiangu*, 37.278.

The Mozi: The Origin of Disorder

whatever arguments the text happens to be making. The ubiquity of this rhetorical strategy, this persistent recourse to the past, substantiates the essential role that historical knowledge is supposed to play in its own method. I am of course not alone in having made this observation. Mark Edward Lewis once remarked that "the Mohist canon routinely, indeed obsessively, inscribes its social program in an imagined antiquity and appeals to the authority of past writings."[73] Miranda Brown expanded on this point much further, and made a provocative, persuasive suggestion that the early Mohists may have in fact remade "ancient authority," by strategically expanding the field of antiquity and elaborating on the legendary sage-kings (*shengwang* 聖王) of the distant past for their own argumentative ends.[74] In the Core Chapters, invocations of the past are not only pervasive but also purposeful; they are essential and instrumental to the text's arguments.

This is admittedly a simple observation to make. One only needs to read through the text to discover the ubiquity of the past in the *Mozi*. The more difficult questions would be, as we had asked of the *Analects*, what is the content of the past in the *Mozi*? What, out of the infinitude of the past, was singled out to be recounted as persuasive historical evidence for its arguments? How was the past imagined in the *Mozi* and to what end? And in this respect, how does it compare to the models in the Western Zhou materials and the near-contemporary *Analects*? Let us now address these larger questions, by an examination of how the past is represented and made to function in the Core Chapters of the *Mozi*.

Reading the passages concerning the past in the *Mozi*, one predominant theme becomes immediately apparent. It is the text's celebratory invocations of legendary kings and sages from antiquity. References to their civilizing innovations and enlightened conduct in antiquity dominate the accounts of the past in the text. Sometime, these past legendary figures are unspecified, simply referred to as "sages" (*sheng* 聖) and "kings" (*wang* 王) from time past (*xian* 先, *xi* 昔, or, more commonly,

---

[73] Lewis, *Writing and Authority*, 111.

[74] Miranda Brown, "Mozi's Remaking of Ancient Authority," in Defoort and Standaert, *The Mozi as an Evolving Text: Different Voices in Early Chinese Thought*, 143–174. Brown offers a persuasive argument that it was likely the early Mohists who were responsible for the widespread use of the term "sage-kings" (*shengwang* 聖王) beginning in the fourth century, for the elaborate promotion of their accounts for political debates in this period.

58 *Time out of Joint*

gu 古). Out of the many such passages in the *Mozi*, the most elaborate would certainly be Chapter Six, "On Eschewing Faults" ("Ciguo" 辭過). It is almost entirely devoted to recounting the civilizing progress made by the "sages" (*shengren* 聖人) in antiquity, through their introduction of the ideas of shelter, clothing, agriculture, and transportation. In each case, the rationale behind the sage's invention, his intent to improve the human condition, is described in an approving and laudatory language, followed by a critique against contemporary perversion of the same practices through their superfluous extravagance harmful to the people and the state at large.[75] Elsewhere in the *Mozi*, these unnamed "sages" are celebrated not only for their introduction of civilizing initiatives, but also for their enlightened conduct and proper rulership. Various Mohist virtues – such as frugality (*jie* 節) and impartial caring (*jian'ai* 兼愛) – are said to have been championed by these figures in the distant past. For instance, in the chapter "Moderation in Use II" ("Jie yong zhong" 節用中), the argument for the virtue of frugality was made not only in theoretical terms but also in historical terms through these legendary past figures. It suggested that this virtue was embraced by certain "enlightened kings" (*mingwang* 明王) and "sages" (*shengren*) in antiquity, which in turn account for their supposed effectiveness as rulers of their subjects.[76] The implicit but unmistakable criticism is that rulers in the present day had long lapsed into self-indulgent immoderation.

These past sages and kings that appear in the pages of the *Mozi* are not always unidentified. Occasionally, we do encounter definite historical personalities. For instance, in the following passage from the chapter "Exalting the Worthies III" ("Shang xian xia" 尚賢下), the idea of meritocracy, one of the key Mohist virtues, was said to have been embraced by historical figures from distant antiquity through the Xia dynasty to the early Zhou:

For what reason did I previously regard as honorable the way of Yao, Shun, Yu, Tang, Wen, and Wu? It was because they were in touch with the

---

[75] After the entries on shelter, clothing, agriculture, and transportation, the fifth and last entry is not an invention per se, rather the virtuous conduct of having a limited harem. In the words of the text, the sage-kings had no "retained women" (*gounü* 拘女). Moreover, the chapter concludes with the argument that the four inventions, and this one virtuous conduct, exemplify the more general principle of frugality of the sage-kings. Sun Yirang, *Mozi xiangu*, 6.37–38.

[76] Sun Yirang, *Mozi xiangu*, 21.163.

The Mozi: *The Origin of Disorder* 59

multitude in issuing their decrees and bringing order to the populace, which meant that those in the world who were good could be encouraged and those who were evil could be stopped. It is in such a manner that exalting worthiness is identical with the way of Yao, Shun, Yu, Tang, Wen and Wu.

然昔吾所以貴堯舜禹湯文武之道者，何故以哉？以其唯毋臨眾發政而治民，使天下之為善者可而勸也，為暴者可而沮也。然則此尚賢者也，與堯舜禹湯文武之道同矣。[77]

This passage is fairly typical of how the *Mozi* invokes past historical figures as exemplars of the virtues that it espouses. Moreover, even though this passage cites just six historical figures, namely Yao, Shun, Yu, Tang 湯, Wen, and Wu, this is in fact the entire canon of the legendary "kings" and "sages" in the *Mozi*. In most passages, only the last four – Yu, Tang, Wen, and Wu – are mentioned, and only in some instances, such as this passage, would the even more ancient Yao and Shun be added to this limited canonical cast.[78] These were all great founders of states in antiquity to the time of the Zhou. Other cultural figures outside or peripheral to the history of the states, such as the likes of Boyi and Shuqi who were celebrated in the *Analects*, are notably absent in the *Mozi*. That is not to say that the text mentions no other historical individual besides these few legendary kings and sages. On the rare occasions when the text does mention them, usually either famous personalities from the past or individual rulers in the present, they are almost always noted for their negative impact rather than virtuous deeds.[79] In the Core Chapters of the *Mozi*, we find sustained attention to "sages" and "kings" from antiquity, specifically this sextet from the very distant past to the time of the founding of the Zhou dynasty.[80] The vast expanse of the past is invoked in the *Mozi* through their historic achievements, be they civilizing innovations or enlightened rulership, for the advancement of the human condition.

This attention to the civilizing innovation and enlightened rulership of past figures carries with it the implication that humanity, as it was in the time before these sagely interventions, was originally disorderly. It required deliberate interventions in order to achieve a semblance of

[77] Ibid., 10.66.   [78] For an example, see ibid., 8.47–48.
[79] For an example, see ibid., 4.23.
[80] There is a very useful tabulation of the distribution of these six sage-kings in the different chapters of the *Mozi*, in Brown, "Mozi's Remaking of Ancient Authority," 163.

order. The work of these past sage-kings, therefore, was not just gratuitous improvement over an otherwise orderly humanity, but rather essential interventions without which humanity would have lapsed into, or reverted back to, the primitive chaos and brutishness of its original condition. This abiding interest in the civilizing works of the past sage-kings in the *Mozi* is directly informed by its subscription to the idea of humanity being originally disorderly. The civilizing progress and political order established by sage-kings of the past are but momentary relief from immanent disorder.

This dismal vision of humanity is evident in its many passages on historical declines and the origin of disorder in antiquity. Besides those celebratory accounts of past sage-kings, these account for the majority of the passages concerning the past in the text. No doubt, for the *Mozi*, the present age is one that has lapsed into chaos (*luan* 亂), having either abandoned or perverted the sagely innovations and enlightened rulership of the past. "Now, when we come to the present time, the sage-kings of the Three Dynasties of former times are already dead and the world is bereft of righteousness," (今逮至昔者三代聖王既沒，天下失義), as the text says time and again before it goes on to detail the specific maladies afflicting the present-day world (e.g. 25.169, 31.221).

This is quite a harrowing vision of ourselves; it sees humanity as perpetually bound and susceptible to various forms of disorder of our own making, with only occasional respite thanks to the few accidental sage-kings of the past. It is perhaps a depressing idea to accept, but according to the *Mozi* it is also a problem that we can ultimately overcome. How would we do that exactly? We begin by understanding the *causes* of our disorder. Then, with that knowledge, we can devise appropriate solutions to address and overcome them. In other words, the text argues for the utility and necessity of understanding the etiology of disorder:

A sage who takes the order of the world as his business must know what disorder arises from, and then he can bring order to it. If he does not know what disorder arises from, then he is not able to bring about order.

聖人以治天下為事者也，必知亂之所自起，焉能治之，不知亂之所自起，則不能治。[81]

---

[81] Sun Yirang, *Mozi xiangu*, 14.99.

The Mozi: *The Origin of Disorder* 61

Then, following this passage, the text drives the point home with a medical analogy:

It is, for example, like a doctor treating a person's illness. He must know what the illness arises from, and then he is able to treat it. If he does not know what the illness arises from, then he is not able to treat it. How can bringing order to disorder be the only thing not like this? One must know the source of the disorder, and then one is able to bring about order. If one does not know the source of the disorder, then one is not able to bring about order. A sage, in taking the ordering of the world to be his business, must examine what disorder arises from.

譬之如醫之攻人之疾者然，必知疾之所自起，焉能攻之；不知疾之所自起，則弗能攻。治亂者何獨不然，必知亂之所自起，焉能治之；不知亂之所自起，則弗能治。聖人以治天下為事者也，不可不察亂之所自起。[82]

This medical analogy, likening our chronic disorder to cases of illness, is quite revealing for the text's larger vision of the basic problems of humanity. As human beings, we are prone to become sick from time to time; one may even say that it is in our very constitution to be susceptible to various forms of illness over time. Yet being sick is certainly not the proper way for us to live; it is something that should be treated, as much as possible, if not altogether, once and for all. To extrapolate from this metaphor, therefore, humanity may be constitutionally susceptible to chaos harmful to itself, yet it is not something that we should accept as part of our natural condition. Instead, it is an aberration from our proper historical course that impedes our flourishing over time. These periodic episodes of disorder must be overcome, and just as with any form of illness, we treat it by understanding its causes. There is a subtle identification here between the nature of disorder and the origin of disorder. To put this differently, the implicit claim here is that a knowledge of a thing's origin is equivalent to understanding its nature. In the case of an illness, an observation of the physical symptoms in the present would lead to a diagnosis of the causes, and that in turn would lead to a prescription for the appropriate cures. Similarly, disorder in the world today is the apparent effects of a more fundamental, underlying dysfunction, whose proper diagnosis

[82] Ibid., 14.99.

62   *Time out of Joint*

is essential as a first step in finding solutions that will restore order and put us back on the right path towards a more civilized world.

So, for the *Mozi*, what is this etiology of disorder? On first reading, the text seems to suggest more than one answer to this question. It accuses the rulers of its time of failing at many things; they are not frugal, their systems of government are not meritocratic, or they fail to understand the importance of impartial caring, to name just a few examples. The ignorance and stupidity of the rulers, however, are not the root causes. If only it were that simple, then educating or removing the rulers would have fixed the world. The *Mozi* does offer a more radical diagnosis, one based on a narrative of antiquity:

> Master Mozi spoke, saying: "Ancient times, when people first came into being, were times when there were as yet no laws or government, so it was said that people had differing principles. This meant that, if there was one person, there was one principle; if there were two people, there were two principles; and if there were ten people, there were ten principles. The more people there were, the more things there were that were spoke of as principles. This was a case of people affirming their own principles and condemning those of other people. The consequence of this was mutual condemnation. In this way, within a household, fathers and sons, and older and younger brothers were resentful and hostile, separated and dispersed, and unable to reach agreement and accord with each other. Throughout the world, people all used water and fire, and poisons and potions to injure and harm one another. As a result, those with strength to spare did not use it to help each other in their work, surplus goods rotted and decayed and were not used for mutual distribution, and good doctrines were hidden and obscured and not used for mutual teaching. So the world was in a state of disorder comparable to that amongst birds and beasts."

子墨子言曰：古者民始生，未有刑政之時，蓋其語人異義。是以一人則一義，二人則二義，十人則十義，其人茲眾，其所謂義者亦茲眾。是以人是其義，以非人之義，故 文相非也。是以內者父子兄弟作怨惡，離散不能相和合。天下之百姓，皆以水火毒藥相虧害，至有餘力不能以相勞，腐朽餘財不以相分，隱匿良道不以相教，天下 之亂，若禽獸然。[83]

---

[83] Ibid., 11.74–75. A similar passage is seen at the beginning of Chapter 12, "Exalting Unity II" ("Shang tong zhong" 尚同中) (12.78). Bryan W. van Norden compares this passage to the idea of the "state of nature" in Thomas Hobbes's *Leviathan*. See Van Norden, *Virtue Ethics and Consequentialism in Early Chinese Philosophy* (New York: Cambridge Unviersity Press, 2007), 162–166.

The Mozi: The Origin of Disorder

The problem, therefore, is the lack of "shared norms," as Chris Fraser put it in his recent study of the philosophy of the *Mozi*.[84] Before we enjoyed the benefits of sagely interventions, we were originally prone to quarrel with others, as each of us was naturally committed to our own idiosyncratic standards. That is a fundamental cause of our disorder, once upon a time in antiquity, according to the *Mozi*. To draw out the significance of this argument, it would be helpful to contrast this to the texts that we looked at earlier, namely the Western Zhou materials and the *Analects*. That would also allow me to further delineate the landscape of the past in the *Mozi*, and begin to circle back to the larger theme of this chapter, namely the transition in how the past was imagined from the Western Zhou of the late Bronze Age to the early Warring States period in the *Analects* and the *Mozi*.

A comparison between what we have seen in the *Mozi* so far and the Western Zhou texts is relatively straightforward, for they are largely diametrically opposite. In the latter, as I argued earlier, the focus is on the origins of order; they tended to valorize the founding moment of a new order, such as the actions of the first Zhou kings, and translate their originary nature into a paradigmatic status for the later generations. One identifies and studies the origins of order in the past in order to emulate them and maintain the same order in the present. In the *Mozi*, however, the focus has shifted from the origins of order to the origins of disorder. Establishing order in the present is no longer a matter of knowing and perpetuating a founding order from a certain point in the past; rather, it depends on understanding the original disorder of humanity. If history figures as a collection of exemplary actions of one's ancestors for faithful emulation in the Western Zhou world, it is now, at least in part, a series of etiological cases awaiting proper diagnoses in the *Mozi*.

One might object to this argument by pointing out that the *Mozi* also focuses on the sage-kings and their civilizing work. So it is not only concerned with etiological moments in history, but also attends to what was positive and exemplary. While it is true that the *Mozi* does celebrate a small cast of past sage-kings, including King Wen and King Wu, who figure prominently in Western Zhou texts, the way that it contextualizes their historical significance still betrays its etiological

---

[84] Chris Fraser, *The Philosophy of the Mòzǐ: The First Consequentialists* (New York: Columbia University Press, 2016), 77–103.

64   *Time out of Joint*

investment, with a clear emphasis on the primacy of recognizing and diagnosing disorders. Take, for example, the aforementioned chapter "On Eschewing Faults" ("Ciguo"), which surveys the various civilizing innovations introduced by the sage-kings in antiquity. In each case, whether it was shelter, agriculture, transportation, or clothing, the narrative always begins with the sage-king discerning a particular deficiency in the way that human beings were living, and having understood the cause of that deficiency, he devised an appropriate solution for its fulfillment.[85] These acts of the sage-kings are not meant to be repeated ad infinitum – the idea of transportation only needed to be introduced once. The lesson that we are supposed to learn from these cases of the ancient sage-kings is that we must recognize the particular deficiencies or disorderliness of our own time, in order to arrive at the appropriate measures to create or restore proper order. These achievements of the sage-kings were ultimately grounded in their etiological approach to the world in which they found themselves. They became the sage-kings that we now celebrate precisely because they understood the causes of the disorder they saw in their own time. Both the Western Zhou materials and the *Mozi* capitalize the past for their respective political visions, but one invests in exemplarity while the other emphasizes etiology.

And what about the *Analects*? How does it compare to the *Mozi*? In these two bodies of materials, which are likely near-contemporaries of each other, we see an interesting point of convergence. It is the figure of deliberative individual that we first encountered in our discussion of the *Analects*. In the last passage that we read from the *Mozi*, on the cause of disorder in antiquity, the text identifies as the culprit literally *everyman*. Each of us is born with our own idiosyncratic standard, according to

---

[85] For instance, in the case of transportation, this is how the *Mozi* described its introduction: "In the times when the people of old still did not know how to make boats and carts, they could not transport heavy loads or reach distant roads. Therefore, the sage-kings brought about the making of boats and carts to facilitate the affairs of the people. The boats and carts they made were perfectly solid, swift and convenient so they could carry what was heavy and travel far. Moreover, in their making, the use of materials was slight, but their being of benefit was great, so the people were happy and benefited from them. Orders and decrees did not spur them, yet they acted. The people were not worn out, yet the ruler had enough for use, therefore the people returned to him" (古之民未知為舟車時，重任不移，遠道不至。故聖王作為舟車，以便民之事。其為舟車也，全固輕利，可以任重致遠。其為用財少而為利多，是以民樂而利之。故法令不急而行，民不勞而上足用，故民歸之). Sun Yirang, *Mozi xiangu*, 6.37.

The Mozi: *The Origin of Disorder* 65

the text, and conflicts always arise when two or more individuals interact. "People had differing principles" (*ren yi yi* 人異義), as the text emphatically remarks.[86] We always choose to privilege our own "principle" over that of others. That is simply our nature. This understanding of human beings as idiosyncratic ideologues, I would argue, implies an attribution of deliberative capacity to individuals that is comparable to the same process that we saw in the *Analects*. Both texts subscribe to this figure of the deliberative individual, who chooses between alternatives and decides on one course of action over another, sometimes with great historical consequences for the world.

The question of individualism or the individual subject has received relatively little attention in the scholarship on the Core Chapters of the *Mozi* in past decades.[87] In a rare exception, Erica Brindley argued recently that there is a radical conception of individuals in the *Mozi* as authoritative agents capable of independent "decision-making" and "self-determination," so much so it may have constituted one of the roots of individualism in early China.[88] I very much agree with Brindley's argument for the centrality of this figure of the deliberative individual in the *Mozi*. And for the text, it is a problem that must be resolved. The question is not whether this or that individual arrives at the right or wrong standard; the fact that individuals are deliberating at all on their own, formulating their own standards, already constitutes incipient disorder. The authors of the *Mozi* see this individual and his deliberative capacity, but they hold a fundamentally negative view of them. This is the root cause of disorder in the world. It must be

---

[86] Ibid., 11.75.

[87] Much of the scholarship on the philosophy of the *Mozi* in the past decades was preoccupied with the question of utilitarianism (or consequentialism), as well as with how its objectivist outlook can be reconciled with its religiosity. There has been very little discussion of its notion of selfhood or individual subjectivity. See Dennis M. Ahern, "Is Mo Tzu a Utilitarian?", *Journal of Chinese Philosophy* 3.2 (1976), 185–193; Rodney L. Taylor, "Religion and Utilitarianism: Mo Tzu on Spirits and Funerals," *Philosophy East and West* 29.3 (1979), 337–346; David E. Soles, "Mo Tzu and the Foundations of Morality," *Journal of Chinese Philosophy* 26.1 (1999), 37–48; Daniel M. Johnson, "Mozi's Moral Theory: Breaking the Hermeneutical Stalemate," *Philosophy East and West* 61.2 (2011), 347–164; and most recently, Fraser, *The Philosophy of the Mòzǐ*.

[88] Erica Brindley, "Human Agency and the Ideal of *Shang Tong* (Upward Conformity) in Early Mohist Writings," *Journal of Chinese Philosophy* 34.3 (2007), 409–425, esp. 412–413, 417. See also the expanded treatment in her monograph *Individualism in Early China Human Agency and the Self in Thought and Politics* (Honolulu: University of Hawaii Press, 2010).

66   *Time out of Joint*

overcome, as the sage-kings once did in the past, before good order can arise and flourish for the benefit of all.

This brings us back to the comparison with the *Analects*, for this point marks a striking divergence between the two texts. Recall that the *Analects*, with its dismissal of the privilege of the originary, exemplary models within the genealogical past, turns to this deliberative capacity of individuals as a potential new source for establishing order. Reflecting on the cultural practices of the past, an individual deliberates on the appropriate model to be creatively adopted in the present. The *Mozi* similarly leaves behind the genealogical past of the Western Zhou, and recognizes the presence and agency of deliberative individuals. However, while the *Analects* sees this deliberative capacity of individuals as a new source of creating order, the *Mozi* sees it as the exact opposite, the original source of disorder in the world. In the *Analects*, this deliberative capacity is one of our endowed faculties that we must cultivate; in the *Mozi*, it is an innate liability of being human that has to be controlled or perhaps even eradicated altogether.

In other words, both texts recognize the same, new political subject, namely the deliberative individual, but they diverge in their interpretations. The *Analects* calls on this person to exercise his deliberative capacity to reflect upon the cultural practices of the past in order to imagine a viable new path for the present; the *Mozi*, on the other hand, chastises this same figure for his idiosyncratic standard and reckless deliberations as the very source of disorder in antiquity, and again now in the early Warring States. The solution that the *Analects* has discovered is considered to be the very problem in the *Mozi*.

To fix this problem, the *Mozi* appeals to the idea of an impersonal, objective standard, denoted in the text by the term "Heaven" (*tian* 天). Individual principles, cultivated within the recesses of our minds, must be abandoned, by referring to this supra-human standard external to all subjective calculations. In the triad of chapters entitled "Heaven's Intention" ("Tianzhi" 天志), this idea of "Heaven" is given this description:

So Master Mozi's having Heaven's intention is no different to a wheelwright having compasses or a carpenter having a square. Now a wheelwright takes hold of his compasses in order to determine whether things in the world are round or not, saying: "What accords with my compasses is called round and

The Mozi: The Origin of Disorder   67

what does not accord with my compasses is called not round." In this way the roundness or non-roundness of all things can be ascertained and known. Why is this so? It is because the standard for roundness is clear. Also, a carpenter takes hold of his square in order to determine whether things in the world are square or not, saying: "What accords with my square is called square and what does not accord with my square is called not square." In this way the squareness or non-squareness of all things can be ascertained and known. Why is this so? It is because the standard for squareness is clear.

是故子墨子之有天之，辟人無以異乎輪人之有規，匠人之有矩也。今夫輪人操其規，將以量度天下之圜與不圜也，曰：「中吾規者謂之圜，不中吾規者謂之不圜。」是以圜與不圜，皆可得而知也。此其故何？則圜法明也。匠人亦操其矩，將以量度天下之方與不方也，曰：「中吾矩者謂之方，不中吾矩者謂之不方。」是以方與不方皆可得而知之。此其故何？則方法明也。[89]

This metaphor of compasses and squares for the idea of Heaven drives home the notion that it represents an objective standard that lies outside, and therefore can serve as a corrective to, our own almost always wrongheaded individual deliberations.[90] Much of the Core Chapters of the Mozi is, therefore, an elaboration on how the world should be organized, and how we should conduct ourselves within it, according to an understanding of this objective standard dispensed from Heaven. In order to arrive at an understanding of this "Heaven's intention," the text recommended the methodology of the "three criteria" (san fa 三法), as we discussed earlier (i.e. historical exemplars, collective senses, and a calculus of effectiveness). The end result is essentially a hierarchical, but meritocratic, bureaucratic system of laws and punishments designed to provide material subsistence for the maximum number of people at the same time.[91] It is headed by the Son of Heaven (tianzi 天子), who comprehends and maintains Heaven's intention in the world. "It is only that the Son of Heaven is able to make uniform the principles of the world; this is how there is

---

[89] Sun Yirang, Mozi xiangu, 27.207.

[90] This metaphor of compasses and squares for the idea of Heaven is also in 4.20–21, 26.197, and 28.213.

[91] This ideal system envisioned by the Mozi is elaborated throughout the Core Chapters of the Mozi; a detailed description can be found in the "Exalting Unity" ("Shang tong" 尚同) triad (Sun Yirang, Mozi xiangu, 11–13.74–98). See also Fraser, The Philosophy of the Mòzǐ: The First Consequentialists, for a good summary of this political and ethical program.

68 *Time out of Joint*

order in the world" (天子唯能壹同天下之義，是以天下治也).[92]
Unlike the barbaric chaos in antiquity with each individual having his
or her own principle, we now have only "shared norms," a single
impersonal principle for the entire world upheld by the Son of
Heaven. A system consistent with Heaven's intention will flourish,
while ones that deviate from it inevitably breed disorder and create
the conditions for their own doom, in addition to incurring natural
calamities as negative responses from Heaven.[93]

Finally, this metaphor of the compasses and squares is also notable
for the ahistoricism that it implies. A square is a square no matter when
or where; likewise, "Heaven's intention," this objective set of standards for establishing order, is presented as constant across historical
contexts. Its efficacy is universal and therefore transhistorical. It means
that the various virtuous principles that the text espouses, such as
meritocracy, frugality, and impartial caring, all perfectly align with
the objective standards of Heaven. They worked at least once before,
and will always work in the future. Orders are historically realized, and
humanity does fluctuate between times of relative chaos and relative
peace, but the idea of order and the means of its constitution have no
historical dimension in the *Mozi*.

This, again, stands in contrast to the *Analects*. There is an entrenched
historical dimension in the imagination of the order of the present in the
Analects; every measure we decide to adopt in the present should be
a creative, reflective adaptation of a historical precedent.[94] The very
notion of a transhistorical order is inconceivable in the *Analects*, while
it is the very ideal that drives the political vision of the *Mozi*. The *Mozi*
promises what the *Analects* precludes: an objective standard for establishing good order that is not susceptible to the corruption of time. This
desire for a transhistorical order, however, does not diminish the significance of history in the text. In fact, it plays an essential role in the
overall political vision of the *Mozi*. It is, after all, in the study of
antiquity that the *Mozi* discovers the true origin of disorder, namely
the contentious arbitrations of men. The past is relevant as a field of

---

[92] Sun Yirang, *Mozi xiangu*, 11.76.

[93] For a description of this, see, for instance, the conclusion of Chapter 11,
"Exalting Unity I" ("Shang tong shang" 尚同上). Sun Yirang, *Mozi xiangu*,
11.77–78.

[94] Recall, for instance, the emphasis on the idea of *shu* 述 ("transmission") over
zuo 作 ("innovation") in the *Analects* (Yang Bojun, *Lunyu yizhu*, 7.1).

The Mozi: The Origin of Disorder

etiological investigations; it allows us to see the causes of our disorder, as the *Mozi* did itself.

Moreover, history is also where we can observe the efficacy of following the intentions of Heaven, through the work of the sage-kings, those who were able to diagnose the problems of their own age, and arrived at the correct solution by appealing to Heaven:

[This being so, then] what can be taken as a standard for bringing about order? It is said that there is no standard like Heaven. Heaven is broad and unselfish in its actions, and is generous in its bestowing without considering itself virtuous. Its radiance is enduring and does not decay. Therefore, the sage-kings took it as the standard. If Heaven is taken as the standard, then all one's actions must be measured against Heaven. What Heaven desires should be done and what it does not desire should not be done.

然則奚以為治法而可？故曰莫若法天。天之行廣而無私，其施厚而不德，其明久而不衰，故聖王法之。既以天為法，動作有為必度於天，天之所欲則為之，天所不欲則止。[95]

Later on, in the conclusion of the same chapter, the text refers to specific cases of the four sage-kings, Yu, Tang, Wen, and Wu:

Formerly, the sage-kings Yu, Tang, Wen, and Wu were universal in loving the world's ordinary people, leading them to venerate Heaven and serve ghosts, and their benefiting people was very great. Therefore, Heaven brought them good fortune, established them as Sons of Heaven, and the feudal lords of the world all respected and served them.

昔之聖王禹、湯、文、武，兼愛天下之百姓，率以尊天事鬼，其利人多，故天福之，使立為天子，天下諸侯皆賓事之。[96]

Conversely, historical figures who went against Heaven's intentions suffered accordingly:

The tyrannical kings Jie, Zhou, You, and Li were universal in hating the world's ordinary people, leading them to revile Heaven and insult ghosts, and their harming people was very great. Therefore, Heaven brought them misfortune, caused them to lose their countries, to be themselves killed, and to be held in contempt in the world so that posterity continues to vilify them unceasingly to the present day.

---

[95] Sun Yirang, *Mozi xiangu*, 4.22.   [96] Ibid., 4.23.

暴王桀、紂、幽、厲，兼惡天下之百姓，率以詬天侮鬼，其賊人多，故天
禍之，使遂失其國家，身死為僇於天下，後世子孫毀之，至今不息。[97]

The past in the *Mozi*, therefore, is an etiological field, and the study of history allows us to observe the causes of disorder as well as their remedies. More pragmatically, it is also a series of case studies of historical figures who either accorded with or deviated from the intentions of Heaven. The negative cases demonstrate the horrific consequences of going against Heaven; the positive examples, namely the actions of the sage-kings in the past, are specific, partial instantiations of the standards of Heaven. A comprehensive knowledge of sagely deeds from the past may aggregate to a rough outline of the order that Heaven has always intended for us. It is an inferential approximation of Heaven through a survey of exemplary and unexemplary figures and their deeds in history.[98]

Finally, let me conclude this section with a speculation on the reason behind the relatively limited canon of sage-kings in the *Mozi*. Only a handful of dynastic founders are noted in the text, namely the sextet Yao, Shun, Yu, Tang, Wen, and Wu, while many other cultural heroes such as Boyi and Shuqi celebrated in the *Analects* (and elsewhere in the Warring States corpus) are absent. In light of our argument about the text here, it is not hard to see why the *Mozi* would find nothing to celebrate about someone such as Boyi or Shuqi. The *Analects* may see the forceful exercises of their deliberative capacity as evidence of virtue, but the *Mozi* would certainly regard such stubborn commitment to one's own arbitrary standard as precisely the seed of disorder. The only ones who are truly worthy of celebration and adherence are the few individuals in history who, in the view of the *Mozi*, recognized the objective standards of Heaven, and subjugated their own arbitrary principles, in order to create governing institutions that gave the world a proper order. Moreover, only the works of these sages, and perhaps those who gave them significant assistance, provide accurate access to the objective order intended by Heaven. The rest are either

---

[97] Ibid., 4.23.
[98] This can be contextualized as an instance of "non-deductive argumentation," to use Paul R. Goldin's phrase, through historical anecdotes in early China. See Paul R. Goldin, "Non-deductive Argumentation in Early Chinese Philosophy," in *Between History and Philosophy: Anecdotes in Early China*, ed. Sarah A. Queen and Paul van Els (Albany: State University of New York Press, 2017), 54–77.

Conclusion   71

irrelevant or negative examples, which the text does occasionally note, as in the case of the "tyrannical kings" (*baowang* 暴王) in the very last passage cited above.[99]

The *Mozi* recognizes the historical agency of deliberative individuals – they can make or break the order of the world. The good ones, however, are those who exercise their deliberative capacity only to realize that they should subjugate it in order to yield to the objective standards of Heaven outside themselves. What the text demands, therefore, is more than just relinquishment, but a willful subjugation of our deliberative selves.

Conclusion

In the late Bronze Age period, the political elite of the Western Zhou saw the past largely as a genealogical field. It starts from the founding moments of the dynasty and marches forward to the present. Exemplary acts by the founders of the dynasty were the stuff of history. They are to be emulated by the later generations, so that the original order of the dynasty will be perpetuated. With the fall of the dynasty, and with it the hereditary aristocratic order of the political elite, this predominance of the genealogical imagination of the past also declined. In the divided world of the early Warring States, a few centuries after the Western Zhou, we begin to see alternative ways to imagine the past. In this chapter, I discussed two particularly powerful examples, namely the *Analects* and the *Mozi*. They are vastly different texts, yet interesting dialogues emerge when they are read together, with a view to their respective capitalization of the past for their political visions.

Both the *Analects* and the *Mozi* engaged with this figure of the deliberative individual. In the former, the past has become a repertoire of cultural practices; an individual evaluates and decides which is the most exemplary and efficacious for the present. In the *Mozi*, on the other hand, the past is where one goes in search of the causes of our disorder, the false and disastrous deliberations of individuals past, in order to surmise the universal, objective standards that will restore order to the world. The *Analects* sees a powerful resource in this deliberative capacity of men, while the *Mozi* considers it a key source of our trouble.

[99] Sun Yirang, *Mozi xiangu*, 4.23. For an alternative answer to this question, see Brown, "Mozi's Remaking of Ancient Authority."

72   *Time out of Joint*

In other words, there were three different figurations of the past: genealogical, cultural, and etiological. Given their relative chronological proximity, we can consider the last two – the cultural past and the etiological past – as two competing voices in the debates of the early Warring States period over a range of political and ethical concerns. They both saw few resources in the old model of the genealogical past, but the trajectories of their departures are different. With the *Mozi*, we can discern a morphological resemblance between its idea of "Heaven" and the originary exemplary actions of the ancestors in the Western Zhou materials. Both represent pre-existing, incontestable ideals external to oneself that predefine the realm of proper action for the present. Perhaps with the ebbing of the genealogical past, and along with it the ideal of an objective standard embodied in the exemplary actions of the ancestors, the *Mozi* turns to this idea of Heaven as a way to preserve or even radicalize this ideal of an external objective standard.

This preservation of an old ideal through a proxy concept in the *Mozi* makes the *Analects*, in comparison, a much more radical departure from the Western Zhou model. The entire edifice built on the foundation of a genealogical past in the Western Zhou has completely vanished in the *Analects*. There is no genealogical continuity, no exemplary founding moments, or any external objective standard that any individual may rely on. Instead, we have only ourselves, with our reflective minds, looking back on the repertoire of past cultural practices for guidance on what to do in the present. There is a lot more deliberative freedom at the individual level in the *Analects*, compared to both the Western Zhou paradigm and the *Mozi*, but with it there is also an uncertainty over the rectitude of one's choices.

Finally, I would like to briefly comment on an issue that has only been implied but never explicitly discussed throughout this chapter. It is the issue of historical continuity and discontinuity. In the Western Zhou materials, there is a presumption of historical continuity between the past and present. Or, more precisely, there is a tacit understanding that the present order is continuous to the original order inaugurated by one's ancestors at a particular moment in the past. The task is to maintain a historical knowledge of the founding moments in order extend the original paradigmatic order into the present.

In the early Warring States period, however, at least in these two bodies of materials the *Analects* and the *Mozi*, we no longer see this comforting belief in a continuum of order between past and present. If

Conclusion   73

anything, they are both committed to the exact opposite, namely the idea of historical ruptures. The orderly existence that once flourished – whether in the early Zhou or in distant antiquity – was so fully corrupted that we are now completely disconnected from it. It was never a matter of inheriting or restoring an old order, for it is beyond repair by this point in time. This is a time of rupture from a superior past. Historical course was radically disrupted; past and present are disjunct.

Time is out of joint, from the perspectives of both the *Analects* and the *Mozi*. In this light, we can appreciate the politics of both texts as driven by a desire to overcome this perceived historical discontinuity. In the *Mozi*, the exhortation to deduce and abide by the intentions of Heaven comes with the promise that we will be reunited with a long line of sage-kings who succeeded in doing so from distant antiquity. By adhering to the exact same transhistorical standard that they too discovered in the past, we will simply be re-establishing and furthering the order that they created. A new genealogy of sagely individuals is therefore forged, stretching from the distant past to the present. Its membership is not defined by blood ties but by one's proper understanding of Heaven.

The *Analects*' attempt at re-establishing historical continuity is subtler and more circumscribed in its scope. If its strategy is to look back in time and deliberate upon a particular cultural practice to follow, the present would always be an extension of particular pieces of the past. The text does valorize a certain idea of historical continuity, as Confucius himself declares a preference for transmission (*shu*) over creation (*zuo*).[100] Compared to the *Mozi*, however, this re-established historical continuity in the *Analects* is much more tenuous and fragmentary. It is contingent on particular individuals, mediated by their idiosyncratic preferences for historical precedents. And in the end, even in the most ideal scenario, there can never be a perfect continuity between the past and present. This is because, for the *Analects*, the past was always already broken into many separate pieces, an imperfectly recollected repertoire of disparate cultural forms and practices. It does not appeal to anything like the idea of Heaven in the *Mozi*, which enables the identification and integration of specific historical moments and individuals into a single overarching genealogy that we can help extend into the present. In the *Analects*, the best that one can hope for is

[100] Yang Bojun, *Lunyu yizhu*, 7.1.

a modular type of historical continuity, where the present is informed by an individual's interpretation of a choice piece of the past.

Pervasive angst over this perceived historical rupture between the past and present informed the politics of the *Analects* and the *Mozi*. In their attempts to re-establish some sense of historical continuity for their world, and to imagine a more orderly and flourishing future, they both looked to the past. In the cultural past of the *Analects*, we are directed to curate past practices for emulation in the present; in the etiological past of the *Mozi*, we act as investigators in search of the root cause of our affliction and the components of a good order as dictated by Heaven. Neither saw much use anymore in the genealogical past that was once instrumental to the cultivation of political authority of the late Bronze Age aristocratic order of the Western Zhou.

2 | A Parenthetical Past

Deep History and Anti-history in the Late Warring States

Both the *Analects* and the *Mozi*, despite their vast differences, subscribe to a rhetoric of antiquity. They both invoke antiquity as a field of exemplary acts, a time when political and ethical ideals were perfectly realized. Such backward gazes connote nostalgia for a once flourishing past as well as regret for the degenerate present. They also suggest a perception of disjuncture between past and present; somewhere along the way, history has gone off course. Time is out of joint, and the world is not quite the way it is supposed to be.

This rhetoric of antiquity was much more widespread beyond the *Analects* and the *Mozi*. It was absolutely pervasive, in fact, and persisted in the literature of the period well into the late Warring States period from around the mid-fourth century to the late third century BCE. "Venerating the past and disparaging the present – this is typical among scholars" (夫尊古而卑今, 學者之流也), as a later chapter of the *Zhuangzi* 莊子 would testify.[1] In both the received and excavated materials of this period, it is indeed difficult to find a single text that does not somehow play with this rhetoric of antiquity. It was obviously a widely shared consensus that the past constituted an instructive field. What lessons we can or should draw from our inevitably scattered knowledge of the past, however, was a much more contentious subject. Besides invocations of an exemplary antiquity, we also saw in this period the compilation of various historical anecdotes, most notably the *Zuozhuan* 左傳 as well as the *Guoyu* 國語 and the *Zhanguo ce* 戰國策, that pursued these questions over the proper lessons of the past in

---

[1] Wang Xianqian 王先謙, *Zhuangzi ji jie* 莊子集解 (Beijing: Zhonghua, 1987), 26.242. This particular passage is from one of the "Miscellaneous Chapters" (*za pian* 雜篇) of the *Zhangzi* and plausibly dates to the last century of the Warring States period. For the dating of the *Zhuangzi*, I refer to A. C. Graham, "How Much of *Chuang Tzu* Did Chuang Tzu Write?", in *Studies in Chinese Philosophy and Philosophical Literature* (Singapore: Institute of East Asian Philosophies, 1990), 283–321. The translation is my own.

76   *A Parenthetical Past*

a much more sustained manner. They represent deliberate attempts to "make arguments" about the past, to offer competing interpretations of historical events, as Li Wai-yee has so richly demonstrated in her monograph on the *Zuozhuan*.[2] In the masters texts of the late Warring States, such as the *Xunzi* 荀子, *Han Feizi* 韓非子, and the *Lüshi chunqiu* 呂氏春秋, historical anecdotes circulate as narrative tokens that invite and demand meaningful interpretations and contextualization. The past – or at least some parts of it – was widely accepted as exemplary, and now more and more stories were being told about it. The landscape of the past expanded, one anecdote at a time, in this period.

This compilation and circulation of historical anecdotes during the late Warring States period has received a fair amount of scholarly attention in recent years, especially among scholars of early Chinese historiography.[3] The *Zuozhuan*, in particular, has been invested with much significance as a depository of some of the earliest historical narratives in anecdotal form in the tradition. It may not be the earliest work of history per se, a distinction that is often assigned to the speeches preserved in the *Classic of Documents*, but it is nevertheless often considered the "earliest extant piece of extended and detailed historical narrative."[4] In many ways, this escalating desire to narrate and interpret historical anecdotes over the course of the late Warring States, as best exemplified by the expansive narratives in the *Zuozhuan*, is resonant and consistent with the paradigm for mobilizing the past in the *Analects*.[5] The past is perceived as a field of diverse cultural practices, and we evaluate them with our ever more refined deliberative capacity. As David Schaberg put it, in the *Zuozhuan* an anecdote

---

[2] Li, *The Readability of the Past in Early Chinese Historiography*.

[3] See, for example, Sarah A. Queen and Paul van Els, eds., *Between History and Philosophy: Anecdotes in Early China* (Albany: State University of New York Press, 2017); and the body of works by David Schaberg, such as "Chinese History and Philosophy," in *The Oxford History of Historical Writing, Volume 1: Beginnings to AD 600*, ed. by Andrew Feldherr and Grant Hardy (Oxford: Oxford University Press, 2011), 394–414.

[4] Burton Watson, *Early Chinese Literature* (New York: Columbia University Press, 1962), 52.

[5] While the *Zuozhuan* may contain materials that date back to the Spring and Autumn Period (722–749), the "present consensus holds that *Zuozhuan* was largely complete by the end of the fourth century B.C.E.," noted in the "Introduction" of Durrant, Li, and Schaberg, *Zuo Tradition = Zuozhuan*, xxxviii.

A Parenthetical Past

always "ends with an invitation to judgment."[6] Those whom we deem exemplary become candidates for models of emulation in the present, and conversely, we learn to avoid repeating deplorable acts from the past. To arrest the meaning of a historical event by situating it in a complex narrative is one strategy to deliberate upon its ethical import and complexity. It is no accident that the narratives of the *Zuozhuan* – and to some extent the *Guoyu* – are thoroughly informed by the basic ethical vocabulary that also runs through the *Analects*. The "gentleman" (*junzi* 君子) figure, who offers critical judgment on historical events throughout the *Zuozhuan*, is also resonant with this particular model of engagement with the past that was articulated in the *Analects*; we are supposed to do precisely what the "gentleman" does, which is to appreciate the complex historical circumstances and then arrive, confidently, at an ethical evaluation of the actions of the individuals involved after careful deliberation.[7] There is a clear affinity between the historical vision that we found in the *Analects* and the narratives of the *Zuozhuan*.[8]

But this was certainly not the only type of historiography, the only way that the political elite engaged with the historical field, in the latter half of the Warring States period. Instead of elaborating on the *Zuozhuan* and the broader phenomenon of the compilation and circulation of historical anecdotes in this period, I will discuss another development that is, in many ways, antithetical to this argument for the edifying utility of the past. These are late Warring States texts that, despite their diverse ideological persuasions, share a great deal of

---

[6] Schaberg, *A Patterned Past*, 183.

[7] The *junzi* is sometime identified as Confucius. Eric Henry, "'Junzi Yue' versus 'Zhongni Yue' in *Zuozhuan*," *Harvard Journal of Asiatic Studies* 59.1 (1999), 125–161.

[8] David Schaberg, *A Patterned Past*, 257, argues that "the narrators of the *Zuozhuan* and *Guoyu* considered themselves followers of Confucius. It would not be enough to note that their characters generally uphold values associated with Confucius' name; narrators need not agree with their characters. But these narrators quote Confucius as an authority on several occasions and never openly challenge his judgments." To be a follower of Confucius does not necessarily mean that one must subscribe also to the ideas in the *Analects*, but nevertheless, I mention this here as further circumstantial evidence of the affinity between "Confucian" ideas and the *Zuozhuan*. See also Yuri Pines, *Foundations of Confucian Thought: Intellectual Life in the Chunqiu Period, 722–453 BCE* (Honolulu: University of Hawaii Press, 2002); Li, *The Readability of the Past in Early Chinese Historiography*.

78 A Parenthetical Past

ambivalence, and sometimes even antagonism, towards the very idea of history as a useful thing. If the proliferation of historical anecdotes and narratives in this period attested to a continual commitment to the idea of the past as a source of moral edification and political imagination, there was also a vigorous, deeply antihistorical countercurrent that we can recover from the extant writings of the period. While the former has garnered much scholarly attention, as a key moment in the history of early Chinese historiography, the latter has remained a largely obscure phenomenon.

One reason why this development of antihistorical thought has received so little attention is, I suspect, due to a certain hermeneutic blind spot within the old paradigms for the study of early Chinese historiography, as I had discussed at length in the Introduction. If reverence for the past was an ingrained cultural attitude, then there just would not be antihistorical ideas in early China. In the early Chinese cultural world, according to this view, it would have been a constitutional impossibility for such a thing even to exist. I have already offered some arguments against this in the Introduction, and in this chapter I hope to offer further evidence for its reconsideration. This vast landscape of the past came into being not as an expression of a cultural attitude that reveres tradition and history, but through lively dialogues and debates over a wide range of political and ethical concerns which mobilized the past as their argumentative capital. In the last chapter, we looked at cases that took the field of the past as a positive resource, in different ways, for their ethical and political visions. In this chapter, I will turn to other more ambivalent voices that responded to this growing prevalence and authority of the rhetoric of antiquity with great skepticism.

The textual remains from the late Warring States are relatively rich. The world had remained politically divided since the fall of the Western Zhou.[9] With escalating state violence across the Central Plain, more and more worried voices offered their proposals for restoring order to the world. Some built on earlier ideas, like those that we have already seen in the *Analects* and the *Mozi*, while others sought to come up with novel solutions. Voices that expressed ambivalence about the utility of

[9] For a summary account, see Mark Edward Lewis, "Warring States Political History," in *The Cambridge History of Ancient China: From the Origins of Civilization to 221 B.C.*, ed. by Michael Loewe and Edward L. Shaughnessy (Cambridge: Cambridge University Press, 1999), 587–650.

Guodian Laozi 79

the past can be found in a variety of texts from this period. In this chapter, for a sketch of this development of antihistorical imagination, I will focus on two bodies of writing from the late Warring States period.

One is the cosmogonic narratives that we find in both the received and the recently excavated corpuses, including texts on bamboo slips discovered in the Guodian tomb and the Shanghai Museum collection. In particular, I will devote most of my attention to the *Laozi*, the Guodian (郭店) tomb version of this popular text, as a key example of this cosmogonic literature, with an ambivalence towards the idea of history that is very much paradigmatic to this entire body of cosmogonic texts. The other body of writings are the ethical theories from this period, with the *Mengzi* as a key example. Notwithstanding the complex ideological ties that the *Mengzi* may have to ideas in the *Analects*, there is a definite and radical rupture between the two in their respective relationship to the past. Its famous argument for an ethical system fundamentally rooted in the biological constitution of men, as I will argue, is a deliberate flight from history. If the Guodian *Laozi* evinces a deep ambivalence towards the idea of history, the *Mengzi* is indifferent or even at times hostile to it.

These are admittedly two disparate bodies of materials from the late Warring States. Their politics and ethics are vastly different. And yet, as I hope to demonstrate, they both participated, separately in their own way, in this countercurrent that questioned the political relevance of the field of the past in the late Warring States period. In this chapter, I will occasionally draw on other cosmogonic and ethical tracts from this period, but for the most part, I will focus on the *Laozi* and the *Mengzi* as two of the richest expressions of this development. As we shall see, they both came to the conclusion that to restore order to the world, the past should not matter all that much – or perhaps not at all. They did not want to forget or run away from the past; they wanted to put it in parentheses.

Guodian *Laozi:* Cosmogony, Deep History, and a Feminine Genealogical History

There is very little scholarship on the conception of the past in the *Laozi*. This is true for the received version of the text; it is also true for the two excavated versions of the text, one on bamboo strips from the

80   *A Parenthetical Past*

Guodian tomb and the other a silk manuscript from the Mawangdui tomb. In the voluminous scholarship on these different versions of the *Laozi* across all the major research languages, few scholars have pursued the question of the idea of the past in these texts. Relatedly, the *Laozi* is rarely mentioned in the scholarship on early Chinese historiography or the early Chinese ideas of history.[10] In contrast to the other more conventionally historiographical texts such as the *Zuozhuan* or *Shiji*, the mystical aphorisms of the *Laozi* appear to be decidedly anything but historiographical. If one wishes to study the idea of history in early China, the *Laozi* would seem hardly relevant at all.

As one reads through the different versions of the *Laozi*, this seems entirely justifiable at first. The *Laozi* is one of those rare texts since the end of the Western Zhou that do not refer to any named sage-kings from antiquity. Almost every single text would mention one sage-king or another, if only for rhetorical effect. The Great Yu or King Wen, for instance, appear quite regularly across most texts throughout the ideological spectrum. But the *Laozi*, interestingly, does not contain a single named sage-king. The popular legendary figures Yao, Shun, Yu, Wen, or Wu are conspicuously absent. Furthermore, there is no reference at all to any specific past event or figure, historical or legendary. For these reasons, it is easy to see why generations of scholars have felt justified in excluding it from discussion of the idea of the past in the history of the late Warring States or early China at large. It simply does not seem to be historically interested in any significant way at all.

Yet the past is not entirely absent in the *Laozi*. Given that this chapter is intended to be an account of the late Warring States period, I will begin with and largely focus on the Guodian version of the *Laozi*. Discovered in 1993 in the village of Guodian, Jingmen, Hubei Province, this version of the *Laozi* is generally dated back to around

---

[10] One exception would be the brief survey of the idealized past in the chapter "Lao Tzu and the Taoist Conception of History" in Ames, *Art of Rulership*, 6–9.
The historical sensibility of the text simply has not been a focus in the scholarship on the text. See the great overviews of scholarship on the text in
Mark Csikszentmihalyi, "Thematic Analyses of the Laozi," in *Dao Companion to Daoist Philosophy*, ed. by Xiaogan Liu (Dordrecht: Springer Netherlands, 2015), 47–70; and Isabelle Robinet, "The Diverse Interpretations of the Laozi," in
Religious and Philosophical Aspects of the Laozi, ed. by Mark Csikszentmihalyi and P. J. Ivanhoe (Albany: State University of New York Press, 1999), 127–159.

Guodian Laozi   81

the year 300 BCE. It is divided into three bundles (A, B, and C), the
majority of which correspond, roughly or exactly, to passages in the
received version of the *Laozi*. In this version, the earliest that we have as
of today, despite how terse it is, we can nevertheless see that the idea of
the past is not entirely absent. Specific historical figures or events are
conspicuously absent, but it is not at all oblivious to the idea of the past.
To begin with, it shares with the other texts of this period this rhetoric of
antiquity that I discussed at the beginning of this chapter: "In antiquity,
men who excelled in official services were always subtle, marvelous,
ingenious, and penetrating"[11] (古之善為士者，必微妙玄達) (5, R5).[12]
The passage continues to elaborate on the sagely demeanors and qualities of these men in antiquity. Situating ideal types and exemplary figures
in an unspecified antiquity, *gu*, is typical of the literature of this period of
the late Warring States. So, at the very least, we can say that the voice of
the Guodian *Laozi* is not entirely historically unmoored.

Despite the openness, the vagueness, of the chronology, there is
clearly a temporal dimension to the various pronouncements of the
text; the author situates himself in the present vis-à-vis distant
antiquity, a time when the world was simply good. So the
Guodian *Laozi* is a text with an awareness of time, a historical
distance between antiquity and present, at the very least. But reading further in this fortuitously preserved collection of bamboo strips
with passages of the *Laozi* on them, we soon realize that in fact it
has an extremely expansive view of the past, as we can see in the
following passage:

> There was a form that came to be, chaotically
> And it came before the birth of Heaven and Earth.

[11] For the Guodian *Laozi*, I refer to the editions in Scott Cook, *The Bamboo Texts
of Guodian: A Study and Complete Translation* (Ithaca, NY: Cornell University
Press East Asia Program, 2012). Unless otherwise noted, translations of both the
received and Guodian versions of the *Laozi* are my own. I did consult and
occasionally adapt from Cook's translation in the aforementioned *Bamboo
Texts of Guodian*; and Robert G. Henricks, *Lao Tzu's Tao Te Ching:
A Translation of the Startling New Documents Found at Guodian* (New York:
Columbia University Press, 2000); and D. C. Lau, *Tao Te Ching* (London:
Penguin Books, 2003).
[12] Cook, *The Bamboo Texts of Guodian*, 5 (R5). Citations from the Guodian
Laozi follow the numbers in Cook's edition. I also include the corresponding
chapter number in the received version, indicated by the letter "R." For the
received edition, I refer to Qianzhi Zhu 朱謙之, *Laozi jiaoshi* 老子校釋 (Beijing:
Zhonghua shuju, 1984).

82 *A Parenthetical Past*

Pure and solitary, it can be considered the mother of all under Heaven.
I do not yet know its name;
I will style it the "Way."

有狀混成，先天地生，清寥，獨立不亥，可以為天下母。未知其名，
字之曰道。[13]

This is a well-known passage, even before the discovery of the Guodian tomb; it also appears in the received version of the *Laozi* (Chapter 25) and over the past two millennia or so has generated much commentary. Much of these exegeses focused on explicating the concept of the Way, or the *dao* 道, as the singular primordial source of all things, a metaphysical entity that precedes and procreates Heaven and Earth and all things therein.[14] Few, however, have explored the obvious fact that this is also a particular statement about the past. While it may not refer to specific events or individuals from the past, it is nevertheless very much a narrative about the past, one that recounts significant changes from one point in time to another. It is a narrative that relates deep time to the present. Moreover, what we have here is a very specific kind of historical narrative. It is a cosmogonic history.[15] It is an account of no less than the birth of the cosmos and all things within it. It is an account of the deepest time, a narrative of deep history in just twenty-eight words.[16]

In the Guodian version of the *Laozi*, this is the only overtly cosmogonic narrative that we have. In the received version, there are several

[13] Cook, *The Bamboo Texts of Guodian*, A.12 (R25).
[14] See, for example, Kristofer Schipper, "The Wholeness of Chaos: Laozi on the Beginning," in *China's Creation and Origin Myths: Cross-cultural Explorations in Oral and Written Traditions*, ed. by Mineke Schipper, Shuxian Ye, and Hubin Yin (Boston: Brill, 2011), 135–152.
[15] In this chapter, I refer to the different versions of the *Laozi* as "history" in the very broad sense of the term that they contain narratives about the past. It is not a work of historiography per se, of the same order as the *Zuozhuan* or the *Shiji*; unlike these other works, the authors of the *Laozi* did not set out to write an account of the past as an end in itself. The text, however, does mobilize the past to articulate its political and ethical ideals through various cosmogonic narratives which, I would argue, are fundamentally historical. Cosmogonic accounts are a type of historical writing. It is in this context that I use the term "history" when referring to the narratives in the different versions of the *Laozi*.
[16] I borrow the terms "deep time" and "deep history," as opposed to the "shallow past," from Andrew Shryock and Daniel Lord Smail, *Deep History: The Architecture of Past and Present* (Berkeley: University of California Press, 2011), 3–20.

Guodian Laozi

more, all fairly consistent with one another in describing the Way as the progenitor of all things, the singular substance that precedes and generates all things in the world, even Heaven and Earth. The one such passage that has generated the most amount of commentary is perhaps Chapter 42:

> The Way gave birth to one;
> One gave birth to two;
> Two to three;
> And three to the myriad things.

> 道生一，一生二，二生三，三生萬物。

This is more elaborate and detailed than what we see in the Guodian version, but they are very similar cosmogonies. They attribute the origin of the cosmos and all things within it – "all under Heaven" (in the Guodian version) or the "myriad things" (in the received text) – to this one entity, the "Way." The entire world, therefore, shares a single historical origin, a common creative substance that came before all things and continues to generate them. It is a cosmogonic narrative that posits a monogenesis of the world. In the deep past, at the very first moment in history, there was only one thing, the Way. From it, all things came.[17]

But what, one may ask, is the point of this cosmogonic narrative? What does this engagement with the deepest history of all enable the *Laozi* to achieve? To begin answering this question, let us now read the second half of this Guodian *Laozi* passage:

> I force upon it [the Way] the name Greatness.
> Greatness is tantamount to Departure.
> Departure is tantamount to Alternation.
> Alternation is tantamount to Returning.
> Heaven is great; Earth is great; the Way is great, and the king is also great.
> In the realm, there are these four great [things], and the king is one of them.
> Man models himself after Earth;
> Earth models itself after Heaven;
> Heaven models itself after the Way;
> And the Way models itself after what is naturally so.

---

[17] Paul R. Goldin, "The Myth That China Has No Creation Myth," *Monumenta Serica* 56 (2008), 1–22, offers a great discussion of this passage as a "creation story."

84   *A Parenthetical Past*

吾強為之名曰大。大曰折，折曰轉，轉曰返。天大，地大，道大，王亦大。域中有四大，而王居一焉。人法地，地法天，天法道，道法自然。[18]

Like most passages of the *Laozi*, it is hard to say whether this is supposed to be descriptive or prescriptive. Is it suggesting that we, as human beings, should model ourselves after earthly patterns? Or is it saying that we are already bound by the patterns of the earth, since we all share a single origin? Either way, the overall structure of the passage is clear; while the first half gives us a cosmogonic narrative of our primordial origin, the latter half demonstrates the intimate connection between the world of men (*ren* 人) and the Way, which the text says is informed by what is "naturally so" (*ziran* 自然). It is a singular entity in itself, not dependent upon another. It is our shared historical origin, yet it is still operative in the present. It continues to be connected to the whole world, including us.

This refines our understanding of this cosmogony, but falls short of answering the question that I posed earlier: what does a commitment to this cosmogonic understanding of the world enable one to accomplish? For this question, let us venture outside this one passage and read other passages from these Guodian bundles of the *Laozi*:

> The Way is permanently in a state of nonaction.
> If lords and kings can guard it,
> then the myriad things will transform on their own.
> Transformed, and then they desire to create;
> To rectify them with the nameless uncarved block.
> One also attains knowledge;
> Know what is sufficient and then become tranquil,
> And the myriad things will settle on their own.

道恒亡為也，侯王能守之，而萬物將自化。化而欲作，將正之以亡名之樸。夫亦將知，知足以靜，萬物將自定。[19]

The cosmogonic Way in the *Laozi* is not just idle knowledge about the origin and nature of the world, but it is something that a person in a position of power, namely kings and lords, can "guard" (*shou* 守) in order to effect proper transformation of things in the world. It is a knowledge, a positioning of oneself in relation to this monogenetic, cosmogonic source of the world, that can afford one an effective

---

[18] Cook, *The Bamboo Texts of Guodian*, A.12 (R25).   [19] Ibid., A.7 (R37).

Guodian Laozi

mastery of the world in the present. Things are not only "transformed" but "rectified" (*zheng* 正) because their ruler is embracing and committing to the knowledge of this monogenesis of the world.[20] These gnomic definitions of the Way are not just idle ontological speculation but cosmogonic apprehension that can potentially lend one great political power. It is a deep historical knowledge that can empower those who have mastered it and acted according to it.

Elsewhere in the Guodian *Laozi*, we see specific, further elaboration on the power that a sage (*shengren*) can gain from "guarding" this procreative cosmogonic Way. Towards the end of the first bundle (A) of the Guodian *Laozi*, we read,

> One who embodies virtue is similar to a newborn infant.
> Vipers, scorpions, insects, and snakes do not bite him.
> Birds of prey and ferocious beasts do not attack him.
> His bones are soft, sinews are supple, and his grip is firm.

> 含德之厚者，比於赤子。蜂蠆虺蛇弗螫，攫鳥猛獸弗搏，骨弱筋柔而捉固。[21]

An enlightened individual, presumably someone who is one with the Way, is physically healthy and at the same time does not invite attack from others. The passage continues to elaborate on the great vitality of an enlightened individual:

> He does not yet know the union of the male and female sexes, yet his
> phallus rouses.
> This is our essence in its most perfect form.
> To the end of days, he is free of worries.
> This is the most perfect harmony.
> What is harmonious we call "constancy";
> Harmony is constancy;
> Understanding harmony is called "enlightenment."

> 未知牝牡之合朘怒，精之至也。終日乎而不憂，和之至也，和曰常，知和曰明。[22]

But then the passage ends abruptly with a surprising conclusion, on what happens when one is no longer with the Way:

---

[20] Michael J. Puett, *To Become a God: Cosmology, Sacrifice, and Self-Divinization in Early China* (Cambridge, MA: Harvard University Press, 2012), 165–167.

[21] Cook, *The Bamboo Texts of Guodian*, A.18 (R55).　　[22] Ibid., A.18 (R55).

86   *A Parenthetical Past*

What promotes life we call "propitiousness";
As for the mind directing this vital energy, we call it "strength."
When things grow strong, they become old;
And this is called being off the Way.

益生曰祥，心使氣曰強，物壯則老，是謂不道。[23]

So one who "embodies virtue" is naturally strong and vital. Hostile animals and elements in the rest of the world cannot do it any harm. But for those who have veered off course, no longer one with the Way, they may feel invigorated at the moment but eventually they will grow old. The implication here seems to be that if one is with the Way, one remains unharmed to such a degree that he will simply not age. Just as he would be safe from the attacks of unfriendly beasts and the stings of pestilent insects, he would also be immune to the ravages of time. Aging, the growing decrepitude of the body, is a sign of our failed appreciation of and positional deviance from the cosmogonic Way. This emphasis on longevity and endurance can be seen elsewhere in the Guodian *Laozi*:

Therefore, if you know what is sufficient, you will fall into disgrace.
If you know when to stop, you will not be met with any peril,
And you will be able to long endure.

故知足不辱；知止不殆：可以長久。[24]

In the second bundle of bamboo strips (B), we see a reiteration of this theme of what can "long endure" (*changjiu* 長久). The first passage in this bundle begins by arguing that an enlightened individual would have accumulated such an abundance of virtue that he would be limitless in his power, and for that reason he would be able to assume the leadership of the country. And it concludes with the following lines:

One who understands the mother of the country can long endure.
Therefore, having deep roots and a strong foundation,
Is the way of longevity and enduring vision.

有國之母，可以長久。是謂深根固柢，長生久視之道也。[25]

Once again, we see the same argument. Sages, properly cultivated and guarding the Way, will be unharmed and able to perpetuate their flourishing existence indefinitely. In this passage, the use of the word

---

[23] Ibid., A.18 (R55).   [24] Ibid., A.19 (R44).   [25] Ibid., B.1 (R59).

Guodian Laozi   87

mu 母 ("mother") is particularly pointed and resonant, as the Way was described elsewhere in the text precisely as the "mother of all under Heaven," as we saw earlier (i.e. A.12). So understanding the origin of a state, or "possessing" (*you* 有) it, in the language of the text, enables one to "long endure" (*changjiu*). This is a pronounced theme in the Guodian *Laozi*, as it is in the transmitted version. In the latter, the language is sometimes even stronger and more explicit, as in Chapter 52:

> There is a beginning to all that is under Heaven;
> It is the mother of all under Heaven.
> Once you apprehend the mother,
> You therefore know the children.
> Once you know about the children,
> You return to guard the mother.
> To the end of times, you will never be harmed.

> 天下有始，以為天下母。既得其母，以知其子，既知其子，復守其母，
> 沒身不殆。

This direct, causal relation between understanding the Way and the possibility of a perpetual existence that is free from harm is made even more explicit in this passage.

At this point, let us sum up our reading of the *Laozi*, which is primarily based on the Guodian version. We began with the simple observation that it is very much a cosmogonic text, and for that it clearly engages with the past and its relationship to the present. It concerns itself with the deepest past of all, that of the origin of the cosmos, and it postulates the idea of a cosmogonic Way, a primordial monogenesis of the entire cosmos, from which all things originate.[26] But this is no idle ontological speculation. It is a particular history of the universe that lends great power to those who have understood it. Behaving in ways that emulate and position oneself close to this cosmogonic Way, an individual can achieve a certain effectiveness over the present order of things and can contribute to their positive transformation. Since the Way is ontologically a priori to all things in the world (and therefore the precondition for their existence and flourishing), sages who are able to "possess" the Way will naturally be able to

---

[26] Cf. Franklin Perkins, "The *Laozi* and the Cosmogonic Turn in Classical Chinese Philosophy," *Frontiers of Philosophy in China*, 11.2 (2016), 185–205.

88   *A Parenthetical Past*

safeguard themselves from conflict with all things. They are able to preserve themselves from harm and enjoy a perpetual existence. Failing that, one will be ravaged by the passage of time, grow old, and die (as most of us do).

To truly understand the past, therefore, according to the *Laozi*, is to gain the ability to transcend history. The text invites us to look into the past; not the shallow past of the age of human affairs, as most texts of the late Warring States did, but the deep past going all the way back to the beginning of the universe. We look backwards to the earliest historical moments in order to discover and understand the one thing that stands outside history, namely the cosmogonic Way. In the here and now, confronted with a multitude of things in an apparently fragmentary world, the text exhorts us to discover this common historical origin, shared substance, among all things, an apprehension of which will allow us to gain mastery over them. Insofar as the Way is forever unchanging and not susceptible to the ravages of time, it transcends history. Each of us, even though we are necessarily a creation of the Way like all things in the world, can nevertheless cultivate ourselves and conduct ourselves in a manner that positions ourselves close to the Way, "guarding" and "possessing" it, and when we do that, we partake of some of its essential qualities, including its resistance to change over time. Those sages in the past who achieved this had "long endured," as the text claims, because, like the Way, they finally managed to stand (almost) outside history. In this reading, we see that the *Laozi* is in fact an invitation to study the deep past, to reflect upon the earliest history, only in order to discover the one thing that stands outside it. It is a playfully self-destructive deep history that is designed to undermine the meaningfulness of all other histories, which are just epiphenomena of the Way. It is a radical instruction to transcend history by way of a cosmogonic investigation into our deepest past.

Finally, I would like to build on this reading of the *Laozi* and situate it in a broader context. More specifically, it is instructive, I would argue, to relate it to the genealogical past that had informed the historical imagination of the political elite of the Western Zhou, as I argued in the last chapter. In that model, as I gathered from the various bronze inscriptions as well as received materials from the *Poetry* and the *Documents*, one studies and emulates the exemplary actions of one's patrilineal ancestors, not in distant antiquity but from

Guodian Laozi

the founding moments of the Western Zhou dynasty. Those in the here and now study and emulate the founding accomplishments of their respective ancestors, with the conceit that their repetitions, generation after generation, will perpetuate the original good order that their ancestors had so well established. The past is therefore always a genealogical one, with an emphasis on the work of the patrilineal ancestors at the founding moment of the present political order. With this in mind, the *Laozi* and its engagement with the past may seem very far removed, with its cosmogonic musing and metaphysical speculation. But I would argue that, in fact, we can read the Laozian cosmogony as a purposeful, systemic inversion of the patrilineal familial history of the Western Zhou.

In the discussion of the Western Zhou materials, I argued that for this late Bronze Age political elite, there is no history outside family history. The only history that truly matters is family history. This, one can say, is also true for the *Laozi*. For its commitment to the idea of the Way as the cosmogonic monogenesis of the world, all things in the world must be related to one another genealogically. The Way is, according to the Guodian *Laozi*, the "mother of all under Heaven" (*tian xia mu* 天下母).[27] Moreover, both models prescribe that we should emulate the good examples of our ancestors. While the Western Zhou texts point to the patrilineal ancestors from the founding period of the dynasty in the recent past, the *Laozi* suggests that we should look much more deeply into the past, all the way back to the very first moment of the universe. The genders of the ancestral models for emulation are also distinct; the *Laozi* substituted a feminine ancestor – "mother of all under Heaven" – for the male ancestors in the Western Zhou texts. Putting all these pieces together, we may argue that the *Laozi* appropriated the genealogical model of history of the Western Zhou materials, and then deconstructed it through a gendered inversion of its elements.

Yes, one should emulate the exemplary acts and attributes of one's ancestors. Not those in the recent past within the patrilineal line, but the feminine cosmogonic entity of the entire universe. That way, we not only perpetuate the original good order created by our recent male ancestors, which are just ephemeral instantiations of the Way anyhow, but stand close to the feminine cosmic origin so that we can be in

---

[27] Cook, *The Bamboo Texts of the Way*, A.12 (R25).

a position to effectively transform all things in the present. It is a radical expansion of the old genealogical model to a cosmic scale, arguing for an ambition beyond perpetuating the old world order, but to gain the power to effect new orders in the present. In this gendered inversion of the Western Zhou genealogical model of seeing the past, the *Laozi* offers a critique of what it perceives to be the parochialism of the Western Zhou genealogical model of history. Against the shallow past of the Western Zhou, the *Laozi* argues for a genealogical history on a cosmic scale.

We can place this cosmogonic past in the *Laozi* alongside the cultural past of the *Analects* and the etiological past of the *Mozi* as yet another deliberate departure from the genealogical history of the Western Zhou period, in the centuries after the collapse of the political order that sustained that late Bronze Age elite. This deep past in the *Laozi*, however, is not simply an abandonment of the Western Zhou familial history but a feminine inversion of it. It appropriated the idea of a genealogical past but undermined the type of familial history seen in Western Zhou texts as pitifully parochial. Similarly, it calls for an emulation of our ancestors, though not the patriarchs in recent history, but the ultimate matriarch of all, the Way that is the "mother of all under Heaven." In this inversion of a masculine genealogical past into a feminine cosmogony, we no longer simply re-create the good order of our forebears, but we may also be able to help effect the positive transformation of all things in the present. The specific mechanics of this are largely left unsaid in the text itself; it simply calls for one to "guard" or "possess" the Way, taking after this greatest maternal ancestor of all, and the rest will follow.

Finally, it must be noted that the *Laozi* is not alone in offering this cosmogonic reimagining of our past in the late Warring States period. In both the received corpus and the recently excavated materials, we see a variety of these cosmogonic texts, each with its own idiosyncratic speculation on the origin of the universe and the monogenesis of all things. In the same Guodian tomb, there is the *Taiyi sheng shui* 太一生水, which was in fact bundled together with parts of the *Laozi* (C), and discusses not the Way but something called the "Great One" (*taiyi* 太一) as the common progenitor and substance of all things. Referred to as the "mother of the myriad things" (*wangwu mu* 萬物母), a knowledge of it will allow

Guodian Laozi

an individual to remain "unharmed" (*bu shang* 不傷).[28] In the collection of Shanghai Museum bamboo slips, we also have two cosmogonic tracts, namely the *Hengxian* 恆先 and the *Fan wu liu xing* 反物流行. The latter refers to this cosmogonic entity as the "One" (*yi* 一), while the former imagines the beginning as a state of "Constancy" (*hengxian* 恆先).[29] These cosmogonies are never entirely the same, but the basic arguments are very comparable. In their cosmogonic narratives, they ascribe a single origin for all things, and armed with this knowledge of the monogenesis of the world, one gains a great, effective mastery over the entire world. They all promise an empowering knowledge of the deep past of the world.

This flurry of cosmogonic literature has inspired scholars such as Franklin Perkins, in his recent article on the *Fan wu liu xing*, to refer to a "cosmogonic turn" in the late Warring States period, where he argued for competitive cosmogonies between this text and the *Laozi*.[30] It was a race, as Perkins convincingly demonstrated, for who can discover the deepest past, the true origin of the universe, and therefore grants the most power to those in the present. Indeed, this was a rather peculiar episode in the history of the past in early China, where cosmogonic texts, such as the *Laozi*, joined the chorus of voices that called for a study of the past in order to prompt its readers to discover the one thing that stands outside history. What truly matters to them is this one thing, this cosmogonic entity that transcends history, but ironically we can only discover it by way of history. In this sense, the *Laozi* and these other cosmogonic texts embody a profound ambivalence towards

---

[28] See the discussion in Sarah Allan, "The Great One, Water, and the Laozi: New Light from Guodian," *T'oung Pao* 89.4–5 (2003), 237–285; and in Goldin, "The Myth That China has No Creation Myth," 16–21.

[29] See the translation and discussion in Erica Brindley, Paul R. Goldin, and Esther Klein, "A Philosophical Translation of the Heng Xian," *Dao* 12.2 (June 2013), 145–151. I have also found helpful Yu Qiang, "The Philosophies of Laozi and Zhuangzi and the Bamboo-Slip Essay *Hengxian*," *Frontiers of Philosophy in China* 4.1 (2009), 88–115. See also Shirley Chan, "Oneness: Reading the 'All Things Are Flowing in Form (Fan Wu Liu Xing) 凡物流形' (with a Translation)," *International Communication of Chinese Culture* 2.3 (2015), 285–99.

[30] Franklin Perkins, "*Fanwu Liuxing* ('All Things Flow into Form') and the 'One' in the Laozi," *Early China* 38 (2015), 195–232; and "The *Laozi* and the Cosmogonic Turn in Classical Chinese Philosophy," *Frontiers of Philosophy in China* 11.2 (2016), 185–205.

92   *A Parenthetical Past*

the idea of history. History is a very useful thing that will help us escape
from it.

The *Mengzi*: Bioethics, Moral Potentiality, and the Antihistorical Imagination

This profound ambivalence towards the idea of history,
a countercurrent against what appeared to have been a pervasive rhetoric of antiquity in the late Warring States, not only articulated itself in
cosmogonic texts such as the *Laozi*, but also expressed itself in an even
more radical, contentious way in ethical writings from around the same
period. This was particularly pronounced in what I refer to as the
bioethical literature of this period, by which term I simply refer to
writings that ascribe an inherent moral technology to the biological
constitution of individuals.[31] There are numerous examples of such
texts in both the transmitted and excavated corpuses. In this section of
the chapter, I will use the *Mengzi* (孟子) as a key example to elaborate
on this development of antihistorical imagination in the late Warring
States. It is certainly one of the most prominent, popular texts from the
entire early Chinese corpus, but that is not the reason why I chose it for
discussion here. Rather, it is because the *Mengzi* embodies one of the
most hostile, antithetical stances towards the possibility of the utility of
history in the late Warring States. If the *Laozi* suggests that we invest in
one kind of history, namely a deep, cosmogonic past, in order to
transcend all history as mere ephemeral permutation of the same substance that is the Way, then the *Mengzi* advances a more radical
proposal that we may actually just want to, or even need to, do away
with history. For the *Laozi*, at least one piece of the past does matter,
namely the cosmogonic moment; for the *Mengzi*, history is at best idle
knowledge.

---

[31] Deviating from the more usual sense of the term in referring to the ethics of
biological work, I use it here to refer to an ethics that is founded on the biological
constitution of men, similar to what Mark Csikszentmihalyi calls "material
virtue" in his monograph *Material Virtue: Ethics and the Body in Early China*
(Leiden: Brill, 2004). Cf. Ole Döring, "Exploring the Meaning of 'Good' in
Chinese Bioethics through Mengzi's Concept of 'Shan'," in *The Book of
Mencius and Its Reception in China and Beyond*, ed. by Junjie Huang,
Gregor Paul, and Heiner Roetz, Veröffentlichungen des Ostasien-Instituts der
Ruhr-Universität Bochum, Bd. 52 (Wiesbaden: Harrassowitz, 2008), 189–201.

The Mengzi 93

This thesis about the *Mengzi*, that history ultimately does not matter, may seem rather improbable to the many readers familiar with this text. How can this be? Doesn't Mengzi (fl. late fourth century BCE) often invoke historical exemplars and celebrate the achievements of past sages, especially the historical Confucius? In the *Laozi*, there was a conspicuous absence of named historical individuals, as if the text is trying to turn our attention away from those shallow histories, but in the *Mengzi* historical figures well populate the elegant prose of the text. In what follows, I will demonstrate that this apparent deference towards the past is merely superficial; it is a common rhetorical device that Mencius must have been familiar with and sometimes used to great effect, but throughout the text he consistently evinces a profound skepticism about, and at times an outright hostility to, the creeping tyranny of history as an authoritative resource towards our moral development and political imagination. It was not mere indifference to the idea of history, but a deliberate, measured distancing from it.

To begin with, let us ask the question of what history do we actually see in the *Mengzi*? For this, we can turn to the very last passage of the *Mengzi*, where he gives us one of the most elaborate historical narratives in the entire text. It begins with the following: "Mengzi said, 'From Yao and Shun to the time of Tang, it was more than five hundred years'" (孟子曰。由堯舜至於湯。五百有餘歲).[32] The narrative continues to say, from Tang to King Wen, it was another 500 years or so; from King Wen to Confucius, it was yet another 500 years, he continued. And between the time of Confucius and the present, his own time, it had been more than 100 years. And he finally concluded with the following:

---

[32] Unless otherwise noted, translations from the *Mengzi* are my own. I consulted, with much benefit, D. C. Lau's translation, *Mencius* (London: Penguin, 1970); and Irene Bloom, *Mencius* (New York: Columbia University Press, 2009). For the original text, I refer to Yang Bojun 楊伯峻, *Mengzi yizhu* 孟子譯注 (Beijing: Zhonghua, 1983), 14.38. Citations of the *Mengzi* are based on this edition. I assume that the received version of the *Mengzi* does largely contain materials that date back to the late Warring States. Sometimes, in the discussion in this chapter, I refer to the person Mengzi, as a shorthand for the author(s) of the ideas found in the *Mengzi*. I am not committed to the idea that there had to be such a person, and that, if he did exist, the ideas in the text are necessarily his. It simply does not matter to the arguments here. See the relatively dated but still accurate history of the text by D. C. Lau in Loewe, *Early Chinese Texts*, 331–335.

94 *A Parenthetical Past*

It seems that we are not far removed from the age of sages. It also appears to be the case that we are not far removed from where the sages dwelled. But yet, how is it that no one is there? Is there really no one?

去聖人之世。若此其未遠也。近聖人之居。若此其甚也。然而無有乎爾。則亦無有乎爾。[33]

It is one of the broadest historical narratives in the entire *Mengzi*, with almost the entire cast of sages that recur throughout the text. But it was hardly an elaborate historical narrative by any measure. There is no particular sense of historical evolution or devolution, and in the end the point is simply that the time is ripe for the emergence of another sagely individual, and yet, somehow, disappointingly, it has not happened. Perhaps a subtle plaint against the lack of recognition of his virtue in his own time, the passage ends simply with a melancholic note on his pining for the overdue arrival of a sage.[34]

This awareness of the past, a recognition of the common legends of the various sages, together with a palpable disinterest in history as such, the ways in which things had changed significantly from one point in time to another, is fairly typical of the historical narratives in the *Mengzi*. He was certainly well versed in various historical lore, yet his engagement with it seemed deliberately superficial. How do we account for this attitude towards historical knowledge and the past at large? To begin to think of an answer, let us turn to the one thing on which Mengzi expended most of his argumentative capital, namely his ethical theory centered around the idea of the mind (*xin* 心), this moral muscle that Mencius believed each of us is naturally endowed with at birth. As we will see in just a moment, this argumentative center, key to the entire philosophy of the text, directly informs and relates to its studied indifference, and sometime even outright hostility, towards the idea of the possible utility of history in one's moral cultivation.

Famously, Mengzi argued that each of us, as a human being, must feel a sense of panic and alarm if we see that a child is about to fall into

---

[33] Yang Bojun, *Mengzi yizhu*, 14.38.

[34] There is relatively little scholarship on the idea of history in the *Mengzi*. Much of the scholarship has focused on its moral theory rather than its actually very peculiar historical views, as I shall discuss in the rest of this chapter. One notable exception is the discussion by David Nivison, "Mengzi as Philosopher of History," in *Mencius: Contexts and Interpretations*, ed. by Alan K. L. Chan (Honolulu: University of Hawaii Press, 2002), 282–304.

The Mengzi 95

a well.[35] This is entirely spontaneous, according to him, without any calculation on our part. This furnishes proof that in fact we are all endowed with this moral intuition, and though it is often obscured given our own ethical perversion, it does come forth under great stress. It is a moral muscle, or "compassionate mind" or "compassionate heart" (*ce yin zhi xin* 惻隱之心), that "all men must possess" (人皆有之). The virtues that we should cultivate, namely "benevolence, righteousness, ritual propriety, and wisdom," are not "struck onto me from without, but are something that I already had within me" (仁義禮智。非由外鑠我也。我固有之也).[36] For Mengzi, the possession of this moral muscle, endowed at birth with the potential to develop into these proper virtues, is the very definition of being human. It is a moral potentiality inherent in all of us; it is a part of our bioethical constitution as human beings.[37]

Importantly, for Mengzi, this bioethical constitution of all men is not historically contingent. It is simply a fact of nature and has always been true across all time and space. For as long as there have been human beings, from great antiquity to the present, we all must have possessed this moral muscle essential to our humanity. This is not something Mengzi explicitly stated but is nevertheless abundantly clear in the numerous metaphors that he used to elaborate on the nature of this inborn moral potential of ours. "Human nature tending towards good is like water falling downwards" (人性之善也，猶水之就下也), as he

---

[35] Yang Bojun, *Mengzi yizhu*, 3.6.   [36] Ibid., 11.6.

[37] For this relationship between biology and ethics in the *Mengzi*, see Irene Bloom, "Human Nature and Biological Nature in Mencius," *Philosophy East and West* 47.1 (1997), 21–32; and Irene Bloom, "Biology and Culture in the Mencian View of Human Nature," in Chan, *Mencius: Contexts and Interpretations*, 91–102. For a challenge to this view of an essential human nature in the classical Confucian tradition, see Roger T. Ames, "Recovering a Confucian Conception of Human Nature: A Challenge to the Ideology of Individualism," *Acta Koreana* 20.1 (2017), 9–27. For the ethical philosophy in the *Mengzi*, see James Behuniak, *Mencius on Becoming Human*, SUNY Series in Chinese Philosophy and Culture (Albany: State University of New York Press, 2005), esp. 73–99; Bryan W. van Norden, "The Virtue of Righteousness in Mencius," in *Confucian Ethics: A Comparative Study of Self, Autonomy, and Community*, ed. by Kwong-Loi Shun and David B. Wong (Cambridge and New York: Cambridge University Press, 2004), 148–182; Philip J. Ivanhoe, *Ethics in the Confucian Tradition: The Thought of Mencius and Wang Yang-ming*, 2nd edn (Indianapolis: Hackett, 2002); Kwong-Loi Shun, *Mencius and Early Chinese Thought* (Stanford: Stanford University Press, 1997).

96   *A Parenthetical Past*

famously argued.[38] The fact that water does naturally fall downwards is not a historical fact but a natural phenomenon that is universally valid. Similarly, the fact that we, as human beings, are endowed with this moral muscle, the "compassionate mind," is a natural fact of our humanity. It has absolutely nothing to do with history.

This ethical theory leads Mencius to make one of the most radical – and interesting – claims about the great sages of the past. It is true that those sages had cultivated their moral muscles more than others, and therefore they were able to accomplish so much more for the benefit of all with their moral charisma, but in the end, there is really no essential difference between the sages and us. We are all human beings after all, and by definition we all have the same naturally endowed "compassionate mind." This is a point that Mencius reiterates time and again. "Sages and I belong to the same category [of being]" (聖人與我同類者), as he declared at one point.[39] When Duke Wen of Teng (*Teng wen gong*滕文公) passed through the state of Song, he heard that Mencius was known for his teaching on our moral potentiality, that our endowed nature tends towards good, and that he was often laudatory of the sages Yao and Shun. He was doubtful that this teaching was correct, and in response, Mengzi argued that "the Way is one and that is it" (夫道一而已矣), and that as Yan Hui 顏回 once said, "Who is Shun, really? And who am I? Those who accomplished things are all [the same] like this" (舜何人也？予何人也？有為者亦若是).[40] Even though Mengzi was seemingly laudatory of these past sages, the lesson that he drew from them is not about the particular things that they accomplished, but the fact that their achievements delineate for all of us the realm of possible human achievements, since we are all essentially the same human beings endowed with the same moral potential. It is less about learning from the work of the past sages, than about discovering what we ourselves are capable of through an examination of their past achievements. As he quoted this earlier saying of a past minister to his duke, "You are a person, and I too am a person; why would I be fearful of you?" (彼丈夫也，我丈夫也，吾何畏彼哉).[41] Or, even more bluntly, he once declared that "Shun is a human being; I too am a human being" (舜人也，我亦人也).[42] Mengzi assumes a fundamental moral identity between all individuals. It is an ethical constitution, rooted in our

---

[38] Yang Bojun, *Mengzi yizhu*, 11.2. [39] Ibid., 11.7. [40] Ibid., 5.1.
[41] Ibid., 5.1. [42] Ibid., 8.28.

The Mengzi 97

biological being, that is common to all. And for that reason, there is no essential distinction between anyone and the sages: "what sets apart a gentleman from others is his preservation of the heart" (君子所以異於人者，以其存心也); we all have the same moral muscle, and what distinguishes a gentleman from the rest is simply his "preservation" (*cun* 存) of it.[43]

To see this identity between ourselves and the sages of the past, for Mengzi, leads not to elevated attention to their exemplary works in the past. In fact, the effect is the opposite; precisely because the sages are exactly like us, in the sense that we all share the same natural endowment and are all equally morally capable, our knowledge of them is not at all essential to our own cultivation. It may be edifying to study the past, especially to appreciate the great accomplishments of past gentlemen that demonstrate for us the extent of our human potential, but at the same time, it is just idle knowledge not necessarily integral to our cultivation. All that we need to know, all that we need to draw on, is already inherent within us in our natural-born ethical constitution. Or in his own formulation, "The myriad things are already there within me" (萬物皆備于我矣).[44] We have all that is necessary within our morally inclined self for our proper cultivation; all external instructive forces, including an education in history, are at best supplementary but never essential. There is no particular reason to valorize the past over the present, or to think of ourselves as subservient to, and therefore always having to learn from, the supposed moral superiority of the sages in the past. "As for those individuals who surpassed others in antiquity, there was no special reason why; they simply benevolently extended their actions, and that was that" (古之人所以大過人者。無他焉。善推其所為而已矣).[45] The ancients exercised their moral muscle, just as we can and must do the same today to achieve the same result.

David Nivison, in one of the few sustained treatments of the idea of history in the *Mengzi*, offers a very well-observed argument that it often took great creative license when retelling the stories of past sages, sometimes even inventing details to make them "live up to his, Mengzi's, ideal of sagehood."[46] This resonates with my reading of the *Mengzi*; the point of departure in one's moral training is always

---

[43] Ibid., 8.28. [44] Ibid., 13.4. [45] Ibid., 1.7.
[46] Nivison, "Mengzi as Philosopher of History," 302.

98 *A Parenthetical Past*

oneself in the *Mengzi*. To learn about the sages of the past is never to subjugate ourselves to the authority of antiquity, but only to have those lessons help us animate and realize our innate moral potential. Of course, then, one can invent or embellish accounts of the past for his own moral edification.

To claim that the myriad things are already inherent within oneself, as Mencius did, is to obviate the need for the assistance of any external forces or sources, including the historical field, for our moral edification. Living in a time in which the rhetoric of antiquity was obviously pervasive, Mencius recoiled in horror sometimes when his interlocutors dogmatically valorized the past. King Hui of the Liang (*Liang hui wang* 梁惠王) told Mengzi that he indulges in the vulgar pleasure of the music of today, and is incapable of appreciating the "music of the former kings" (先王之樂); Mencius was quick to correct him that "the music of today is like the music of antiquity" (今之樂猶古之樂也).[47] The fact that King Hui was fond of music, in the here and now, is already a sufficient condition for the development of his moral virtue; he need not think that he must listen to the "music of antiquity" in order to be properly cultivated. In another instance, Mengzi was asked if he could re-create the governing success of the historical Guan Zhong 管仲 (*c.*725–645 BCE) and Yanzi 晏子 (*c.*578–500 BCE), and he responded by pointing out his interlocutor's parochial understanding of good governance. Trust not popular sources of authority from the past, but apply your own deliberative capacity, guided by this endowed moral muscle, the "compassionate heart," to arrive at proper moral understanding of the world. "If you entirely trust the *Documents*, then it is better not to have the *Documents* at all" (盡信書則不如無書), as he famously advised.[48] This very much encapsulates his profound wariness regarding historical knowledge. Yes, it could be helpful, but one must engage with it very cautiously. It is potentially harmful to our moral selves, if we defer to the authority of the past uncritically.

In this sense, Mengzi is consistent with the idea of cultivating your own deliberative capacity that was articulated in the *Analects*, but what

[47] Yang Bojun, *Mengzi yizhu*, 2.1.

[48] Ibid., 14.3. Cf. his attitude towards the *Classic of Poetry*, as discussed in Chaoying Chen, "Text and Context: Mencius' View on Understanding the Poems of the Ancients," in *Interpretation and Intellectual Change: Chinese Hermeneutics in Historical Perspective*, ed. by Jingyi Tu (New Brunswick, NJ: Transaction Publishers, 2005), 33–45.

The Mengzi 99

is new here is this profound skepticism towards historical exemplars and the utility of the past.[49] In the *Analects*, Confucius gently insisted on a study of the past as a way to identify exemplary acts to emulate in the present, but in the *Mengzi*, this historical field is no longer integral to one's self-cultivation. All that we really need to know is already within us. History, in the hands of Mengzi, has been rendered idle knowledge.[50] Heiner Roetz, in a recent study, made the insightful observation that in the late Warring States, there was a "paradigm shift" from thinking historically to thinking anthropologically in "normative discourse"; reacting to the "breakdown of the traditional Zhou institutions," there was a loss in faith in history, the old habits of "unreflected appeal to the past," followed by a search for "a new foundation unaffected by history's imponderabilities – a foundation in the imagined reciprocal generalization of basic desires of human beings as such, and in an ahistorical moral disposition (*xing* 性)." What we have seen in the *Mengzi* can be contextualized as a powerful instance of this general pivot from history to anthropology in the late Warring States.[51]

Finally, to conclude this reading of the *Mengzi* as a text with a deliberately cultivated antihistorical tendency, I should note its resonance with the late Warring States cosmogonic texts, such as the *Laozi*, that we discussed in the first part of this chapter. While it is true that the *Mengzi* does not engage in cosmogonic speculation, its strategy in circumscribing the significance of the historical field has much in common with the *Laozi* and the other cosmogonic texts. The *Laozi* offers

---

[49] I accept Michael Hunter's argument that Mengzi – or whoever was responsible for the content of the *Mengzi* – likely did not see the version of the *Analects* that we have today. The comparison I make here between the two is purely ideological, with no implication for the historical relationship between these bodies of ideas or bundles of texts. Michael Hunter, "Did Mencius Know the Analects?", *T'oung Pao* 100.1–3 (2014), 33–79. For the difference between the *Analects* and the *Mengzi* on the concept of humaneness, see Ming Chen 陳明, "The Difference between Confucian and Mencian Benevolence," *Journal of Chinese Humanities* 2.2 (2016), 217–235.

[50] For a different assessment, see Franklin Perkins, "No Need for Hemlock: Mencius's Defense of Tradition," in *Ethics in Early China: An Anthology*, ed. by Chris Fraser, Dan Robins, and Timothy O'Leary (Hong Kong: Hong Kong University Press, 2011), 65–81.

[51] Roetz, "Normativity and History in Warring States Thought," 85–86. While I consider this turn to anthropology to be a phenomenon distinct to the bioethical writings of this period, Roetz considers it to be a much broader paradigm shift that cuts across all intellectual traditions.

100 *A Parenthetical Past*

the idea of the Way as the cosmogonic origin, the singular primordial entity, from which all things arose. The *Mengzi*, on the other hand, suggests that our bioethical constitution, our moral potential, embodied in our "compassionate heart," has within it the "myriad things." It is not a cosmogonic source but an embryonic moral coherence, naturally endowed within each of us, that allows us to situate ourselves properly within the cosmos. In both cases, namely the *Laozi* and the *Mengzi*, there is this appeal to an entity, the Way in one case and the "compassionate heart" in the other, that stands resolutely outside history. And it is precisely because they stand outside history that they matter. A proper knowledge or a proper cultivation of them potentially translates to great power. In the *Laozi*, there is still an investment in the idea of history, as a method to discover what stands outside it, namely the Way, but in the *Mengzi*, the engagement with history is at best superficial. It engages with the rhetoric of antiquity, eloquently so, but time and again it warns us not to indulge in the past but discover what lies outside history, this moral constancy deep within ourselves, in the here and now.

Conclusion

The *Laozi* and the *Mengzi* make for an unlike pairing, but as two bodies of ideas that circulated among the late Warring States political elite, they do share a similar sense of unease with the increasingly elevated authority of the historical field across the ideological spectrum.[52] Both aimed to construct an idea, a certain entity, that not only stands outside history but also above it. The *Laozi* and other cosmogonic texts from this period decided to undermine the authority of historical knowledge with the simple argument that, logically, all history must take place (and is only perceptible to us) against an ahistorical background; there has to be a beginning and therefore a cosmogonic origin of all things. It is the original progenitor that has been giving birth to all things, and to which we all ultimately return; it is simultaneously everywhere and nowhere. The *Mengzi*, on the other hand, devised an alternative strategy; it did not appeal to a deep history but to our supposed bioethical constitution. Instead of delving into the

---

[52] Cf. ibid. Roetz saw this shift as an erosion of the faith in history in this period, while I consider it to be a reaction against the growing importance of history.

Conclusion   101

distant past, it invites us to consider what is close and very near to our sense of the self. The end game for both, however, is the same. It is to discover the one thing in the world that stands outside history. The *Mengzi* was not alone in this endeavor. One may cite, for examples, the *Neiye* 內業 or the *Wuxing* 五行 from the Guodian tomb, as other late Warring States texts that aimed for an ethical understanding of men that allows us to imagine humanity outside the strictures of history.[53] History had come to matter a great deal for many, as the authors of both of these texts were warily aware, and in response they argued for why perhaps it should matter less or not at all. Not forgetting or running away from the past, they wanted to put it in parentheses.

The pervasiveness of the rhetoric of antiquity in the early Chinese corpus was never evidence for any cultural habit that compelled deference to the authority of the past. Rather, as we have seen in this and the previous chapters, it was just a thin veneer that points to a mobilization of the field of the past for lively disputations over a wide range of political and ethical concerns from the late Bronze Age to the centuries after its collapse. History came to matter a great deal for some, such as Confucius in the *Analects*, while others like Mengzi grew increasingly ambivalent about its supposed utility and growing authority. Should the past matter, and how? That was truly an open question in early China.

---

[53] For the *Wuxing*, see the discussion of "material virtue" in Csikszentmihalyi, *Material Virtue*. For the *Neiye*, see Harold Roth, *Original Tao: Inward Training (Nei-yeh) and the Foundations of Taoist Mysticism* (New York: Columbia University Press, 1999); and Puett, *To Become a God*, 109–117.

3 | Specter of the Past
Bureaucratic Amnesia under the Rise of the Qin Empire

This chapter is concerned with the changing politics of the past under the rise of the Qin empire (221–207 BCE) from the middle of the fourth century to the end of the third century BCE. In the previous two chapters, we saw diverse approaches to capitalizing the past to lend support to different political relations and ethical imaginations; first, it was under the aristocratic order of the Western Zhou, then it was in the hands of different political and cultural elites – as collected in the texts the *Analects, Mozi, Laozi,* and *Mengzi,* among others – in the centuries after the collapse of that late Bronze Age regime. This long period of political division finally came to an end when the Qin empire was founded in the year 221 BCE. It annexed – or unified, depending on one's perspective – the entire civilized world known to them with authoritarian bureaucracy supported by laws and punishments of its own dictates. How did this empire regime capitalize the past for its novel political order? How did the Qin empire situate itself in history? The answers to these questions will be the subject of this chapter.

To do that, we will read texts that came from the hands of the ruling elite of the Qin empire itself, including the First Emperor of Qin (Qin shi huangdi 秦始皇帝, 259–210 BCE; r. 221–210 BCE). We will also discuss writings by (or that have been attributed to) prominent Qin officials from the time of its unifying conquest of the realm, most importantly Shang Yang's (d. 338) *Shangjunshu* 商君書 (*The Book of Lord Shang*) and the eponymous collection of Han Feizi's (*c.*280–233 BCE) writings.[1] When I discuss the ideas in these late Warring States texts associated with the rise of the Qin state, I will be using the term "Legalism" to refer to the "intellectual current," to borrow Yuri

---

[1] It may be worthwhile pointing out that Han Fei served the Qin court only for less than a year, despite the fact that he is often associated with this regime. See Sima Qian 司馬遷, *Shiji* 史記 (Beijing: Zhonghua shuju, 1959), 63.2155 and 6.232.

102

Specter of the Past 103

Pines's judicious phrasing, of which they are a part.[2] The term "Legalism" is typically understood by the scholarly community as a direct translation of the Chinese term *fajia* 法家, an anachronistic, tendentious term invented during the Former Han dynasty that none of these writers would have used themselves. It implies a degree of coherence – ideological and institutional – that did not exist in these texts.[3] Nevertheless, I am going to follow the example and advice of Yuri Pines and adopt the use of this term "merely for heuristic convenience" in this study.[4] It works as a placeholder for a broad intellectual current that we have retrospectively identified, one that includes the ideas of Shang Yang and Han Fei as well as several others in the late Warring States that articulated their political ideals through the multivalence of the term *fa* 法 and its many implications.[5]

The discussion in this chapter will be relatively circuitous. By way of preamble, I will begin with a discussion of the notorious bibliocaust

[2] Yuri Pines, *The Book of Lord Shang: Apologetics of State Power in Early China* (New York: Columbia University Press, 2017), 3.

[3] For a most thorough critique of the use of this term, see Paul R. Goldin, "Persistent Misconceptions about Chinese 'Legalism'," *Journal of Chinese Philosophy* 38.1 (2011), 88–104. See also the older but still relevant critique in Herrlee G. Creel, "The Fa-Chia: 'Legalists' or 'Administrators'?", in *What Is Taoism? And Other Studies in Chinese Cultural History* (Chicago: The University of Chicago Press, 1970), 92–120. More recently, Kai Vogelsang offered another critique and suggested using the term "political realism" as a translation of the original Chinese term *fajia*. See Kai Vogelsang, "Getting the Terms Right: Political Realism, Politics, and the State in Ancient China," *Oriens Extremus* 55 (2016), 39–71.

[4] Yuri Pines, "Legalism in Chinese Philosophy," *The Stanford Encyclopedia of Philosophy*, 2017, https://plato.stanford.edu/archives/spr2017/entries/chinese-legalism, accessed May 31, 2018.

[5] The typical "Legalist" canon would include *Shenzi* and *Shen Buhai*, in part because the intellectual lineage that Han Fei had constructed for himself included these two earlier figures. See Eirik Lang Harris, *The Shenzi Fragments: A Philosophical Analysis and Translation* (New York: Columbia University Press, 2016); P. M. Thompson, *The Shen Tzu Fragments* (Oxford and New York: Oxford University Press, 1979); and Herrlee G. Creel, *Shen Pu-Hai: A Chinese Political Philosopher of the Fourth Century B.C.* (Chicago: The University of Chicago Press, 1974). One may also include passages from the *Guanzi* 管子 (e.g. chapters 16, 45, 46, 52, 53, 64, and 67) or the *Lüshi chunqiu* 呂氏春秋 (e.g. chapters 14.4 and 15.8). Chen Qiyou 陳奇猷, *Lüshi Chunqiu jiaoshi* 呂氏春秋校釋 (Shanghai: Xuelin chubanshe, 1984); and Li Xiangfeng 黎翔鳳, *Guanzi jiaozhu* 管子校注 (Beijing: Zhonghua shuju, 2004). For a discussion of the idea of *fa*, see the excellent article by Jeffrey L. Richey, "Lost and Found Theories of Law in Early China," *Journal of the Economic and Social History of the Orient* 49.3 (2006), 329–343.

104   *Specter of the Past*

historical episode from the Qin empire in the year 213 BCE. Then, I will
move back to the Warring States period to discuss the conception of the
past in various Legalist writings. Then, I will return to the Qin empire,
with a discussion of the disquieting career of the past under the rule of
the First Emperor.

Preamble: Bibliocaust, or Empire and Time

In the year 221 BCE, the Qin empire was founded. That marks the end
of more than half a millennium of interstate warfare from the collapse
of the Western Zhou aristocratic order. The Qin state, one of the
domains (*guo* 國) on the far western edges of the Zhou world, annexed
all the others and incorporated their territories into its bureaucratic
order. It divided this newly unified country into thirty-six command-
eries (*jun* 郡), each administered by a governor and his subordinates
appointed by the central government.[6] Rulers of the old domains and
their aristocratic clans were dispossessed of their territories, rendered
mere subjects of the Qin empire. This effort to demolish the old aristocracy for a new authoritarian bureaucratic order extended even to
the ruling family itself. In 213 BCE, almost a decade after the founding
of the empire, an academician (*boshi* 博士) at the Qin court raised his
concern over precisely this matter.[7] At a festive occasion hosted by the
First Emperor, a certain academician named Chunyu Yue 淳于越
expressed his concerns that the emperor did not enfeoff his sons and
younger brothers, rendering them practically commoners of the
empire. This is a deviation from past practices of the Shang and Zhou
dynasties and for that, he alleged, Qin may not be able to maintain its
order for long. "I have never heard of any undertaking that failed to
imitate the example of antiquity and yet was able to endure for long"
(事不師古而能長久者，非所聞也).[8] The First Emperor did not

---

[6] See Michael Loewe, *The Government of the Qin and Han Empires: 221 BCE–
220 CE* (Indianapolis: Hackett, 2006). Also Michael Loewe, "The Operation of
the Government," in *China's Early Empires: A Re-appraisal*, ed. Michael Nylan
and Michael Loewe (Cambridge: Cambridge University Press, 2010), 308–319.

[7] I follow Burton Watson in translating the term *boshi* as "academician." Burton
Watson, *Records of the Grand Historian: Qin Dynasty* (Hong Kong and New
York: Chinese University of Hong Kong and Columbia University Press, 1993), 53.

[8] Sima Qian, *Shiji*, 6.254. Translations from the *Shiji* are adapted from Burton
Watson's translations: *Records of the Grand Historian: Han Dynasty*, Records
of Civilization, Sources and Studies, no. 65, rev. edn (Hong Kong and New York:

Preamble: Bibliocaust, or Empire and Time 105

respond immediately, but instead, he went to consult with the Chancellor Li Si 李斯 (d. 208 BCE), the highest-ranking official of the Qin government.[9]

Li Si's response was fast and furious. He was greatly incensed by Chunyu Yue's admonition. Governance, according to him, was not a matter of aping past successful measures; times are always changing, and new historical circumstances always require new measures. Chunyu Yue was a conservative fool who failed to recognize that the new order of the Qin was appropriate for its own time. As he said:

The Five Thearchs did not imitate each other; the Three Dynasties did not carry on each other's ways, yet each was well governed. It was not that they rejected one another, but that the times changed. Now Your Majesty has initiated this great undertaking, establishing merit that will last ten thousand generations. This is not the sort of thing a stupid scholar [i.e. Chunyu Yue] would understand!

五帝不相復，三代不相襲，各以治，非其相反，時變異也。今陛下創大業，建萬世之功，固非愚儒所知。[10]

Li Si did not stop at this rebuke. There was more here that troubled him, namely the fact that a courtier would criticize the new empire for its deviation from the supposedly exemplary standards of antiquity. Even though the Qin state was the one that had finally put an end to the centuries of warfare and chaos, there were still courtiers like Chunyu Yue who, "instead of looking to the present, study antiquity in order to criticize their own age, misleading and confusing the people" (今諸生不師今而學古，以非當世，惑亂黔首).[11] To put an end to this once and for all, Li Si proposed that all publicly historical records, those that retained traces of the past, be destroyed by burning:

I therefore request that all records of the historians other than those of the state of Qin be burned. With the exception of the academicians whose duty it is to possess them, if there are persons anywhere in the empire who have in their possession copies of the *Poetry*, the *Documents*, or the writings of the hundred schools of philosophy, they shall in all cases deliver them to the

---

Columbia University Press, 1993); and Burton Watson, *Records of the Grand Historian: Qin Dynasty*.

[9] Paul R. Goldin, "'Li Si, Chancellor of the Universe," in *After Confucius: Studies in Early Chinese Philosophy* (Honolulu: University of Hawaii Press, 2005), 66–75.

[10] Sima Qian, *Shiji*, 6.254. [11] Ibid., 6.255.

106   *Specter of the Past*

governor or his commandant for burning. Anyone who ventures to discuss the *Poetry* or *Documents* shall be executed in the marketplace. Anyone who uses antiquity to criticize the present shall be executed along with his family. Any official who observes or knows of violations and fails to report them shall be equally guilty. Anyone who has failed to burn such books within thirty days of the promulgation of this order shall be subjected to tattoo and condemned to wall construction labour. The books that are to be exempted are those on medicine, divination, agriculture, and forestry. Anyone wishing to study the laws and ordinances should have a law official for his teacher.

臣請史官非秦記皆燒之。非博士官所職，天下敢有藏詩、書、百家語者，悉詣守、尉雜燒之。有敢偶語詩書者棄市。以古非今者族。吏見知不舉者與同罪。令下三十日不燒，黥為城旦。所不去者，醫藥葡筮種樹之書。若欲有學法令，以吏為師。[12]

The First Emperor assented to this proposal of an empire-wide bibliocaust. Scholars today continue to debate the veracity of this historical event.[13] Regardless of the extent of the execution of this order, it is indicative of the sort of absolutist power that the Qin court imagined for itself. It serves as a vivid illustration of the supposed authoritarian instinct of the Qin officialdom, especially its intolerance of dissenting voices against the state. In the context of this study, however, what is most interesting about this episode is that what seemed to have truly rattled Li Si was the subversive potential of a knowledge of the past. He did not even deign to respond to the specific proposal about royal enfeoffment but reacted only and furiously to Chunyu Yue's valorization of past practices as exemplary for the present. This aggressive response of an empire-wide bibliocaust was

[12] Ibid., 6.255.

[13] At issue here is how reliable is the *Shiji* account of this incident, the first and most important source of this event. See Jens Østergård Petersen, "Which Books Did the First Emperor of Ch'in Burn? On the Meaning of *Pai Chia* in Early Chinese Sources," *Monumenta Serica* 63 (1995), 1–52. On two different assessments on the reliability of the *Shiji*, see Hans van Ess, "Emperor Wu of the Han and the First August Emperor of Qin in Sima Qian's *Shiji*," in *Birth of an Empire: The State of Qin Revisited*, ed. Yuri Pines, Lothar von Falkenhausen, Gideon Shelach, and Robin D. S. Yates (Berkeley: University of California Press, 2014), 258–279; and Yuri Pines, "The Messianic Emperor: A New Look at Qin's Place in China's History," in Pines et al., *Birth of an Empire*, 258–279. See also Yuri Pines, "Biases and Their Sources: Qin History in the *Shiji*," *Oriens Extremus* 45 (2005–2006), 10–34. The weight of my argument concerning the uses of the past under the Qin empire in this chapter largely rests on the stele inscriptions, not the historicity of the Qin bibliocaust.

Preamble: Bibliocaust, or Empire and Time

conceived in order to eliminate, pre-emptively, all potentially subversive traces of the past.

In this episode, we see that it was not enough for the Qin to have annexed the domains and established an effective authoritarian bureaucracy. To maintain its political authority, the Qin also found it necessary to establish dominion over the past. The rise of the Qin was therefore not only a reorganization of spatial relations (e.g. territorial organization and physical relations between things), but also a remaking of past time. It was an imperialist project that situated itself in both space and time.

Building on this point, this episode also brings our attention to one issue that I think is often overlooked in the study of empires, not only in the context of early China but also world history. It is the different ways that temporality figures in imperial politics. In the voluminous scholarly literature on the idea of empires, there is a tendency to understand empires, as a form of political organization geared towards expansion, as spatial entities first and foremost.[14] There have been numerous definitions given for "empires," and common to all of them is this implicit emphasis on the spatial dimension. Take, for example, these qualifications of an empire by Charles Maier:

An empire in the classic sense is usually believed, first, to expand its control by conquest or coercion, and, second, to control the political loyalty of the *territories* it subjugates. It may rule these subject *lands* directly or it may install compliant native leaders who will govern on its behalf, but it is not just an alliance system among equal partners. Note that the first qualification for empire refers to the historical process by which it is formed, whereas the second describes its ongoing structure.[15]

These two general features of all empires are both spatially conceived, based on land and territorial relations. Burbank and Cooper, in a subtler example, argue that empires are defined by their politics and

[14] On empires as entities driven by imperialism, I follow Michael Doyle's observation: "Empire, then, is a relationship, formal or informal, in which one state controls the effective political sovereignty of another political society. It can be achieved by force, by political collaboration, by economic, social, or cultural dependence. Imperialism is simply the process or policy of establishing or maintaining an empire." Michael W. Doyle, *Empires* (Ithaca, NY: Cornell University Press, 1986), 45.

[15] Charles S. Maier, *Among Empires: American Ascendancy and Its Predecessors* (Cambridge, MA: Harvard University Press, 2006), 24–25, emphasis added.

108   *Specter of the Past*

integration of differences, "self-consciously maintaining the diversity of people they conquered and incorporated."[16] What remains implicit in this formulation is the presumption that such "differences" are only imaginable and observable over a geographical expanse. Even in the most deterritorialized definition given for an empire in recent literature on the subject, by Michael Hardt and Antonio Negri in *Empire*, it is still defined by an expansion of networks, both informal and formal, across the boundaries of sovereign entities.[17] This emphasis on territorial conquest and geographical expansiveness, common to virtually all definitions of empires, betrays a privileging of the spatial dimension in their understanding of what an empire is.

To be sure, empires are spatial entities; there is no such thing an empire of nowhere. However, by way of this bibliocaust episode of the Qin, I would like to draw attention to a more elusive but equally constitutive aspect of imperial formation, namely the remaking of temporal relations, in addition to spatial reorganization. While empires unify terrains and introduce a new spatial intelligibility over originally disparate regions, they must also rework the past in order to find a proper place for themselves in history. To create a new empire is not only to create a new space but also a new past, present, and future for itself.[18]

In the rest of this chapter, I will study how the past was reimagined under the rise of the Qin, as an illustrative case for how temporality figures in the the process of imperial formation. We begin in the middle of the fourth century, with various Legalist writings, and will conclude with the rise and fall of the Qin empire at the end of the third century.

---

[16] Jane Burbank and Frederick Cooper, *Empires in World History: Power and the Politics of Difference* (Princeton, NJ: Princeton University Press, 2010), 2.

[17] Michael Hardt and Antonio Negri, *Empire* (Cambridge, MA: Harvard University Press, 2000).

[18] Outside the scholarship on empires and imperial formations, there have been important discussions on the politics and history of temporality. See, for instance, Vanessa Ogle, *The Global Transformation of Time: 1870–1950* (Cambridge, MA: Harvard University Press, 2015); and the classic article E. P. Thompson, 'Time, Work-Discipline, and Industrial Capitalism', *Past & Present* 38 (1967), 56–97. There are considerably fewer works on this topic in the ancient world; see the important study, Denis Feeney, *Caesar's Calendar: Ancient Time and the Beginnings of History* (Berkeley: University of California Press, 2007); and in the field of early China, Michael Nylan, "Mapping Time in the *Shiji* and *Hanshu* Tables 表," *East Asian Science, Technology, and Medicine* 43 (2016), 61–122.

The Legalist Premise of a Discontinuous Past

At the end of the first chapter, I noted that by the early Warring States period, there was a prevailing sense of historical discontinuity between the past and present. Both the *Analects* and the *Mozi* recognized a disjuncture between antiquity and the present. In the Legalist writings of the late Warring States period, their authors too saw moments of rupture when they looked back upon the past. However, unlike the authors of the *Analects* and the *Mozi*, who tried to overcome this and reconnect with exemplary antiquity somehow, the Legalist thinkers assumed a very different gesture. They simply accepted disjuncture as inevitable.

The world is constantly changing. It never remains the same. This idea can be found in many texts of the Warring States, not just the Legalist corpus, especially by the end of the third century BCE.[19] Yet it is certainly a most prominent theme that characterized much of the Legalist writings. For example, the *Han Feizi* declares:

Past and present have different customs; new and old adopt different measures. To try to use the ways of a generous and lenient government to rule the people of a critical age is like trying to drive a runaway horse without using reins or whip. This is the misfortune that ignorance invites.

夫古今異俗，新故異備，如欲以寬緩之政、治急世之民，猶無轡策而御駻馬，此不知 之患也。[20]

Elsewhere in the *Han Feizi*, and other Legalist texts, we can find various elaborations of this basic position. Typically, they would take a historical form. To demonstrate that the past and present are in fact disjunct, they would turn to elaborate historical narratives. One of the best examples of this is the chapter "Huace" 畫策 of the *Shangjunshu*.[21] It begins with this broad historical narrative:

Of old, in the times of the Great and Illustrious Ruler, people found their livelihood by cutting trees and slaying animals; the population as sparse and

---

[19] Kern, *The Stele Inscriptions of Ch'in Shih-Huang*, 173–174.

[20] Chen Qiyou 陳奇猷, *Han Feizi jishi* 韓非子集釋 (Hong Kong: Zhonghua shuju, 1974), 49.1051. All citations of the *Han Feizi* refer to this edition. Unless otherwise noted, translations from the *Han Feizi* are adaptations from Burton Watson, *Han Feizi: Basic Writings* (New York: Columbia University Press, 2003).

[21] Yuri Pines concludes that it is impossible to date this chapter of the *Shangjunshu*. For the textual history of this text, see Pines, *The Book of Lord Shang*, 25–58.

110   *Specter of the Past*

trees and animals numerous. In the times of the Yellow Emperor, neither young animals nor eggs were taken; the officials had no provisions and when the people died, they were not allowed to use other coffins. These measures were not the same, but that they both attained supremacy was due to the fact that the times in which they lived were different.

昔者昊英之世，以伐木殺獸，人民少而木獸多。黃帝之世，不麛不卵，
官無供備之民，死不得用椁。事不同，皆王者，時異也。[22]

Then, the *Shangjunshu* drives home the point with the following account of the past sages:

In the times of Shennong, men ploughed to obtain food, and women wove to obtain clothing. Without the application of punishments or governmental measures, order prevailed; without the raising of mailed soldiers, he reigned supreme. After Shennong had died, the weak were conquered by force and the few oppressed by the many. Therefore the Yellow Emperor created the ideas of prince and minister, of superior and inferior, the rites between father and son, between elder and younger brothers, the union between husband and wife, and between consort and mate. At home, he applied sword and saw, and abroad he used mailed soldiers; this was because the times had changed (*shibian* 時變). Looking at it from this point of view, Shennong is not higher than Huangdi, but the reason that his name was honored was because he suited his time.

神農之世，男耕而食，婦織而衣，刑政不用而治，甲兵不起而王。神農
既沒，以彊勝弱，以眾暴寡。故黃帝作為君臣上下之義，父子兄弟之禮，
夫婦妃匹之合；內行刀鋸，外用甲兵，故時變也。由此觀之，神農非高
於黃帝也，然其名尊者，以適於時也。[23]

This acceptance of and submission to the inevitability of historical change, or *shibian* 時變 in the language of the *Shangjunshu*, is a consistent theme in the Legalist corpus.[24] Problems of each age are unique,

---

22   Zhu Shiche朱師轍, *Shangjunshu jiegu dingben* 商君書解詁定本 (Beijing: Guji chubanshe, 1956), 18.64. Citations from the *Shangjunshu* all refer to this edition. Unless otherwise noted, all translations are adapted from J. J. J. L. (Jan Julius Lodewijk) Duyvendak, *The Book of Lord Shang: A Classic of the Chinese School of Law, Translated from the Chinese with Introduction and Notes* (London: A. Probsthain, 1928); with consultation of the more recent translation in Pines, *The Book of Lord Shang*.
23   Zhu Shiche, *Shangjunshu jiegu dingben*, 18.64.
24   See also a great example of this term *shibian* 時變 in Book 15, chapter 8, "Cha jin" 察今, of the *Lüshi chunqiu* 呂氏春秋; whenever we see a reference to the ideal of *fa*, there is likely a reference to this idea of *shibian*: "Now, those who would not

The Legalist Premise of a Discontinuous Past
111

and therefore the solutions needed would also need to be new. History, therefore, for the Legalists, is understood as a series of irrevocable ruptures. It is not possible that ideas and practices of a bygone age would still be efficacious in the present, contrary to the models in both the *Analects* and the *Mozi*. "I follow Zhou" (吾從周) can only be the utterance of a quixotic fool like Confucius, for the Zhou belongs wholly to the domain of the past.[25] For their insistence on the inevitability of historical change, one may say that the Legalists were profoundly historically minded. They were acutely aware of the power of the temporal dimension, the ravages of time in the world of things. To illustrate this, the *Shangjunshu* as well as the *Han Feizi* often resorted to historical narratives such as the one we just saw above. The truth of historical discontinuities was demonstrated, time and again, by elaborate narratives about radical transformations in the past. History has a pronounced presence in the Legalist corpus.[26]

Despite their historical-mindedness, however, the Legalist writings are rather disinterested in the question of historical causation. There is no obvious commitment to any particular way of explaining how one period made the transition to the next; there never emerged a predominant narrative, within a single text or across the corpus, on the overall shape or direction of the past across the various points of rupture. Here, one may cite the famous Malthusian argument in the *Han Feizi* as a counterexample, which is clearly a devolutionary view of the human condition.[27] But for all the power of that argument, there is no obvious

---

presume to debate laws are the multitude. Those who die preserving the laws exactly as they are hold the offices charged with managing them. Those who rely on the times (*yin shibian* 因時變) to reform the laws are worthy rulers. This is why the seventy-one sages who have possessed the empire each had different laws. This was not because they overturned those of their predecessors, but because the times and situations were different" (夫不敢議法者，眾庶也；以死守者，有司也；因時變法者，賢主也。是故有天下七十一聖，其法皆不同，非務相反也，時勢異也。) Translation by John Knblock and Jeffrey R. Riegel, *The Annals of Lü Buwei* (Stanford: Stanford University Press, 2000), 370.

25 Yang Bojun, *Lunyu yizhu*, 3.14.

26 Yuri Pines, "From Historical Evolution to the End of History: Past, Present and Future from Shang Yang to the First Emperor," in *Dao Companion to the Philosophy of Han Fei*, ed. Paul R. Goldin (Dordrecht: Springer Netherlands, 2013), 25–46.

27 Exponential increases in population from antiquity to the present create an increasing scarcity of natural resources. Consequently, there has been a historical transition from rule by virtue in antiquity to rule by force in the present. Chen Qiyou, *Hanfeizi jishi*, 49.1040–1041.

112   *Specter of the Past*

commitment to it as the one correct way to understand the shape of the past in the *Han Feizi*. It is never referred to as a basis for any other argument elsewhere in the *Han Feizi*, and more than that, the text readily offers alternative, parallel historical narratives for the same span of time from antiquity to the present.[28] In the end, it is just one among many arguments in the text about historical causation for a demonstration of the verity of a discontinuous past. The emphasis is on proving the truth that past and present are in fact disjunct, but not on the historical mechanism behind the passage from one era to the next. To not commit to a particular mode of historical causation is to pre-empt a historical narrative's predictive capability; the result is a past that is broken up into many pieces, with no obvious overarching narrative that embodies certain historical logic or points towards a possible *telos*. In this sense, despite the writings' repeated invitation to contemplate the past, it is the condition of the present that demands our most immediate and important attention in the end.

This point brings us close to the intent behind their commitment to this idea of the inevitability of historical change. It is an idea that supports their argument for a new form of political order based on the idea of *fa*, an authoritarian set of rules or methods, and by extension an authoritarian bureaucratic order based on laws and punishments according to the dictates of the state.[29] Legalist writers were keenly aware that what they were proposing would be perceived as a radical political innovation.[30] Specifically, it represented a stark

---

[28] For the most elaborate example, see the narrative from "high antiquity" (*shanggu* 上古) to "middle antiquity" (*zhonggu* 中古) to the present in the chapter "Five Vermin." Chen Qiyou, *Han Feizi jishi*, 49.1040–1041.

[29] The term *fa* has a long and complicated history that preceded the beginning of the Legalist intellectual current. See Yuri Pines, "Legalism in Chinese Philosophy," *The Stanford Encyclopedia of Philosophy*, 2017, https://plato.st anford.edu/archives/spr2017/entries/chinese-legalism, accessed 31 May 2018; Richey, "Lost and Found Theories of Law in Early China"; Goldin, "Persistent Misconceptions about Chinese 'Legalism';" R. P. Peerenboom, *Law and Morality in Ancient China: The Silk Manuscripts of Huang-Lao*, SUNY Series in Chinese Philosophy and Culture (Albany: State University of New York Press, 1993), 48–49; A. C. Graham, *Disputers of the Tao: Philosophical Argument in Ancient China* (La Salle, IL: Open Court, 1989), 267–291.

[30] I am referring to the *rhetoric* of innovation here in the Legalist writings, not the historical reality of the actual innovativeness of these bureaucratic institutions. See Kern, *The Stele Inscriptions of Ch'in Shih-Huang*, esp. 154–196, for an argument on the continuity between Qin institutions and those of the earlier periods. Also see the recent reflections in Pines, "The Messianic Emperor."

departure from the last viable political order in history, namely the Zhou. Now, instead of creating enfeoffed kingdoms shared between a small number of aristocratic families, the Qin would govern the country through a bureaucratic administration with stringent laws and harsh punishments. No longer a world organized around kin-based groups and their relations to the ruling family, the Qin would be an authoritarian state, under the dictates of a ruler and his ministers, who govern through a bureaucratic machine.

The founding assumption of *shibian*, or historical discontinuities, works directly for the Legalist argument for this political innovation. Things are constantly changing, and presently, in the late Warring States, they are confronted with new problems that require new solutions. And one new solution, according to the Legalists, is neither the cultivation of humaneness (i.e. the *Analects* and the *Mengzi*), nor an approximation of Heaven's standards (i.e. the *Mozi*), nor an investigation into our cosmogonic origins (i.e. the Guodian *Laozi*), but the idea of *fa*, specifically a form of authoritarian bureaucratic government, with a clear set of rules, compulsory by physical force, dictated by a ruler and his ministers.[31] There is no direct historical precedent for such a radical measure, but that is just the way it should be. Given that the late Warring States, just like any other historical period, represented a new, unique constellation of problems, the solution for them could not possibly be found in the repertoire of political practices from the past. Seeing the past as a series of radical ruptures, the Legalists argued that they had absolutely no choice but to innovate.

Legalists and Their Trouble with History

While this assumption of the inevitability of historical change served the Legalists' argument for *fa* as a new political ideal, it also entailed a series of intellectual complications that subtly militate against the coherence of the Legalist paradigm. The tension that resulted was productive at times but also potentially destabilizing for the various Legalist ideological constructs. It is in the context of these intellectual complications, arising out of their commitment to seeing historical discontinuities, that we can begin to understand the specific ways in

---

[31] See, for example, the passages Zhu Shiche, *Shangjunshu gujie dingben*, 1.1–4; Chen Qiyou, *Han Feizi jishi*, 49.1040–1042.

which the Qin empire, when it was founded in 221 BCE, remade the past for its political legitimacy. In this section, we will survey the said intellectual complications within the Legalist intellectual current; in particular, I will focus on three issues: the ambivalent status of historical knowledge, the legitimacy of the idea of an authoritarian bureaucracy, and finally the historicity of the laws. Together, they will convey the vexing relationship between the notion of *fa* and the past within the Legalist tradition.

First, the ambivalent status of historical knowledge. This issue might already be apparent in the last section on the Legalists' assumption of historical discontinuities. As I noted then, in order to demonstrate the radical differences between past and present, the Legalists often had to turn to elaborate historical narratives as their main evidentiary ground. Moreover, as I also also noted earlier, this insistence on the irreversible course of time, the inevitable ruptures from one period to the next, also made the Legalist texts some of the most historically minded texts in the early China corpus. History, as narratives on changes over time in the past, has a pronounced presence throughout the Legalist corpus.

However, because the goal is to demonstrate historical discontinuities, the lesson at the end of each of these historical narratives in Legalist texts is always that what once worked before is not going to work anymore in the present. In the *Analects*, when an old exemplary act is cited, it is considered a potential candidate for emulation in the present. In a Legalist text, this can never be the case. When the *Han Feizi* cited the "humane" and "righteous" (*renyi* 仁義) governance of King Wen of the Zhou, the point was that this rule by virtue is sadly no longer feasible in the present. Those who tried to emulate it in the present, such as one King Yan of Xu 徐偃王, would predictably fail. "This is because humaneness and righteousness served for ancient times, but no longer serve today" (是仁義用於古不用於今也).[32] Past exemplary acts should never be emulated; in fact, we must actively work against the temptation to reduplicate old practices in the present. Past historical acts, effective measures in their own times, when cited in the texts, are only meant to convey the great distance between then and now, and we are constantly reminded of their categorical uselessness in the present.

[32] Chen Qiyou, *Han Feizi jishi*, 49.1042.

Legalists and Their Trouble with History 115

As such, historical knowledge is both necessary and useless in the Legalist corpus. They must be recited in order to discover the unbridgeable gap between one historical period and another, between the past and present. But at the same time, whatever knowledge about the past we may have gained in the process cannot have any utility in the present. Therefore historical knowledge is only useful and relevant in a negative sense. It is necessary only to the extent that it helps us realize it is ultimately useless (for us in the present). If we truly understand history, we will understand that everything that happened before is no longer meaningful and relevant to the here and now.

This ambivalent status of historical knowledge can be characterized as a specter of the past in the historical imagination of the Legalists. Just as the visibility of a specter signals the very immateriality (i.e. death) of its subject, the very presence of history in a Legalist text signals its meaninglessness within the order of the present.[33] Knowledge about the past is therefore to be cultivated and repressed at the same time. The level of engagement with history is persistently indeterminate throughout the Legalist corpus. This spectral quality of history indicates less a contradiction within the Legalist corpus than an unsettling presence of the past in the Legalist political imagination. If the past and present are truly disjunct, then how is it that the past continues to be intelligible to us and even figures integrally in argumentation? There is a persistent sense of unease over this ghostly presence of history, for it can neither be fully expelled nor legitimately integrated.[34]

Now, let us move on to the second intellectual complication, namely the legitimacy of an authorian bureaucratic order, supported by laws and punishments dictated by the state. While this Legalist vision of history as a constant series of ruptures liberates them and obliges them to innovate a new political order for the present, it also introduces a new epistemological burden. If every age requires unique solutions to its unique problems, then how do we know with any certainty that this

---

[33] For this definition of the term "specter," I follow Jacques Derrida, *Specters of Marx: The State of the Debt, the Work of Mourning and the New International* (New York and London: Routledge, 1994), 6–7.

[34] In the *Han Feizi*, we can almost describe the situation as a schizophrenic one. Alongside its categorical dismissal of the governance of the past, we also see frequent references to the past (*gu* 古) as a repository of exemplary acts (e.g. the chapters "Guan xing" 觀行, "Yong ren" 用人, "Da ti" 大體).

idea of *fa*, as advocated by the Legalists, is in fact the right measure for the present day? In both the *Analects* and the *Mozi*, references to past exemplary acts are self-justifying – what had worked once before may work once again in the present. In the *Analects*, it is the creative adoption of a past exemplary practice by a deliberative individual that ensures its continual effectiveness in the present; in the *Mozi*, it is one's approximation of the universal standards of Heaven, as sage-kings had done in the past, that ensures success. The Legalists, however, did not have the luxury or convenience of referring to the past as evidence of efficacy. They pre-empted that possibility with their very own founding assumption in a discontinuous past. It behooves them to demonstrate that the idea of an authoritarian bureaucracy, founded on laws and punishments, is in fact the most appropriate and effective political measure for their dire times.

And it is a burden that was never truly relieved, at least not from what we can see in the extant corpus of the Legalists. There is no clear consensus on how this proof of the efficacy of *fa* is to be delivered. In one of the earlier texts, the *Shangjunshu*, the argument is mostly a positive description of the order that will allegedly arise once the laws and bureaucracy are established.[35] So the argument for the efficacy of *fa*, as convincing as it may have been to some, was largely in the realm of hypotheticals. By the end of the third century BCE, when we get to the *Han Feizi*, there were still many such idealized descriptions and hypothetical conjectures, but in addition to that, we also see a tentative attempt to legitimate the idea of *fa* by situating it within a metaphysical context.[36] In a couple chapters in the *Han Feizi*, the laws and the rulers who execute them are said to be consistent with a certain metaphysical Way (*dao*), described in a language reminiscent of the *Laozi* 老子 as "the beginning of all things and the measure of right and wrong"

---

[35] For examples, see Chapter 3, "Nong zhan" 農戰; Chapter 4, "Qu qiang" 去強; Chapter 5, "Shuo min" 說民; and Chapter 17, "Shang xin" 賞刑 of the *Shangjunshu*.

[36] For examples, see Chapter 6, "You du" 有度; Chapter 7, "Er bing" 二柄; Chapter 25, "Anwei" 安危; Chapter 53, "Chi ling" 飭令; and Chapter 55, "Zhi fen" 制分 of the *Han Feizi* for idealized descriptions of this Legalist political order. For attempts at legitimating this new order, see its Chapter 5, "Zhu dao" 主道; and Chapter 8, "Yang quan" 揚權. For the issue of legitimacy, see Albert Galvany, "Beyond the Rule of Rules: The Foundations of Sovereign Power in the *Han Feizi*," in Goldin, *Dao Companion to the Philosophy of Han Fei*, 87–106.

Legalists and Their Trouble with History

(萬物之始，是非之紀也).[37] This appeal to a cosmogonic foundation can be read as an attempt by the *Han Feizi* to give the idea of *fa* the legitimacy that it needed. It was an epistemological issue that the Legalists had created for themselves: if no historical precedent can serve as a reliable guide, then how can we be certain that laws and bureaucracy are in fact the right answer?[38]

Finally, let us move on to the third intellectual complication that arises from this Legalist presumption of historical discontinuities. It is the issue of the historicity of the laws. If all things must change over time, and no one period is identical to the next, then our own times should be no exception. They too must give way to the next era at one point or another. So does it mean that this political innovation for the present age, namely an authoritarian bureaucracy based on laws and punishments, is only a temporary institution that must be adjusted, or perhaps even abandoned, as times inevitably change?

It would have to be so according to their own idea of the inevitability of historical change. But if that's the case, how are the laws supposed to change and adapt to new circumstances when they are supposedly unassailable by all and submission to them must be absolute at all

---

[37] Chen Qiyou, *Han Feizi jishi*, 5.67. This association between the laws, the rulers, and the Way (*Dao*) is not limited to the *Han Feizi*. It can also be seen in one of the *Shenzi* fragments: "If, in governing a state, there is no law, there will be disorder; if the laws are [merely] maintained and not reformed [according to the times], then there will be decline. Even if there are laws, if private gains are pursued, it is equivalent to having no laws at all. The people are the ones who serve the laws with their strength; the officials are the ones who follow the laws to death; the leaders are the ones who reform the laws according to the Way" (故治國，無其法則亂；守法而不變則衰；有法而行私，謂之不法。以力役法者，百姓也；以死守法者，有司也；以道變法者，君長也。). Thompson, *The Shen Tzu Fragments*, 278, my own translation. This attempt to associate *fa* with a cosmology that is based on Dao can also be seen in one of the texts recovered from the Mawangdui site, namely the *Jing fa* 經法, which famously opens with the line, "The Way gives birth to the laws" (道生法). See Robin D. S. Yates, *Five Lost Classics: Tao, Huanglao, and Yin-Yang in Han China*, Classics of Ancient China (New York: Ballantine Books, 1997), 50–51. It is perhaps possible to reconstruct a genealogy here of efforts to situate *fa* in relation to the *Dao* from the late Warring States to the early Han dynasty, which would indicate an ongoing search for the legitimacy for the idea of *fa* in the third and second centuries BCE.

[38] There are various attempts to abstract a systematic cosmology out of the *Han Feizi*. See, for example, Zhang Chun 張純 and Wang Xiaobo 王曉波, *Han Fei sixiang de lishi yanjiu* 韓非思想的歷史研究 (Beijing: Zhonghua shuju, 1986), 40–48.

118   *Specter of the Past*

times? The system advocated by the Legalist texts thrives on being inflexible. It works when, and only when, the application of the laws dictated by the state is strict and absolute. But in a world that is supposedly always in a state of flux, wouldn't such a rigid system quickly outdate itself? Wouldn't it create the condition for its own expiration? By what mechanism can the Legalist order adapt to changes over time while it is designed to function irrespective of changing circumstances?

Moreover, this question of the historicity of the laws, arising out of this premise of the inevitability of historical change, is further complicated by the largely theoretical (and therefore ahistorical) language in which the mechanism of the laws is related in the Legalist corpus. Take, for example, the famous account of the "Two Handles" ("Er bing" 二柄) in the *Han Feizi*. Considered a Legalist measure par excellence, the "Two Handles" refers to a ruler's monopoly of the prerogative to mete out rewards and punishments as a means to control his ministers and to establish order at large. The description of its mechanism is formulated in entirely theoretical terms:

The enlightened ruler controls his ministers by means of two handles alone. The two handles are punishment and favor. What do I mean by punishment and favor? To inflict mutilation and death on men is called punishments; to bestow honor and reward is called favor. Those who act as ministers will fear the penalties and hope to profit by the rewards. Hence, if the ruler wields his punishments and favors, the ministers will fear his sternness and flock to receive his benefits.

明主之所道制其臣者，二柄而已矣。二柄者，刑德也。何謂刑德？曰：殺戮之謂刑，慶賞之謂德。為人臣者畏誅罰而利慶賞，故人主自用其刑德，則群臣畏其威而歸其利矣。[39]

This is an entirely theoretical scenario; the mechanism of control described here is unbound to any specific historical context. Later in the chapter, the following conclusion is noted as a result of a ruler relinquishing this prerogative:

Invariably when rulers are intimidated, assassinated, obstructed, or forced into the shade, it has always come about because they relinquished the rights to administer punishment and favor to their ministers, and thus brought about their own peril and downfall.

[39] Chen Qiyou, *Han Feizi jishi*, 7.111.

Legalists and Their Trouble with History 119

故劫殺擁蔽之，主非失刑德而使臣用之，而不危亡者，則未嘗有也。[40]

Here, we see an even stronger claim on the universal validity of this mechanism of governance; it is not a specific measure for a specific time, but a proven mechanism that will never fail. On one hand, the Legalist texts insist on the historicity of political measures; on the other hand, they appear to contradict this by ascribing universal efficacy to this idea of *fa* which they were prescribing for the present. How are these governing mechanisms, such as the "Two Handles," supposed to fare in the long run as the times change? The theoretical language with which they are related implies that they will simply work in perpetuity, but at the same time, that has to be an impossibility under their own founding assumption that political measures are always historically specific. In short, how are we supposed to understand these seemingly ahistorical governing mechanisms in a historical world?

This issue over the historicity of the laws constitutes a major source of tension throughout the Legalist intellectual current in the late Warring States. The only significant solution that has been proffered is the figure of the ruler. From the *Shangjunshu* to the *Shenzi* fragments and the *Han Feizi*, we can see an investment in the figure of the ruler as a solitary individual who, standing obligatorily "outside the laws (*fa*)" (法之外), is uniquely capable of creating—and, even more importantly, modifying – them according to the times.[41] In the *Han Feizi*, as we discussed earlier, the ruler is uniquely associated with the Way, and as a result, rather than submitting himself to the rules and standards that he himself had created, he is capable of instituting and deploying them according to his proper perception of the times. In the *Shenzi* fragments, we also see this description of the ruler as the one uniquely capable of changing the laws.[42] Across these Legalist texts, the ruler occupies the same relative position; in an authoritarian system that commands absolute submission from all, he is the one exception as an extralegal entity, the one element in the entire system that ensures its necessary adaptability. But in the end, this figure of the extralegal ruler is a purely theoretical construct; there is no discussion at all of how such a person would come about and how succession

---

[40] Ibid., 7.111.   [41] Zhu Shiche, *Shangjun gujie dingben*, 1.2.
[42] See note 37 above in this chapter for the passage from *Shenzi*.

120   *Specter of the Past*

would work. For a tradition of persuasion that takes pride in being pragmatic, this is a surprisingly abstract component in Legalist thought.[43]

Now, let me recapitulate. For their commitment to the idea of *shibian*, the inevitability of historical change, which helps justify their political innovation of an authoritarian bureaucratic order enforced by laws and punishments, the Legalist texts incurred a series of intellectual complications that, in various ways, called into question the very coherence and viability of their own proposal. There was the ambivalent status of historical knowledge, the question of the legitimacy of the idea of an authoritarian bureaucracy, and finally the historicity of the laws. Together, they point to a complex, problematic, and contentious relationship between the idea of *fa* and the past in the Legalist tradition. Instead of crippling the tradition, these complications may have served as a source of creative tension that helped further this intellectual current centered around the notion of *fa*, leading to rich elaborations on the cosmological context and the figure of the ruler, as we have discussed. So much of modern scholarship on these Legalist texts has aimed to abstract a system of political thought from them; sometimes, it could be more productive to study where the ideas in the texts become unsystematic and contradictory.[44]

---

[43] The abstract figure of the ruler in the Legalist texts may be related to their agenda to shift the actual ruling power to the ministers. This is especially true in the *Han Feizi*, where we see a very complex relationship between a ruler and his ministers. See, for example, Chapter 27, "Yong ren" 用人; and Chapter 52, "Ren zhu" 人主 of the *Han Feizi*. See Yuri Pines, "Submerged by Absolute Power: The Ruler's Predicament in the *Han Feizi*," in Goldin, *Dao Companion to the Philosophy of Han Fei*, 67–86; and Denecke, *The Dynamics of Masters Literature*, 279–325.

[44] E.g. Léon Vandermeersch, *La formation du légisme: Recherche sur la constitution d'une philosophie politique caractéristique de la Chine ancienne*, Publications de l'École française d'Extrême-Orient, vol. 56 (Paris: École française d'Extrême-Orient: Dépositaire, Adrien-Maisonneuve, 1965); Banroku Ōtsuka大塚伴鹿, *Hōka shisō no genryū* 法家思想の源流 (Tokyo: Sanshin Tosho, 1980); and Wang Xiaobo王曉波, *Xian Qin fajia sixiang shilun* 先秦法家思想史論 (Taipei: Lianjing chuban shiye gongsi, 1991). Or one can also cite the treatment of this body of texts in the narratives of early Chinese intellectual history: Schwartz, *The World of Thought in Ancient China,* 321–349; and Graham, *Disputers of the Tao,* 267–291.

The Qin Resolution: Bureaucratic Amnesia and the End of History

The rise of the Qin empire and the development of the Legalist current of thought are often discussed in conjunction with one another. They bear a positive relationship with each other, according to a great many scholarly narratives of the late Warring States period. Legalist precepts, many of them articulated by those who actually served the Qin, were put into practice by this ambitious state, beginning with Shang Yang under the reign of Duke Xiao (秦孝公, r. 361–338 BCE) in the latter half of the fourth century BCE.[45] Much of the Qin imperial state apparatus was supposedly inspired by one or another tenet of Legalism, most notably the idea of an authoritarian bureaucracy. It follows, also, that the swift collapse of the Qin empire meant that Legalism was by and large a failed tradition of political thought in early China. The Qin empire was a material experimentation of select Legalist theoretical constructs, and in the end, both proved themselves to be miserable failures.

In this final section of the chapter, I will offer a revision of this narrative. While I do recognize the intimate relationship between the history of the Qin and the Legalist intellectual current in the late Warring States, I would suggest that the former was never just a material instantiation of a version of Legalist theories of statecraft. Something a lot more interesting was going on. The Qin empire under the First Emperor did not enact certain Legalist ideas, but it radicalized them. If the Legalist tradition of political thought was sometimes fraught with problematic tension, as I described in the last section, the Qin empire reworked it in a way that resolved many of the long-standing intellectual complications and gave it an ideological coherence that it never had. The result is a radicalized Legalism that culminates in a vision of the Qin as the literal end of history, for having arrived at the final form of government in all human history.

To make this argument, I am going to turn to the series of stele inscriptions commissioned by the First Emperor between 219 and

---

[45] "Qin unification of 221 BCE could have become the triumph of Legalism." This is just a most recent example, in Pines, "Legalism in Chinese Philosophy." For an older example, see Derk Bodde, *China's First Unifier: A Study of the Ch'in Dynasty as Seen in the Life of Li Ssŭ (280?–208 B.C.)* (Leiden: Brill, 1938), 181–222.

122   *Specter of the Past*

210 BCE. There are altogether seven inscriptions, erected at various sites of the newly founded empire at the command of the emperor while he made his inspection tour of the conquered territory.[46] Given the relative paucity of historical sources in this era, these stele inscriptions provide a rare glimpse into the political imagination of the First Emperor and of the Qin political elite at large. They are, as we shall discuss, filled with idealized descriptions of the new imperial order, far removed from the harsh reality of those who actually lived and toiled under the Qin regime. Nevertheless, the language of the inscriptions does allow us to reconstruct how the Qin saw itself and, more pertinently for us, how it reworked the past.

* * *

I will begin with a simple observation. It is that, in the stele inscriptions, we find one of the most fundamental ideas in the Legalist corpus, namely the inevitability of historical change. Times change and things never stay the same. This is a common refrain in Legalist writings, as we discussed in the last section. The inscriptions clearly subscribed to this idea of historical ruptures. But that is not all; they added to it a new, evaluative dimension:

> The people are transformed and civilized,
> Distant and near share unified measures,
> Viewed against the old, [Our times] are absolutely superior.

> 黔首改化，遠邇同度，臨古絕尤。[47]

The past and present are not just distinct, but the present, under the new political order created by the Qin, is in fact superior to the past.

---

[46]   The seven inscriptions are located at Mount Yi, Mount Tai, Mount Langye, Mount Zhifu, Mount Zhifu eastern vista, Jieshi gate, and Mount Kuaiji. The first three were erected in 219 BCE; the Zhifu and the additional one on the eastern vista were erected the next year in 218 BCE; the one on Jieshi gate was erected in 215 BCE; finally, the Mount Kuaiji inscription was erected in either December 211 or January 210 BCE. The texts of the last six inscriptions are all preserved in Chapter 6 of the *Shiji*, while that of the first one, Mount Yi, was preserved in later collections. On the textual history of the Mount Yi inscription, see Yuan Weichun 袁維春, *Qin Han bei shu* 秦漢碑述 (Beijing: Beijing gongyi meishu chubanshe, 1990), 42–49. I also found useful the comprehensive discussion of the stele inscriptions in Kern, *The Stele Inscriptions of Ch'in Shih-huang*.

[47]   Mount Zhifu eastern vista, 218 BCE. Sima Qian, *Shiji* 6.250. Unless otherwise noted, all translations of the stele inscriptions are based on Kern, *The Stele Inscriptions of Ch'in Shih-huang*, 10–49, with some modifications.

The Qin Resolution   123

This self-congratulatory evaluative dimension was a Qin innovation that was absent in the Legalist texts of the late Warring States. If anything, in a text such as the *Han Feizi*, there is nothing to celebrate about the present era; it is only out of necessity that we no longer have recourse to rule by virtue and have to resort to a competition of brute strength.[48] In our earlier discussion of the Legalist texts, we also noted that there was no predominant narrative on the shape of the past, in how one period transitioned to the next and what was the nature of that transition. In the stele inscriptions, however, this evaluative dimension advances a progressive historical narrative. It is not progressive in the sense that each period is necessarily an improvement over the preceding one, but that the present is certainly superior to all that had come before. Right here, right now, we "overlook" (*lin* 臨) the entire field of the "past" (or "antiquity," *gu*), and realize that we are in fact "absolutely superior" (*jue you* 絕尤).

Building on this positively evaluated rupture between past and present, the inscriptions make a further, even bolder, claim for the empire. It is superior to the past because the world that the Qin empire has created pertains to absolute perfection; in fact, it was such a perfect realm that it need not be changed forever into the future:

> The Emperor assumed His position,
> Created the regulations and illuminated the laws;
> ...
> The way of good rule is advanced and enacted;
> The various professions achieve their proper place,
> And all find rule and model.
> His great principle is superb and shining
> To be passed on to later generations
> Who accept this obediently and will not change it.

> 皇帝臨位，作制明法 。。。 治道運行，諸產得宜，皆有法式。大義休明，垂于後世，順承勿革。

And again,

> He [the Emperor] boiled alive and exterminated the violent and cruel,
> Succored and saved the black-haired people [i.e. the commoners],
> And all around consolidated the entire world.
> He universally promulgates the shining laws (*fa*),

---

[48] Chen Qiyou, *Han Feizi jishi*, 49.1042.

Gives standards to all under heaven—
Forever to serve as norm and guide.

烹滅彊暴，振救黔首，周定四極。普施明法，經緯天下，永為儀則。

There is much in these declarations that points to their inheritance from the late Warring States Legalist tradition. First of all, there is a clear echo of the morally dubious injunction from the *Shangjunshu* that it is permissible to stop violence by means of violence.[49] Furthermore, we also see the figure of the ruler as the one who instituted laws (*fa*) in order to create good order for the world. These are all familiar ideas from the Legalist tradition, but at the same time, the inscription introduces something radically new. It is the idea that such a state, once created, can "serve as norm and guide" forever into an indefinite future. With their commitment to the idea of a discontinuous past as well as the inevitability of historical change, the Legalist texts never once declared that the institutions that they envisioned would be everlasting. It was a theoretical impossibility, and perhaps more importantly, it was hardly a concern for them at the time. The most urgent matter was to put an end to the chaos of the late Warring States; the future of these Legalist institutions was something that they could afford to defer to future generations.

The First Emperor, however, thought differently. The world that he had fashioned was not only for the present but for eternity. This is resonant with other early accounts of the Qin empire, outside these stele inscriptions. For instance, in 221 BCE, the First Emperor made the following declaration concerning the titles of the future emperors of the Qin:

An edict was issued, saying: "We have heard that in high antiquity there were titles but no posthumous names. In middle antiquity there were titles, and posthumous names were assigned after the death of a person on the basis of his actions. This results in the son passing judgment on the father, and subjects passing judgment on their ruler. Such a procedure is highly improper and we will have none of it! From now on, this manner of assigning posthumous names shall be abolished. We ourselves shall be called First Emperor (*shi huangdi*), and successive generations of rulers shall be numbered consecutively, Second, Third, and so on for a thousand or ten thousand generations, the succession passing down without end."

[49] Zhu Shiche, *Shangjunshu gujie dingben*, 18.142.

The Qin Resolution

王曰：「去『泰』，著『皇』，采上古『帝』位號，號曰『皇帝』。他如議。」制曰：「可。」追尊莊襄王為太上皇。制曰：「朕聞太古有號毋諡，中古有號，死而以行為諡。如此，則子議父，臣議君也，甚無謂，朕弗取焉。自今已來，除諡法。朕為始皇帝。後世以計數，二世三世至于萬世，傳之無窮。」[50]

The rhetoric of this speech, once again, is reminiscent of the earlier Legalist texts; we see the familiar idea that each historical period had its own unique practices, and that the present day requires its own innovation.[51] At the very end of the statement, we see this grandiose vision where the Qin empire is supposed to rule for ten thousand generations. Once again, we see the same conceit that this new world order will continue in perpetuity.

All these, at first, seem like mere state propaganda – the emperor of an authoritarian government touting the perfection of his own state, declaring the everlasting excellence of his own regime. Upon closer scrutiny, however, I would argue that these ideas represent a careful reworking of the late Warring States Legalist tradition and a powerful consideration of the meaning of history. Specifically, I would now argue, this Qin imperial vision managed to resolve all of the intellectual complications of the Legalist tradition that we discussed earlier. First, there is no longer the issue of the historicity of the laws. Recall that in the Legalist texts, there was the question of how laws should adapt to inevitable changes over time, especially if they are supposed to command absolute submission from all subjects at all time. Moreover, the seemingly universal nature of the Legalist measures also stands in contrast to their own premise that the world is always undergoing change. Under the Qin empire, however, all these issues are rendered meaningless. While the Qin would readily admit that historical changes were constant and persistent in the past, it was no longer the case from this point onwards for they had created a new order so perfectly realized that it could be maintained for perpetuity. The laws wouldn't have to be changed because they were perfect as they were. So while the Qin empire subscribed to the Legalist

---

[50] Sima Qian, *Shiji*, 6.236.

[51] E.g. Chen Qiyou, *Han Feizi jishi*, 49.1040, where he even uses the same periodization, i.e. *shanggu* 上古 ("high antiquity") and *zhonggu* 中古 ("middle antiquity").

126   *Specter of the Past*

premise of the inevitability of historical change, it relegated it to the past and denied its meaningfulness for the future.

Recall, also, that there was the issue of the legitimacy of the idea of an authoritarian bureaucracy. The problem was that if every age is unique and requires its own solutions, then how do we know that *fa*, this idea of a bureaucratic order based on laws and punishments dictated by the state, is in fact the right idea for the present era? For this, the Qin empire only had to point to the fact that they had actually instituted such a Legalist order in the world after a successful conquest of all the domains. It was a *fait accompli* and the proof of the efficacy of this notion of *fa* was in the work of the empire itself. The issue of legitimacy was therefore not so much resolved as it was rendered meaningless.

Finally, there is still the matter of the ambivalent status of historical knowledge. Recall that for the Legalists, historical knowledge had this unsettling, indeterminate status; the past represented an object that was both necessary and ultimately useless at the same time. If the Legalist texts of the late Warring States were haunted by this specter of the past, then this specter had been expelled once and for all under the Qin empire. With its bold claim that we had at last arrived at a perfect order, one that would last indefinitely into the future, historical knowledge would in fact be rendered completely meaningless and useless. Subjects of this empire would live in this perfectly realized world, in accordance with the laws and punishments established by the state, from one moment to the next indefinitely into the future. There would be no need anymore to learn from the past, as the earlier Legalists did, to understand the verity of a discontinuous past; from this point onwards, it would be a steady, eternal present without the need for any further political innovation.

In such a world, if one must inquire about the past, the only significant thing to know was that the past was absolutely an inferior time to ours. And in the stele inscriptions, this is precisely what we find. There are hardly any references to the past at all, except in the very first inscription on Mount Yi erected in 219 BCE:

> Recalling and contemplating the times of chaos:
> When they apportioned the land, established discrete states,
> And thus unfolded the impetus for struggle.
> Attacks and campaigns were daily waged;

The Qin Resolution 127

How they shed their blood in the open countryside—
This had begun in highest antiquity.
Through untold generations
One [rule] followed another down to the Five Divine Kings [*di*],
And no one could prohibit or stop them.
Now today, the Emperor
Has unified all under Heaven under one lineage—
Warfare will not rise again!
Disaster and harm are exterminated and erased,
The black-haired people [i.e. commoners] live in peace and stability,
Benefits and blessings are lasting and enduring.

追念亂世，分土建邦，以開爭理。攻戰日作，流血於野，自泰古始。
世無萬數，陀及五帝，莫能禁止。　乃今皇帝，一家天下，兵不復起。
災害滅除，黔首康定，利澤長久。

In contrast to the obsessive reiterations of historical ruptures in the late Warring States Legalist corpus, this passage is the full extent of the purview of the past in the stele inscriptions. There was indeed a past, a time before the present, but the only thing one needs to know about it is that it was a horrific time, far inferior to the present. There is nothing to be gained, truly, by learning about history. For the less enlightened, learning about the past may even lead them astray into thinking that there is anything at all worthwhile from the past that should be repurposed for the present, like the academician Chunyu Yue whom we discussed earlier in this chapter. Historical knowledge is at best irrelevant, or at worst subversive to the order of the state. It stands to reason that knowledge of the past should be purged or at least contained. In such a world, of course, an idea like the bibliocaust would have been entirely conceivable.

The creation of a perfect bureaucratic order is therefore contingent upon an erasure of history, according to the Qin empire under the First Emperor. The antithetical relation between the past and the idea of *fa* that was kept in a delicate balance in the late Warring States Legalist intellectual current at last found a radical resolution under the Qin empire. To live in this perfectly ordered, self-perpetuating world requires an active forgetting of the past. What the expulsion of the specter of the past exacts is a submission to bureaucratic amnesia. In this sense, we can characterize this Qin imperial ideology, as gathered from the stele inscriptions, in relation to earlier Legalist writings, as one

128   *Specter of the Past*

version of the idea of the end of history. It sees the past as a protracted series of struggles of men, but at long last, out of that long period of strife, we have finally worked out and instituted a political order that will be the very final form of government in human history. Generations will come and go, but the search for the right form of government is now over. With this political innovation by the Qin empire, we as human beings have at long last arrived at an all-encompassing order that is perfectly proper to ourselves from now to eternity.[52]

Conclusion

The supposed end of history did not last very long; the Qin empire collapsed in a spectacular fashion in just about a decade and a half. Nevertheless, despite the brevity of its reign, it did do much to remake the landscape of the past in early China. In the last two chapters, we saw that for the different Warring States texts – the *Analects*, the *Mozi*, the *Mengzi*, the *Laozi*, etc. – there was a common recognition and concern over a rupture between past and present. For the Legalist texts in the late Warring States period and the Qin empire under the First Emperor, they simply embraced historical discontinuity as an inevitable reality and the foundation of their political visions. It was a landscape of the past that was full of holes and gaps. The strong sense of historical continuity in the Western Zhou materials, with its emphasis on the genealogical past and originary moments, eventually gave way to a prevailing sense of historical ruptures by the time of the Warring States period. Time was out of joint, and many took it upon themselves to set it right. The Legalists came along, in the late Warring States, and declared that no, time has always been out of joint. It is just the way of the world. There is no use trying to re-establish continuity with the past – whether through exemplary acts of sage-kings or by emulating the cultural order of the Zhou; these are all dead ends. What

[52] Yuri Pines has written extensively about this idea of the "end of history" in the stele inscriptions of the Qin empire. See his "From Historical Evolution to the End of History." For the idea of the end of history, see Eric Michael Dale, *Hegel, the End of History, and the Future* (New York: Cambridge University Press, 2014); Francis Fukuyama, *The End of History and the Last Man*, Power and Morality Collection at Harvard Business School (New York: Free Press, 1992); and Alexandre Kojève, *Introduction to the Reading of Hegel* (Ithaca: Cornell University Press, 1980).

Conclusion 129

works for this day and age, according to them, is an authoritarian bureaucratic order based on laws and punishments as dictated by the state. Reworked through various hands – from Shang Yang to Han Feizi and finally to the First Emperor of Qin – the Legalist intellectual current finally arrived at the realization that the construction of a perfect empire would require a near total destruction of the idea of a meaningful past. A good empire must always stand on a pivot, between a dark past that need not be known and an amnesiac future that just goes on forever.

4 | *The Rehabilitation of Antiquity in the Early Han Empire*

How does one live within the remains of an empire? That was the question for those involved with the state-building effort in the early years of the Han empire in the early second century BCE. The Qin empire, despite its incredibly successful military campaign that put an end to the warfare of the Warring States, collapsed in spectacularly short order in less than two decades. Following a brief period of civil war between different military leaders, the Han empire under the leadership of Liu Bang 劉邦 (256–195 BCE), the later Emperor Gaozu (Han Gaozu 漢高祖, r. 202–195 BCE), emerged as the legitimate successor of the Qin.

From our standpoint, more than two millennia in retrospect, the early Han is easily seen as the grand beginning of imperial China after the failed start of the Qin. It marks the start of an imperial order that, despite occasional disruptions, would last for more than two thousand years into the early twentieth century. However, suppose we were contemporaries of the early Han, without the benefit of hindsight, then we would perhaps more likely see the early Han as a volatile and uncertain time with a nascent government that was desperately searching for a viable governing model to sustain its authority and legitimacy. The aristocratic order of the Western Zhou had failed over the long run, leading to the centuries of chaos of the Warring States period. Then, amongst all the different proposals to restore peace to the world, the one successful attempt, namely the Legalism-inspired regime of the Qin, experienced a most spectacular collapse in just a couple of decades. Standing at the end of this long line of failed political experiments, there were few viable models of governance for the early Han to chart its way into an uncertain future.

The initial hybrid organization of the Han empire – the western one-third of the territory ruled by a centralized bureaucracy based at the capital, Chang'an 長安, and the eastern two-thirds largely reverting

130

The Rehabilitation of Antiquity in the Han

back to a system of aristocratic enfeoffment – reflected, to a certain extent, its tentative and improvisatory nature.[1] Having inherited much of the Qin bureaucratic institutions and retaining them in the region centered around the new capital, the empire also scaled them back in the east in order to avoid the logistical overreach that had apparently plagued the Qin.[2] On one hand, we can fairly say that the early Han had created a delicate balance, over its large territory, between these two existing models of political organization, namely the aristocratic domains of the Zhou (*fengjian* 封建) and the centralized administration of the Qin (*junxian* 郡縣). On the other hand, given what we know of the tumultuous history between the central court and the regional domains in the eastern part of the empire, it was perhaps less a delicate balance than an unstable amalgam of two historically problematic forms of governance. In this sense, the early Han was less a grand beginning than a reluctant heir to a long line of failed political experiments.

In this ideologically ruinous landscape of the early Han, there was once again a turn to the past as a field of capital for imagining new political orders. From the texts that have survived from the first decades of the early Han, which must have been just a small fraction of what were in circulation at the time, we can gather that there were diverse engagements with the past among the political elite. Many looked back upon the past, but they did not see the same thing. Some emphasized the great urgency of rediscovering the past, while others gave it a more circumscribed role in relation to other forms of knowledge.[3] In this

---

[1] Mark Edward Lewis, *The Early Chinese Empires: Qin and Han* (Cambridge, MA: Belknap Press of Harvard University Press, 2007), 51–74; Denis C. Twitchett and Michael Loewe, *The Cambridge History of China, Volume 1: The Ch'in and Han Empires, 221 BC–AD 220* (Cambridge and New York: Cambridge University Press, 1986), 103–127.

[2] See Ōba Osama大庭脩, *Shin Kan hōseishi no kenkyū* 秦漢法制史の研究 (Tokyo: Sōbunsha, 1982); with the Chinese translation, Ōba Osamu大庭脩, *Qin Han fazhishi yanjiu* 秦漢法制史研究, trans. by Xu Shihong徐世虹 (Shanghai: Zhongxi shuju, 2017); and Bu Xianqun卜憲群, *Qin Han guanliao zhidu* 秦漢官僚制度 (Beijing: Shehui kexue wenxian chubanshe, 2002).

[3] In the cosmological writings of this period, most importantly the *Huainanzi* 淮南子, history as a form of knowledge only has secondary significance. Cf. Michael Puett, "Sages, Creation, and the End of History in the *Huainanzi*," in *The* Huainanzi *and Textual Production in Early China*, ed. by Sarah A. Queen and Michael Puett (Leiden: Brill, 2014), 267–290; and Michael Puett, "Violent Misreadings: The Hermeneutics of Cosmology in the *Huainanzi*," *Bulletin of the Museum of Far Eastern Antiquities* 72 (2000), 29–47. For the

132   *The Rehabilitation of Antiquity in the Han*

chapter, I will focus on two early Han texts that, in different ways, aimed to rehabilitate the past as a meaningful thing after the war against it under the Qin. They also had in common an emphasis on the importance of an education in the classics (*jing* 經). They are the *Xinshu* 新書 by Jia Yi 賈誼 (201–169 BCE) and the *Xinyu* 新語 by Lu Jia 陸賈 (d. 170 BCE). These are two collections of writings by two politicians who once had a flourishing career at the central court at Chang'an. These were ideas that were articulated close to the center of power in the early Han. Invested in the political future of the Han empire, they both discovered much political capital in the landscape of the past that could secure the Han empire a place in history.

Jia Yi's *Xinshu*: Historicizing the End of History

The extant writings attributed to Jia Yi, the question of their authenticity aside, can only be a small fraction of what he once committed to bamboo strips and silk cloth in the first decades of the second century BCE. All his known writings are gathered in a single collection, the *Xinshu*, which, at least as a title, has existed since the Liang 梁 dynasty (502–557) in the sixth century. Modern scholars, following the late imperial textual scholarship, have generally accepted the authenticity of the pieces in this collection, and it is on the basis of this collection that I will discuss his thought on the politics of the past.[4] But first, a brief note about his life. Jia Yi had a tragically short life. He lived for only thirty-three years, and for most of his adult life, he served as a prominent adviser at the court of the second emperor of the Han, namely Emperor Wen (Han Wendi 漢文帝, r. 180–157 BCE). A native of Luoyang 雒陽, he was known as a literary child prodigy of a sort,

---

    Huainanzi, see the discussion of the text and its historical context in John Major, Sarah Queen, Andrew Seth Meyer, and Harold D. Roth, *The Huainanzi: A Guide to the Theory and Practice of Government in Early Han China, by Liu An, King of Huainan* (New York: Columbia University Press, 2010), 1–40.

[4] For the textual history of the *Xinshu*, see Michael Nylan's account in Michael Loewe, ed., *Early Chinese Texts: A Bibliographical Guide* (Berkeley, CA: Society for the Study of Early China, Institute of East Asian Studies, University of California, Berkeley, 1993), 161–170; and the more recent discussion in Pan Mingji 潘铭基, *Jia Yi ji qi Xinshu yanjiu* 賈誼及其新書研究 (Shanghai: Shanghai guji chubanshe, 2017). For the *Xinyu*, I refer to Yan Zhenyi 閻振益 and Zhong Xia 鍾夏, *Xin shu jiaozhu* 新書校注 (Beijing: Zhonghua shuju, 2000).

Jia Yi's Xinshu 133

and when he was just a little more than twenty years old, he had already been appointed an academician (*boshi*) at the Han court.[5] Except for a period of exile in Changsha 長沙 from 177 to 173 BCE, he consistently held prominent positions at the central court. The writings he left behind reflect this official career; the fifty-eight chapters (*pian* 篇) of the *Xinshu* consist mostly of memorials and essays on various issues of state policy. In addition to these writings drawn from his official career, there are also essays on various political matters, as well as lyrical pieces including the famous "Funiao fu" 鵩鳥賦 and "Diao Qu Yuan fu" 弔屈原賦, both of which were written during his exile.

I begin this discussion of Jia Yi with a simple observation: the past has a pervasive presence throughout his writings collected in the *Xinshu*. Given the varied contexts of the different essays in the *Xinshu*, it is to be expected that this collection would have no unified design in respect to the subject matters that it deals with. Despite this heterogeneity of its content, we do see thematic patterns and argumentative strategies that remain consistent across different essays, irrespective of the specific subject matters at hand. And persistent attention to the past is definitely one of the recurring themes in the *Xinshu*.

In contrast to the vision of the Qin empire, which aims to deny the usefulness of a knowledge of the past, Jia Yi argues for its essential role in formulating any political understanding in and of the present. This position on the importance of historical knowledge is explicitly and repeatedly made in his writings. In his famous essay "Guo Qin lun" 過秦論 ("On the Faults of Qin"), for instance, we find the following declaration on the urgent need for a knowledge of the past, especially different historical precedents:

The homely proverb says, "Former affairs (*qianshi* 前事), not forgotten, teach those who come after." That is why, when the gentlemen is given charge of

---

[5] Sima Qian, *Shiji*, 84.2491–2503. This chapter from the *Shiji*, namely the "Qu Yuan Jia sheng liezhuan" 屈原賈生列傳, is the first biography of Jia Yi. Together with the later biography in the *Hanshu*, they constitute the earliest and most important sources of information on the life of Jia Yi. See Ban Gu 班固, *Hanshu* 漢書 (Beijing: Zhonghua shuju, 1962), 48.2221–2266. See also the studies of Jia Yi's biography and the *Xinshu* by Jiang Runxun 江潤勳, Chen Weiliang 陳煒良, and Chen Bingliang Chen 陳炳良, *Jia Yi yanjiu* 賈誼研究 (Kowloon: Qiujing yinwu gong si, 1958); Qi Yuzhang 祁玉章, *Jiazi tanwei* 賈子探微 (Taipei: Sanmin shuju, 1969).

134 *The Rehabilitation of Antiquity in the Han*

a state, he observes how things were done in ancient times (*shanggu* 上古), tests them in terms of the present day, sees how they tally with human concerns, examines into the cause of flourishing and decay, perceives what is fitting in the light of circumstances, initiates actions in the proper order, and changes with the times (*bianhua you shi* 變化有時). As a result, his days as ruler are long and many, and his altars of the soil and grain rest secure.

鄙諺曰「前事之不忘，後事之師也」。是以君子為國，觀之上古，驗之當世，參以人事，察盛衰之理，審權勢之宜，去就有序，變化有時，故曠日長久而社稷安矣。[6]

This argument for the importance of historical knowledge was made in the context of a larger argument on the precipitous fall of the Qin. The question that Jia Yi posed was, why did the Qin empire fall so quickly while the Zhou managed to last for so long? His answer was that the Qin had failed to learn from the good example of the Zhou dynasty, particularly how it was able to adjust to changing circumstances after its conquest of the Shang. The Qin empire's ignorance of the lesson of the Zhou led to its failure to understand that it too needed to adjust its administration, which was designed primarily for military conquest, to one that was more appropriate for peacetime. With its continuation of policies that emphasized stringent rules and harsh punishments, it inevitably prompted popular resentment that led to its unraveling. "In the case of the Qin, however, while it was in a flourishing state, its manifold laws and stern punishments caused the whole world to tremble. But when its power declined, then the people eyed it with hatred and the whole area within the seas rose up in revolt" (故秦之盛也，繁法嚴刑而天下震；及其衰也，百姓怨而海內叛矣).[7] It was for this very reason that the Qin did not at all enjoy the political longevity that the Zhou dynasty had enjoyed. So a fundamental cause of the failure of the Qin was its arrogant ignorance of the lessons of the past. In his own words,

Because the Zhou dynasty set up the five noble ranks and ruled according to the Way, it was able to endure for over a thousand years without break. But

[6] Yan Zhenyi 閻振益 and Xia Zhong 鍾夏, *Xinshu jiaozhu* 新書校注 (Beijing: Zhonghua shuju, 2000), 3.12. Translations of the *Xinshu* are my own, except for the passages from the essay "Guo Qin lun," which are adapted from Watson, *Records of the Grand Historian: Qin Dynasty,* 74–83; and Watson, *Records of the Grand Historian: Han Dynasty I,* 10–13.

[7] Yan Zhenyi and Xia Zhong, *Xinshu jiaozhu,* 3.12.

Jia Yi's Xinshu   135

the Qin had lost its entire foundation, and therefore it did not continue for long. From this we can see that the course of action in times of peace, and that in times of peril, are far apart indeed.

故周王序得其道， 千餘載不絕，秦本末並失，故不 能長。由是觀之，安危之統，相去遠矣。[8]

So, according to Jia Yi, the Qin's failure to adapt to the post-unification condition can be traced back ultimately to its historical ignorance of the history of the Zhou.[9]

This emphasis on the instructive value of historical precedents, or *qianshi* 前事, together with a distinct appreciation for historical changes (*bianhua* 變化) over time, is not limited to his discussion of the Qin empire but can be observed throughout his writings. References to historical episodes constitute the standard evidentiary ground. There are abundant examples in the *Xinshu*. For instance, the essay "Fan jiang" 藩疆, a memorial on the necessity of uniformly weakening the regional domains, begins with the statement that "in studying the traces of past events, in most cases the strong are always the ones who revolt first" (竊跡前事，大抵彊者先反).[10] The chapter "Jieji" 階級 argues for a ritual program that codifies and reflects social and political distinctions, as they were once successfully implemented by the "sage-kings in antiquity" (*gu zhe shengwang* 古者聖王).[11] The chapter "Wu xu" 無蓄 argues that the Han must have abundant provisions in reserve similar to the examples set by Yu 禹, Tang 湯, and other unnamed "men of antiquity" (*guren* 古人).[12] The best example of all is perhaps the chapter "Shu yuan" 屬遠. It begins with a brief description of the exemplary territorial and logistical organization of the states from antiquity, then it offers a criticism of the Qin for its deviance from the past model, and then

---

[8] Ibid., 3.12.
[9] Cf. Elisa Levi Sabattini, "How to Surpass the Qin," *Monumenta Serica* 65.2 (2017), 263–284.
[10] Yan Zhenyi and Xia Zhong, *Xinshu jiaozhu*, 7.20.
[11] Ibid., 15.41. For a recent detailed discussion of the chapter "Jieji," and the political philosophy of Jia Yi at large, see Charles Sanft, "Rituals That Don't Reach, Punishments That Don't Impugn: Jia Yi on the Exclusions from Punishment and Ritual," *Journal of the American Oriental Society* 125.1 (2005), 31–44.
[12] Yan Zhenyi and Xia Zhong, *Xinshu jiaozhu*, 30.87–89.

136 *The Rehabilitation of Antiquity in the Han*

concludes with a specific policy recommendation for the contemporary Han empire.[13]

These invocations of the past, an acute awareness of the vicissitudes of history, point to an insistent call for recognizing not only the temporal dimension in political understanding but also the ceaselessness of historical change from past to present. And on this point, we may also cite the aforementioned poem the "Funiao fu" ("Poetic Exposition on the Owl"), written while Jia Yi was in exile in Changsha. This poem does not so much invoke the past or exemplary precedents, as basically all chapters in the *Xinshu* do, but insists on the constant transformation of all things at all times. It begins with these lines:

> All things of this world move in change
> With never a moment's pause or rest;
> They flow past swirling and away,
> Sometimes forge forward and return,
> Form and force in endless revolution,
> Moving through change as if shedding husks.
> Deep mystery is here that has no end—
> How can I win the full telling?

萬物變化兮，固無休息。斡流而遷兮，或推而還。形氣轉續兮，變化
而蟺。沕穆無窮兮，胡可勝言。[14]

The rest of this short poem expounds, eloquently and elegiacally, on the mutability of all things, including one's sense of self. This insistence on the inevitable transformation of all things is resonant with the historical-mindedness that we see in the *Xinshu*. The term *bianhua* 變化 ("changes") here, which appears no fewer than twice in these opening lines of the poem, also figures significantly throughout the *Xinshu*, as both a descriptive and a prescriptive term: the world is in a constant state of flux, and we must be able to observe and adapt accordingly.[15] "Changes with the times" (*bianhua you shi* 變化有時), as he wrote in

[13] Ibid., 23.116–119.

[14] Fei Zhen'gang 費振剛, Hu Shuangbao 胡雙寶, and Zong Minghua 宗明華, eds., *Quan Han fu* 全漢賦 (Beijing: Beijing daxue chubanshe, 1993), 2. Translation by Stephen Owen, *An Anthology of Chinese Literature: Beginnings to 1911* (New York: W. W. Norton, 1996), 111.

[15] He Lingxu 賀凌虛, *Xi Han zhengzhi sixiang lunji* 西漢政治思想論集 (Taipei: Wu nan tu shu chu ban gong si, 1988), 91–93, also noted this aspect of Jia Yi's political thought.

Jia Yi's Xinshu

the essay "Guo Qin lun," are among the features of a truly sustainable order.[16]

It is interesting that this stance on the constant transformation of all things did not lead Jia Yi to make the claim for historical discontinuity that the Legalists did, as we discussed in the last chapter. His attention to the reality of historical change did not entail a vision of the past as a series of radical ruptures. If anything, the opposite is true. His constant invocation of the past and deferral to the authority of antiquity point to a belief in the potential continuity between past and present through creative adaptations of past exemplary acts. This, of course, is resonant with the way of seeing and using the past in the *Analects*, as we discussed in the first chapter of this book. In fact, I would argue that Jia Yi's basic approach – i.e. studying the repertoire of past cultural practices for their potential adaptations in the present – closely follows the model for capitalizing the past in the *Analects*.

But why this turn to the model of the *Analects* at this particular moment in time in the early Han? How may we contextualize this turn to Confucian hermeneutics of the past in the wake of the fall of the Qin empire? One answer is to read this renewed commitment to the model of the *Analects* as a critical commentary on the failure of Qin. To once again refer to the authority of the past, as a vast repertoire of potentially adaptable models for the present, is to refute the Qin imperial vision which dismissed the field of the past as basically irrelevant. Each time the past is cited in the *Xinshu*, with certain historical precedents valorized as exemplary models for the present, amounts to an implicit criticism of the Qin's dismissal of historical knowledge. In this reading, we may say that this obsessively backward gaze of Jia Yi can be interpreted as an attempt to once again invest potential meaning in the field of the past and reintegrate it into political discourse, as a reaction against the Qin imperial vision which only a generation ago had attempted to divest it of any meaning.

The writings by Jia Yi, as collected in the *Xinshu*, can be read as a document, an exceptionally eloquent one, from a larger movement in the early Han that rebuked the Qin's dismissal of history and searched for ways to see the past anew. Against an empire that saw itself as the end of history, the cessation of all effective historical change, Jia Yi

---

[16] Yan Zhenyi and Xia Zhong, *Xinshu jiaozhu*, 3.12.

138   *The Rehabilitation of Antiquity in the Han*

insisted on the reality of *bianhua*, or changes, in time and in the temporal dimension of all polities at large. In this context, the afore-mentioned essay "Guo Qin lun" is a particularly critical effort. Not only is Jia Yi implicitly discrediting the Qin imperial vision with cita-tions of the past (specifically the positive example of the Zhou dynasty), but in this essay he isolates the history of the Qin as an object of historical inquiry. There is a certain acerbic playfulness here – the polity that once claimed to be the end of history is now fully situated within the domain of the past, being reduced to no more than a disastrous historical episode within the vast expanse of the past. This deliberate act to historicize the end of history was perhaps the most pointed and thorough effort by Jia Yi to demonstrate the absurdity of the Qin's self-perception as the end of history and its failure to see meaning in the past.

I tried, a moment ago, to place Jia Yi's writings within a genealogy of historical thinking that goes back to passages in the *Analects*, based on the observation that for him, too, as it was for Confucius, the past was an adaptable repertoire of exemplary acts. It should be noted that his inheritance of the paradigm first articulated in the *Analects* is actually much more extensive than just this particular attitude towards the past. For instance, throughout the *Xinshu*, one can see an emphasis on the importance of self-cultivation, through "learning" (*xue* 學) and the instructive power of the classics (*jing* 經), that is very resonant with the *Analects*. The chapter "Bao fu" 保傅, for example, details the rigorous ritual and moral education for princes under the Shang and Zhou dynasties; he further attributed the relative longevity of these dynasties to these educational institutions, in contrast to the Qin, which had nothing of the kind.[17] In the chapter "Fu zhi" 傅職, Jia Yi makes a similar argument for the importance of ritual and moral education, but this time, he gives a much more specific curric-ulum; he mentions the *Poetry* (*Shi* 詩), *Documents* (*Shu* 書), *Ritual* (*Li* 禮), *Music* (*Yue* 樂), and *Spring and Autumn* (*Chunqiu* 春秋) as part of an essential curriculum for princes in general.[18] In the chapter "Dao de shuo" 道德說, he adds to these five classics the *Book of Changes* (*Yi* 易), all as part of a self-cultivation curriculum.[19]

Similar to the *Analects*, Jia Yi never gave a systematic account of the origin and nature of the classics; they were simply presented as

[17] Ibid., 33.97–102.   [18] Ibid., 32.93–97.   [19] Ibid., 49.167–168.

Lu Jia's Xinyu

inherited texts and/or traditions that are worthy of our study and reflection. The basic object of one's contemplation is still the vast expanse of the past, that great historical repertoire of exemplary acts, of which the classics are significant, authoritative pieces. Jia Yi, demanding one's reflection upon past exemplary acts for their emulation in the present, was also effectively reintroducing the figure of the deliberative individual that lies at the basis of the political and ethical paradigm in the *Analects*. This is also significant as part of his reaction against the imperial vision of the Qin imperial ideology, for this very deliberative capacity of men is precisely what the Legalist bureaucratic system of laws and punishments under the Qin was designed to circumscribe and ultimately eradicate in favor of an unthinking obedience to the state.

All in all, from the attitude towards the past to this figure of the deliberative individual, we can see many significant traces of the *Analects* in the *Xinshu*. A model of criticism that emerged in a time after the disintegration of a late Bronze Age aristocratic order had now been repurposed to reflect upon the hubris of an imperial authoritarian state and to redress the purging of the idea of a meaningful past under its short-lived rule. Reacting against the Qin's vision of itself as the end of history, early Han thinkers were eager to restore meaningfulness to the past, both as a critical commentary against the Qin and as a new ground for political expression. In the case of Jia Yi, he seems to have largely fallen back on the model that was first articulated in the *Analects*. An expansive landscape of the past was therefore cultivated in his corpus, and with it the figure of the deliberative individual and the imperative for self-cultivation through an education in the classics, especially the authoritative words of the *Poetry, Documents, Music, Changes, Ritual*, and *Spring and Autumn*.

Lu Jia's *Xinyu*: A Classical Encapsulation of the Past

Lu Jia's career slightly preceded that of Jia Yi. While the latter served under Emperor Wen's reign in the 170s BCE, three decades into the early Han, Lu Jia served the founding Emperor Gaozu. From the *Shiji* and the *Hanshu*, we know that he had been a close associate of Emperor Gaozu from the first years of the empire. His official career had remarkable longevity, extending over a few decades into the first

140   *The Rehabilitation of Antiquity in the Han*

years of the reign of Emperor Wen.[20] The careers of Lu Jia and Jia Yi did overlap at the court of Emperor Wen in the 170s, even though there is no record of any direct interaction between the two. Politically, Lu Jia was perhaps best remembered for his successful diplomatic missions to Nanyue 南越 under the reign of Emperor Gaozu, but for our discussion here, we are less concerned about that than about his important intellectual output also from the first decade of Han rule.[21] In a famous anecdote recorded in his biography in the *Shiji* (and the *Hanshu*), Lu Jia was said to have mentioned the classics, specifically the *Poetry* and the *Documents*, in his conversation with Emperor Gaozu. The emperor, so the anecdote goes, had no appreciation for them at all and protested that these classical traditions were useless in matters of military conquest. Lu Jia chastised the emperor for his parochial view of governance and how it might lead to the downfall of the new empire. Not persuaded yet, the emperor asked Lu Jia to write on the causes behind the rise and fall of the Qin empire and other states in history. Lu Jia submitted these essays to Emperor Gaozu, who received them enthusiastically, and so the story goes, they are now collected in the *Xinyu*.[22]

So, unlike the *Xinshu* of Jia Yi, the *Xinyu* was a contemporary collection of essays from the early Han. The *Shiji* account noted that the version at the court of Emperor Gaozu consists of twelve chapters (*pian* 篇), which corresponds exactly to the version we have today. But of course, like any other transmitted text from early China, we can hardly assume that the version that we have today is the same as the one that Emperor Gaozu once held in his hands. On the whole, however, the authenticity of the *Xinyu* has never been seriously challenged; it has been read as a faithful repository or at least a close approximation of Lu Jia's ideas.[23]

---

[20] The two earliest biographies of Lu Jia in the *Shiji* and the *Hanshu* are basically identical to each other: Sima Qian, *Shiji*, 97.2697–2701; and Ban Gu, *Hanshu*, 43.2111–2116. For his biography, see the dated but still accurate Liang Rongmao 梁榮茂, "Han-chu rusheng Lu Jia de shengping ji qi zhushu" 漢初儒生陸賈的生平及其著述, *Kong-Meng Yuekan* 孔孟月刊 7.7 (1969), 21–23.

[21] Ban Gu, *Hanshu*, 95.3828–3853.   [22] Sima Qian, *Shiji*, 97.2699.

[23] Loewe, *Early Chinese Texts*, 171–177, for an overview of its textual history. The argument for the authenticity of the text was made years ago by Miyazaki Ichisada 宮崎市定, *Riku Ka "Shingo" no kenkyû* 陸賈新語の研究 (Kyoto: Kyoto University, 1965), and in my reading, it still stands today.

Lu Jia's Xinyu   141

In any event, the part of the *Xinyu* that I will largely focus on is a relatively unproblematic portion of the text. It is the first chapter, "Daoji" 道基, or "Foundation of the Way." Out of the twelve chapters of the text, it is the most germane to our discussion, for it gives a most detailed and schematic account of the past from antiquity onwards, including the genesis of the classics.[24] It tells a story of our civilizing progress with some rather unexpected twists and turns that, when contextualized against the Qin–Han transition, will have much to tell us about the shifting landscape of the past under the early Han empire.

* * *

The "Daoji" chapter of the *Xinyu* is a historical narrative of how civilization began and developed from the very beginning to the near present. It is, of course, a highly tendentious account with a very specific ideological design. To see what that design is, let us first follow along and see how Lu Jia tells the story of our collective past since the beginning of time.

The narrative begins not with the first human endeavor, but with the cosmological context against which humans and their civilizing progress would soon emerge: "The ancient record says: 'Heaven generated all the myriad things which were nourished by earth, and the sages brought them to fulfillment.' When all these good works and influences merged together, then the Way was generated from them" (傳曰天生萬物，以地養之，聖人成之。功德參合，而道術生焉).[25]

The entire world, and all that happens within it, are the results of dynamic interactions between these three elements, namely heaven, earth, and men. Then, the text goes on to describe the natural patterns in the world, such as the changing of the seasons, and observes that there is a perceptible regularity in their operation. "So changes in the sky can be seen, what is on earth can be measured, changes in nature can be governed,

---

[24] See the discussion of the authenticity of the collection and the paradigmatic significance of this chapter in particular by Miyazaki Ichisada 宮崎市定, "Riku Ka Shingo dōki hen no kenkyū" 陸賈新語道基編の研究, *Tōhō gaku* 25 (1963), 1–10.

[25] Wang Liqi 王利器, *Xinyu jiaozhu* 新語校注 (Beijing: Zhonghua shuju, 1986), 1.1. Unless otherwise noted, translations from the *Xinyu* are adapted from Meikao Ku, *A Chinese Mirror for Magistrates: The Hsin-Yü of Lu Chia*, Faculty of Asian Studies Monographs, new series, no. 11 (Canberra: Faculty of Asian Studies, Australian National University, 1988).

142   *The Rehabilitation of Antiquity in the Han*

what is in men can be diagnosed" (故在天者可見，在地者可量，在物者可紀，在人者可相).[26] With the cosmological staging complete, various life forms now start to emerge.

It is at this point that Lu Jia introduces human beings into the narrative. And it is not men as such but sages. "Thus the sages of antiquity looked upward to the signs of heaven and looked downward on the pattern of earth, and they charted the phenomena in between heaven and earth to fix the way of man" (於是先聖乃仰觀天文，俯察地理，圖畫乾坤，以定人道).[27] To do this—to "fix the way of man"—the sages began to introduce various inventions into the world of humanity. And with these deliberate interventions by the sages, civilization commenced.

The very first step in this civilizing progress, according to Lu Jia, was the introduction of the idea of proper social and political relations: "The people were for the first time enlightened; they recognized the affection between father and son, the correct behavior between ruler and subject, the distinction between husband and wife, the order between elder and younger. So, official positions were appointed and the way of the ruler was established" (民始開悟，知有父子之親，君臣之義，夫婦之別，長幼之序。於是百官立，王道乃生).[28] Following that, then we have the introductions of grain diet by Shennong 神農, shelter by Huangdi 皇帝, agriculture and clothing by Hou Ji 后稷, irrigation by Yu 禹, and transportation and tools by Xizhong 奚仲.[29] In each case, the sage was said to have discerned a material deficiency in the world of men, and then devised an appropriate solution to address it. This brought us closer, step by step, to achieving a fully civilized order.

While these civilizing inventions had elevated the human condition, they also had a corrupting influence on men. "People came to know the relative value of things; everyone liked what was useful and hated what was difficult" (於是民知輕重，好利惡難，避勞就逸).[30] To address this new problem caused by the earlier sagely inventions, another sage, Gaoyao 皋陶, came along and introduced the idea of laws and standards for rewards and punishments. He succeeded in establishing a proper order that "distinguished between right and wrong, and made clear the difference between good and evil, controlled evildoers and exterminated the lazy and lawless" (異是非，明好惡，檢奸邪，消佚亂).[31]

---

[26] Wang Liqi, *Xinyu jiaozhu*, 1.2.   [27] Ibid., 1.9.   [28] Ibid., 1.9.
[29] Ibid., 1.10–15.   [30] Ibid., 1.16.   [31] Ibid., 1.16.

Lu Jia's Xinyu 143

This invention of laws and standards, in turn, prompted yet another sagely invention. It was the introduction of moral education and academic institutions that supported it. It was not enough that people were fearful of punishments by the state, but they must also understand morality and ritual propriety:

At that time the people knew how to respect laws (*fa*) but still lacked propriety and righteousness. And so, the sages of the middle period established education in academies and local schools, and in this way they rectified the decorum between high and low, making clear the correct behavior between father and son, and the right way of action between the ruler and his ministers. In these circumstances they caused the strong not to oppress the weak, the many not to ill-treat the few; they did away with greed and evil ideas, and they encouraged noble actions.

民知畏法，而無禮義；於是中聖乃設辟雍庠序之教，以正上下之儀，明父子之禮，君臣之義，使強不凌弱，眾不暴寡，棄貪鄙之心，興清潔之行。[32]

No specific sages were mentioned as responsible for this last civilizing invention. Instead, it was simply attributed to certain "middle-period sages" (*zhong sheng* 中聖); this was the "middle period" between antiquity and the present. At the very beginning of this narrative, Lu Jia identified the first civilizing invention by "former sages" (*xian sheng* 先聖) as the introduction of the idea of proper social and political relations, i.e. the distinction between father and son, ruler and subject. And now, towards the end of this long civilizing process, having properly domesticated the world by the time of the "middle period," we have come full circle by understanding the morality of these human relationships.

So what happens now after civilization is seemingly complete? Interestingly, for Lu Jia, this was not a self-perpetuating order but only a perfected condition that requires constant, vigilant maintenance. From time to time, people would pervert these various institutions, wittingly or unwittingly, and let civilization go to ruin. And this, according to Lu Jia, was precisely what had happened in more recent times. "Propriety and righteousness were not practiced; laws and regulation were not established. The later ages fell into decay and ruin" (禮義不行，綱紀不立，後世衰廢).[33] But just as the sages in antiquity responded to the challenges of their own time, the sages in the later

[32] Ibid., 1.17.   [33] Ibid., 1.18.

144   *The Rehabilitation of Antiquity in the Han*

ages, the "latter sages" (*hou sheng* 後聖), also took it upon themselves to rectify this deplorable situation. Their solution was to encapsulate all the civilizing principles within a set of classics:

Therefore, the sages of the later age established the Five Classics, elucidated the Six Arts, followed Heaven's wishes to govern things on earth, traced the origin of every event, and scrutinized each tiny thing. They studied human sentiment and established its origins, and thus they arranged the relationships between men, following the model of heaven and earth; they compiled literary works to be passed down to later generations and even extended their influence to birds and beasts. In this way, they obtained relief in a time of decay and rebellion.

於是後聖乃定五經，明六藝，承天統地，窮事察微，原情立本，以緒
人倫，宗諸天地，纂脩篇章，垂諸來世，被諸鳥獸，以匡衰亂。[34]

Unfortunately, Lu Jia did not specify immediately what he meant by the "Five Classics" (*wu jing* 五經) and the "Six Arts" (*liu yi* 六藝), but following the reading by Wang Liqi 王利器, I believe it is safe to assume that they represent two overlapping sets of the classics, namely the *Poetry, Documents, Ritual, Music, Changes,* and the *Spring and Autumn.*[35] These are also the six classics that Lu Jia referred to specifically at the end of this chapter.[36]

This last sagely intervention is very different from the rest. It was not just a solution for a specific problem of the time, but was meant to be the creation of a comprehensive resource, namely a classical canon, that could help us maintain this hard-earned civilized order into the indefinite future. As Lu Jia explains immediately following the passage above:

The affairs of men and the wishes of Heaven are matched. The original way is entirely encompassed [within the classics]. Intelligent people can fully express their intent, and artisans can develop their skills to the utmost. In this way the sages harmonized [the entire world] with the tones of flute and strings, and they established music of bells and drums, dancing and singing, and so they curbed extravagance, rectified customs, and extend proper culture and elegant refinement [throughout the realm].

[34] Ibid., 1.18.
[35] Ibid., 18–19. That is, of course, the same set of classics that Jia Yi also emphasized, as we discussed in the last section. See also Michael Nylan, *The Five "Confucian" Classics* (New Haven: Yale University Press, 2001), 1–72, esp. 19–23.
[36] Wang Liqi, *Xinyu jiaozhu*, 1.34.

Lu Jia's Xinyu 145

天人合策，原道悉備，智者達其心，百工窮其巧，乃調之以管弦絲竹之音，設鐘鼓歌舞之樂，以節奢侈，正風俗，通文雅。[37]

From this point onwards, after the establishment of the classical canon, there need not be any more sagely inventions in history. This was the very last necessary step in our civilizing progress. It is a closed and comprehensive canon that can serve our needs as human beings for all time. Unnecessary addition or deviation from this would only create chaos. And, for Lu Jia, this is precisely what happened in recent ages:

The later ages were licentious and depraved. People added to it the music of the state of Zheng and of Wei; they abandoned the foundation and chased after the frivolous. Excesses appeared in every form, with everyone acting according to his own wishes. They embellished their work with carvings, they applied gum and lacquer, they brushed on valuable colors like red and green, black and yellow, to meet the utmost pleasure of ears and eyes, and to exhaust the skills of the artisan and carpenter.

後世淫邪，增之以鄭、衛之音，民棄本趨末，技巧橫出，用意各殊，則加雕文刻鏤，傅致膠漆丹青、玄黃琦瑋之色，以窮耳目之好，極工匠之巧。[38]

This is where the historical narrative of the chapter ends. In the last part of the chapter, it gives a brief elaboration of the figure of the sages. It explains that sages are defined by their adherence to the foundation of things (*ben* 本), always acting out of principles of humaneness (*ren* 仁) and righteousness (*yi* 義), in order to help maintain proper order in the world. This supposed "foundation of things" (*ben*) is fully identified with the classical canon, namely the "Five Classics" and the "Six Arts":

Now, those who plan affairs, unless they follow both benevolence and righteousness, will surely fail. If you do not make the foundation firm before you erect a high building, then it will certainly fail [in ruins]. Therefore, the sage uses the Classics and the Arts to prevent disorder from emerging, [just as] an artisan uses the marking line to make the crooked straight. The authority of a virtuous person is widespread, while those who rely on force show their pride before many. In this fashion, Duke Huan of Qi prized virtue and became a hegemon, while the Second Emperor of Qin prized punishment and was destroyed.

[37] Ibid., 1.18.   [38] Ibid., 1.21.

夫謀事不並仁義者後必敗，殖不固本而立高基者後必崩。故聖人防亂以經藝，工正曲以準繩。德盛者威廣，力盛者驕眾。齊桓公尚德以霸，秦二世尚刑而亡。[39]

The chapter concludes with a note on the efficacy of each of the classics, and in the very last sentence, he even quotes from the *Guliang zhuan* 穀梁傳, a commentary on the *Spring and Autumn*.[40] His endorsement of this classical canon was emphatic and absolute.

* * *

In the "Daoji" chapter, Lu Jia has given us a historical narrative that begins with the cosmos in antiquity and ends with the establishment of a classical canon in recent times. This is not the first text in the tradition that argues for the authority of the classics, but nevertheless it may well be the earliest text we have that claims that the formation of the classics was the *telos* of our civilizing progress. Sages from one generation to the next built on the work of one another, bringing us closer and closer to civilization, and it all culminated in the creation of the classics in the later ages. This teleological narrative started with an announcement of the beginning of the Way (*dao de sheng yan* 道德生焉) at the conjunction of heaven, earth, and man.[41] The classics represent, then, the *telos* where, in Lu Jia's words, "the designs of Heaven and men are perfectly matched, and the original Way is entirely encompassed" (天人合策，原道悉備).[42] This long and exhausting civilizing process already happened once, and only needed to happen once. Being in the early Han, long after this process that had already been completed, one only needed to study the classics, which contain all essential instructions for the maintenance and perpetuation of this proper order.

It should be noted that there are precedents for this type of civilizational narrative. Similar narratives can be found in a number of late Warring States texts such as the *Xunzi* 荀子 and *Xici zhuan* 繫辭傳; like the "Daoji," they also argued for the necessity of sagely inventions, including the formation of the classics, as part of our civilizing process that would ultimately enable the world at large to achieve its proper order.[43] In the case of Lu Jia, why did he turn to this teleological mode of seeing the past at this particular moment in history? What political implication would such a teleology have in the context of the Qin

---

[39] Ibid., 1.29. [40] Ibid., 1.30–34. [41] Ibid., 1.1. [42] Ibid., 1.18.
[43] Puett, *The Ambivalence of Creation*, 86–90; 152–157.

Lu Jia's Xinyu

debacle and early Han state-building effort? I will now venture a few speculations on these questions.

In the last section on Jia Yi and his *Xinshu*, we noted how his insistence on the utility of the past and emphasis on the inevitability of historical change can be read as a critical refutation of the Qin's dismissal of historical knowledge and the idea of the meaningful past. One can make a similar argument for the "Daoji" chapter. There was a definite effort by Lu Jia to reintegrate the past as an essential dimension for a political understanding of the present.[44] Yet, at the same time, despite this clear presupposition of a meaningful past, we do not see the same broadly ecumenical approach to the past that we saw in Jia Yi's writings. The past, as it was in the "Daoji" chapter, is not the vast repertoire of exemplary acts that it was in Jia Yi's *Xinshu*; instead, it has been ordered into a clearly defined linear trajectory with set historical acts all situated within a definite teleology.

Moreover, at the very end of this teleological history, the result is a set of classics that encompasses all essential principles sufficient for the establishment and perpetuation of this historically realized perfect order. The classics themselves are the product of a historical process, the very end of a teleological movement, but as soon as they come into existence, their comprehensive quality, incorporating all necessary principles into a synchronic whole, renders that entire history that led to their own creation irrelevant. Jia Yi studies the past, including the classics, for models that can be adapted in the present, but for Lu Jia, the existence of the classics obviates the need for such an exhaustive hunt in the historical field. We rely not on our own interpretation of past models, but on proper interpretation of the classics, as the basis for imagining and establishing a proper order for and in the present. The locus of authority for political arguments is not in the expansive, exemplary past, as it was for Jia Yi, but in a past that was encapsulated in the classics.

So, in Lu Jia's case, the past was reintroduced *and* contained at the same time. The classics, as the culmination of the teleological history of the world, were structures that encapsulate the entire past. History did have an essential role to play in producing the classics, but the classics

---

[44] Cf. Zhang Qiusheng 張秋升, "Lu Jia de Lishi Yishi Ji Qi Wenhua Yiyi" 陸賈的歷史意識及其文化意義, *Qilu xuekan* 齊魯學刊 5 (1997), 67–73, for the importance of history in the *Xinyu*.

148 *The Rehabilitation of Antiquity in the Han*

themselves were attributed a universal efficacy that would make that very same history irrelevant in the end. Why should one still study history if all its essential lessons are already perfectly worked out and synthesized in the classics? Why search for exemplary models in fragmentary records of the past while historically proven principles for a well-integrated order are already laid out between the lines of the classics? The classics were the historical end product designed to fully encapsulate that very same history.

But what might have motivated Lu Jia to cultivate such a difficult position? If the idea was to react against the Qin's erasure of history by demonstrating a meaningful past, then why not simply indulge in the vast expanse of the past, appealing to its innumerable models, as Jia Yi had done in the *Xinshu*? The answer, I think, lies in Lu Jia's complex, ambivalent attitude towards the legacy of the Qin empire. His simultaneous reintegration and containment of history, through this classical encapsulation of the past, allowed him to criticize and distance himself from the Qin while preserving its ideal of a singular, normative governing standard for the early Han state. Let me now elaborate on this.

First of all, this appeal to the classics, as a comprehensive set of governing principles that have been historically derived since antiquity, cannot be further removed from the idea of a Legalist bureaucracy, dictated by the ruler and his officials, as espoused by the Qin. Lu Jia's model of classical authority promises a historical continuity between the past and present that was devalued and denied by the Legalist tradition. As we discussed in the previous chapter, the Qin saw a radically discontinuous past, and on that basis, it argued for the innovation of an authoritarian bureaucracy based on laws and punishments as a specific remedy for the chaotic present. Lu Jia's integration of the historical dimension and deferral to the authority of the classics, therefore, can be read as a criticism against what he had diagnosed as a cause behind the precipitous downfall of the Qin. Against Qin's dismissal of the idea of a meaningful past and its radical erasure of history, Lu Jia, like his contemporary Jia Yi, offered an alternative political vision that was fully founded on the past.

Yet, despite this contention of Lu Jia, this idea of an orthodox set of governing principles, embodied in a coherent set of classics, suggests a commitment or sympathy towards the ideal of an authoritarian regime based on the model of the Qin empire. As we discussed in the last chapter, the Qin empire considered itself to have fashioned a perfectly ordered world, made possible by the sagely invention of a centralized bureaucracy, which operated on a normative set of laws. The internal coherence and singular authority of the laws, enforced by rewards and punishments, were what guaranteed a perfect order where, quite literally, everything was in the right place at all time. As the Mount Tai inscription, commissioned by the First Emperor, says, "The emperor assumed his position, and created regulations and illuminated the laws ... The way of good rule is advanced and enacted; the various professions achieve their proper place. And all find rule and model; a great righteousness prevails and shines" (皇帝臨位，作制明法 ... 治道運行，諸產得宜，皆有法式，大義休明).[45] And later in the same inscription: "All receive the sage's will; the noble and the mean are clearly distinguished. Men and women embody compliance; all are cautious and respectful to their professions and duties. Inner and outer spheres are clearly demarcated, and there is nothing that is not clear and pure" (咸承聖志。貴賤分明，男女體順，慎遵職事。昭隔內外，靡不清淨).[46] The orderliness of this world was due to an authoritarian design by a singular source, namely the "will of the sage" (*sheng zhi* 聖志).

Lu Jia's vision that the ideal order must be based upon an orthodox – i.e. singular and normative – set of governing principles, which now happens to be encapsulated in the classics, is strikingly similar to that of the Qin empire. Lu Jia, however, had shifted the source of this governing standard from the figure of the ruler to the set of classics, which also entailed a transposition of political authority from the emperor to classic specialists such as himself. Moreover, in Lu Jia's model, the governing standards were no longer arbitrary creations by the emperor as they were under the Qin, but they were historically realized, morally normative, principles that would perfectly align human society with the rest of the cosmos. In this reading, what Lu Jia had constructed, by way of this classical encapsulation of the past, was essentially a moralized version of Qin authoritarianism. While the Qin imposed a singular order upon the world with admittedly arbitrary laws and punishments, Lu Jia argued that the idea of having singular order was not an imposition at all but natural to the human condition. The Qin demanded that we live in an arbitrary, but perfectly orderly, world

---

[45] Sima Qian, *Shiji*, 6.243.   [46] Ibid., 6.243.

of its own making, while Lu Jia presented this perfect order as a second nature that we should strive to create and inhabit, as sages since antiquity had gradually steered us towards. Accordingly, while the Qin would rely on Legalist state apparatus that forcibly compelled our submission, Lu Jia turned towards moral "instruction" (*jiao* 教) of the subjects through an education in the classics.[47] But in the end, both envisioned a perfectly ordered world, with content subjects, under a singular source of political authority that transcended history.

Lu Jia's reorganization of the past, this classical encapsulation of history as seen in the "Daoji" chapter, is therefore more than just a critical reaction against the Qin empire after its demise, but an effort at inheriting the Qin legacy for the early Han state. It rejected the Qin's dismissal of the past, but aimed to salvage and preserve its ideal of a normative authoritarian regime. It found a solution in this idea of a classical encapsulation of the past. The past is now legitimately reintegrated but at the same time its significance is delimited as secondary to the primary authority of the classics. Perhaps the very suggestion that there can be a historically legitimate, morally grounded, authoritarian rule was sufficient to give the early Han state an ideological cover as it continued to rely on much of the Qin institutions that had crumbled just years ago. After all, in the teleological history of the "Daoji" chapter, the penultimate sagely invention was laws and penal institutions to eliminate all deviant behavior, only to be followed by the introduction of schools to teach the people that proper behavior should not just be motivated by fear of punishments.[48] Perhaps the Qin–Han transition was, or should be, a version of that – the Qin institutions achieved their intended purposes in ending the chaos of the Warring States, and now, building on the same institutions, the Han was meant to take the next step in moralizing those institutions.

Conclusion

In this chapter, we studied two efforts, by Jia Yi and Lu Jia, to reorganize the past in the first decades of the Han. In both cases, the history of the Qin empire loomed large. What sort of history does one, or can one, tell after the fall of an empire that denied the possibility of a meaningful

---

[47] Wang Liqi, *Xinyu jiaozhu*, 1.17.   [48] Ibid., 1.16–17.

Conclusion 151

past and saw itself as the end of history? For both of them, the immediate task was to restore the past as a meaningful dimension for understanding the nature of the present political condition. In other words, they both deliberately worked towards a rehabilitation of antiquity as a meaningful thing. By reasserting the relevance of the past in the present, they repudiated the Qin's vision of history as a series of radical ruptures from one period to the next in a discontinuous past. Similar to certain Warring States texts like the *Analects* and the *Mozi*, Jia Yi and Lu Jia presumed the theoretical feasibility of establishing some form of historical continuity between the past and the present.

More specifically, in the case of Jia Yi, we saw a return to the model of the *Analects*, by opening up a vast expanse of the past in his writings as a virtually limitless repertoire of exemplary acts that can be creatively adapted in and for the present. To reintroduce this model of relating to the past from the *Analects* is also to invite into the picture the figure of the deliberative individual that lies at the very foundation of the *Analects*. This can also be read as part of Jia Yi's reaction against the Qin, for its system of laws and punishments was precisely designed to circumscribe and ultimately eradicate this deliberative capacity of men. Jia Yi's effort at debunking the Qin's vision of history was at its most devastating when he simply applied this old "Confucian" perspective to the history of the failed empire itself. The hubris behind its declaration of the end of history was laid bare when it itself became history.

The case of Lu Jia is more ambivalent. The historical dimension is definitely reintegrated, but at the same time its significance is also curtailed by the existence of the classics, themselves a historical product, which supposedly encapsulate the entire civilizing progress in history into a synchronic whole with universal efficacy. This argument for the existence of such an orthodox governing standard betrays a sympathy towards the authoritarian ideal of the Qin empire, except that for Lu Jia, this orthodox standard encapsulated in the classics was understood as morally normative and historically continuous with the past. In this reading, Lu Jia's classical encapsulation of the past was perhaps less a reaction against the Qin than an effort at working through its problematic legacy. It was a question of fashioning a viable inheritance from the Qin for the early Han state, which in fact persisted with many of the old Qin institutions despite their now discredited, or even defunct, ideological foundation after the fall of the empire.

152 *The Rehabilitation of Antiquity in the Han*

This strategy of classical encapsulation would have a long and varied career for the rest of the Han empire. For instance, in the next generation, at the height of the imperial effort by Emperor Wu (Han Wudi 漢武帝, r. 141–87 BCE), we see a fully fledged classical fundamentalism in the works of Dong Zhongshu 董仲舒 (179–104 BCE) that called for official recognition of this classical orthodoxy at the exclusion of all other traditions.[49] These efforts at relating history and the classics for a viable philosophy of the state stand in contrast to a parallel tradition in the early Han, as represented by the great Sima Qian 司馬遷 (d. 86 BCE), that deployed history not as a means to construct, but to deconstruct and critique, the very concept of a state. This will be the subject of the next chapter.

[49] Ban Gu, *Hanshu*, 56.2523.

5 | *Sima Qian's Critical Past*

In the preceding chapters, we saw a great variety of narratives about the past. There was the genealogical past of the Western Zhou, the cultural past of the *Analects*, and the etiological past of the *Mozi*. In the fourth century, there was the cosmogonic past in the *Laozi* and the parenthetical past, subjugated to the bioethical self, in the *Mengzi*. There was also the spectral past in the writings of the Legalists, leading to its exorcism under the Qin empire, which saw itself as the end of history. Then, in the early Han era, attempts to salvage the field of the past led to renewed attention on the classical canon, among one segment of the political elite at Chang'an.

In this last chapter, we will turn to Sima Qian's *Shiji* from the turn of the first century BCE. In it, we will discover yet another mode in the capitalization of the past. It is what I would call a *critical past*. In the other modes that we have discussed thus far in the earlier chapters, the political elite mobilized the past in order to construct *something*. It could be used to establish aristocratic clan membership, to discover the origins of disorder, or to understand the exemplary acts of the sage-kings of the past, to name just a few examples. In the *Shiji*, however, we have something rather different. Sima Qian, the putative author of the *Shiji*, cast his sight on the past not to construct anything new necessarily, but to stage critiques of the political order of the present. It is a past designed specifically to serve critical ends.

There has been much reflection and debate on the nature and history of the *Shiji* in recent scholarship, not to mention the many different readings of the text in the last two millennia. What I intend to offer here is not meant to be a reading that captures the meaning of the entire text, all 130 chapters of it. It is only one design, one particular mobilization of the past, that we can see in one part of this text (that was possibly mostly written) by Sima Qian. In her recent study of the historical receptions of the *Shiji*, Esther Klein questions the utility of any unitary interpretation of

153

154   *Sima Qian's Critical Past*

the *Shiji* or the authorial intent of Sima Qian.[1] I share the same skepticism and will refrain from extrapolating the conclusion I draw here to the significance of the whole text. What I hope to demonstrate here is only a particular moment in the history of the politics of the past in early China, around the turn of the first century BCE, when we see a new mode of mobilization of the past in relation to the new political condition of the time, namely the aggressively imperialistic reign of Emperor Wu (r. 141–87 BCE).[2] I will use the *Shiji* and the figure of Sima Qian as a window into this particular historical moment, but it is ultimately not about the meaning of the *Shiji* per se.

Such an approach gives me some liberty in choosing which part of the *Shiji* and the Former Han corpus to focus on. After all, I do not have to arrive at a reading that explains all parts of this massive bricolage of a text by Sima Qian. For my argument, I will focus on two chapters of the *Shiji*: the "Huozhi liezhuan" 貨殖列傳 ("Accounts of Commodity Growth") and the "Pingzhun shu" 平準書 ("Treatise on Balanced Standard"). I will draw on other parts of the *Shiji* too occasionally, as well as on other writings from this period. But the focus will be on a close reading of these two texts. These two texts do form a set of a sort; more than other chapters of the *Shiji*, they both deal with the material conditions of the Han empire, especially the history of economic relations in the area governed by the empire under Emperor Wu.[3] While almost all other chapters of the *Shiji* deal with events and personalities that are squarely in the past, the "Pingzhun shu" is one of the few that deal with contemporary history, specifically the military affairs and economic policies of the Han empire, and for that reason it

[1] Esther Sunkyung Klein, *Reading Sima Qian from Han to Song: The Father of History in Pre-modern China* (Leiden: Brill, 2018). For works that tried to offer a broad interpretation of the *Shiji* or Sima Qian from recent decades, see Nylan, "Mapping Time in the *Shiji* and *Hanshu* Tables 表"; Stephen W. Durrant, *The Cloudy Mirror: Tension and Conflict in the Writings of Sima Qian* (Albany: State University of New York Press, 1995); Hardy, *Worlds of Bronze and Bamboo*; Nylan, "Sima Qian: A True Historian?"; and Li Changzhi 李長之, *Sima Qian zhi renge yu fengge* 司馬遷之人格與風格 (Hong Kong: Taiping shuju, 1963).

[2] For a summary account of the reign of Emperor Wu, see Vincent S. Leung, "The Former Han Empire," in *Routledge Handbook of Early Chinese History*, ed. Paul R. Goldin (London: Routledge, 2018), 160–179.

[3] These two texts are often read in conjunction with one another. See Zhang Dake张大可, *Shiji yanjiu* 史記研究 (Beijing: Shangwu yinshuguan, 2011); Wei Wei 韦苇, *Sima Qian jing ji si xiang yan jiu* 司馬遷經濟思想研究 (Xi'an: Shanxi renmin jiaoyu chubanshe, 1995).

"Huozhi Liezhuan" 155

is particularly germane to the question of how the *Shiji* mobilizes the past in relation to the new political condition of the empire. The "Huozhi liezhuan," on the other hand, does not deal with contemporary history but is a sustained discussion of economic matters in the past, and as such it provides an important context for the narratives in the "Pingzhun shu." To draw out this critical past from the *Shiji*, I find these two texts to be an effective means.

The discussion in this chapter will be divided into two halves, each devoted to one of these two texts. First, I will discuss the "Huozhi liezhuan," focusing on its idea of a natural economy and the uselessness of government. Then, in the second half, I will look at the "Pingzhun shu" and look at its account of the imperial expansion and monetary policies of the Han empire under Emperor Wu. Then, at the end, I will bring the two together, and offer a conclusion on Sima Qian's critical mobilization of the past vis-à-vis early Han imperialism.

"Huozhi Liezhuan": Natural Economy and the Futility of Governance

Let's start at the beginning. The chapter "Huozhi liezhuan" begins with what turns out to be a programmatic statement for the entire chapter:

The Grand Archivist remarks: "I know nothing about the times of Shennong and before but, judging by what is recorded in the *Poetry* and *Documents*, from the age of Emperor Shun and the Xia dynasty down to the present, ears and eyes have always longed for the ultimate in beautiful sounds and forms, mouths have desired to taste the best in grass-fed and grain-fed animals, bodies have delighted in ease and comfort, and hearts have swelled with pride at the glories of power and ability. So long have these habits been allowed to permeate the lives of the people that, though one were to go from door to door preaching subtle, wondrous arguments, he could never succeed in changing them."

太史公曰：「夫神農以前，吾不知已。至若《詩》、《書》所述，虞夏以來，耳目欲極聲色之好，口欲窮芻豢之味，身安逸樂，而心誇矜勢能之榮。使俗之漸民久矣，雖戶說以眇論，終不能化。[4]

---

[4] Sima Qian, *Shiji*, 129.3253. For my reading of this chapter, I have greatly benefited from the exposition in Michael Nylan, "Assets Accumulating: Sima Qian's Perspective on Moneymaking, Virtue, and History," in *Views from Within, Views from Beyond: Approaches to the Shiji as an Early Work of*

156   *Sima Qian's Critical Past*

Here, Sima Qian offers an observation based on his reading of the classics. Since the dawn of time, men have always had a natural inclination to desire beautiful things that give them great comfort and pleasure.[5] Then, after this passage, Sima Qian enumerated the key regions in the world and the goods for which they are well known: ginger and cinnamon south of the Yangzi, bamboo and jade in Shanxi, silk and beautiful women in Shandong, and so on. At the end of this inventory, he concluded that "all of them are commodities coveted by the people of the middle kingdom, who according to their various customs use them for their bedding, clothing, food, and drink, fashioning from them the goods needed to supply the living and to bury the dead" (皆中國人民所喜好謠俗被服飲食奉生送死之具也).[6] Later in the chapter, Sima Qian would return to this list and elaborate on them further, with even more commodities and local customs of the people.[7]

In this opening passage of the "Huozhi liezhuan," we see Sima Qian drawing a specific relationship between men and nature. We naturally desire beautiful things, and to satisfy those needs, we appropriate and make use of the resources in the world. "Society obviously must have farmers before it can eat; foresters, fishermen, miners, etc., before it can make use of natural resources; craftsmen before it can have manufactured goods; and merchants before they can be distributed" (故待農而食之，虞而出之，工而成之，商而通之).[8] There arose the different industries and professions, namely agriculture, fishery, crafts, and commerce, to satisfy our material needs. Economic activities thus began in history.

In the encounter between men and the world, human beings and their natural habitat, economic activities naturally arose. To be human is to engage with nature and its resources to satisfy our desire. Divisions of labor naturally arose out of this process – some are farmers, while others may become fishermen, craftsmen, or commodity traders. Moreover, we also start to see the accumulation of wealth in these economic communities. Human beings had moved beyond just

---

Historiography, ed. Hans van Ess, Olga Lomová, and Dorothee Schaab-Hanke (Wiesbaden: Harrassowitz, 2015), 131–170.

[5] I use the name "Sima Qian" as a shorthand to refer to the author(s) of the *Shiji*, who may include Sima Qian himself, his father Sima Tan 司馬談, and others.

[6] Sima Qian, *Shiji*, 129.3253–3254.   [7] Ibid., 129.3261–3270.

[8] Ibid., 129.3254.

"*Huozhi Liezhuan*" 157

satisfying their subsistence needs but a state or a family can now "enrich" (*fu* 富) themselves through these economic engagements with nature:[9]

The *Zhou Documents* says, "If the farmers do not produce, there will be a shortage of food; if the artisans do not produce, there will be a shortage of manufactured goods; if the merchants do not produce, then the three precious things will not circulate;[10] if the foresters, fishermen, miners, etc., do not produce, the treasury will be depleted." And if the treasury is depleted, the resources of the mountains and lakes cannot be exploited. These four different endeavors are the source of the people's clothing and food. If the source is great, they will enjoy abundance. If the source is small, there will be scarcity. In this way, the state became rich above, and individual families became rich below.

《周書》曰:「農不出,則乏其食;工不出,則乏其事;商不出,則三寶絕;虞不出,則財匱少;財匱少,而山澤不辟矣。」此四者,民所衣食之原也。原大則饒,原小則鮮。上則富國,下則富家。[11]

What Sima Qian has outlined here is no less than an account of the origin of wealth in human history. People had natural desires for good things, as they do today, and to satisfy those needs, they domesticated nature and transformed pieces of it for their own pleasure. Specifically, these economic activities fell into four main categories: agriculture, industries, commerce, and crafts. Collectively, they constituted the wealth of that economic community.

Human beings, in this sense, are economic animals by nature. Economic activities are natural acts. Our natural instincts propel us to engage in economic activities. The process starts with the desire within all of us for material comfort and ends with the production and accumulation of wealth. It is a natural process all the way down, as he said:

Each man relies on his ability, uses his strength in order to obtain what he desires. So, things that are cheap would tend to have their price increased,

---

[9] Liang Qichao 梁啓超, "Shiji huozhi liezhuan jin yi" 史記貨殖列傳今義, in *Yinbingshi heji* 飲冰室合集 (Beijing: Zhonghua shuju, 1996), Volume 1, 35–45.

[10] The "three precious things" (*sanbao* 三寶) is generally understood as referring to the products of the three other classes mentioned in this same paragraph, namely farmers, artisans, and foresters, fishermen, miners, etc. See the commentary on this passage in Takigawa Kametarō 瀧川龜太郎, *Shiki kaichū kōshō* 史記會注考證 ([Japan]: Shiki Kaichū Kōshō Kōho Kankōkai, 1958), 129.6.

[11] Sima Qian, *Shiji*, 129.3255.

158　　　　　　　　　　　　　　　　　　　　　　*Sima Qian's Critical Past*

and the expensive ones would incur price reductions. Each man applies himself in his occupation, and takes delight in his works. Like water flowing downward, this flows forth ceaselessly all day and night without being summoned, and the people engage in the production without ever being asked. Does this not tally with the Way (*Dao*), and is this not a testament to what is natural?

人各任其能，竭其力，以得所欲。故物賤之徵貴，貴之徵賤，各勸其業，樂其事，若水之趨下，日夜無休時，不召而自來，不求而民出之。豈非道之所符，而自然之驗邪？[12]

This is all natural, or in his own words *ziran* 自然, literally "self-actualizing," just like "water flowing downward." In addition to this emphatic argument for understanding economic activities and the generation of wealth as an extension of nature, Sima Qian went one step further to claim that this satisfaction of our material needs is in fact a precondition for all other activities that we do, including ritual training and moral cultivation:

Thus it was said, "Only when the granaries are full would people bear on their minds rituals and obligations; and only after they have enough food and clothing would they know glory and shame." Rituals are born of plenty and abandoned in time of want. When a gentleman becomes rich, he delights in practicing virtue; when a petty man becomes rich, he exercises his brute force. If the pools are deep, then the fish would dwell in them; if the mountains are the most secluded, then the wild beasts would travel into them. Likewise, when people become wealthy, benevolence (*ren* 仁) and righteousness (*yi* 義) would then be attached to them.

故曰：「倉廩實而知禮節，衣食足而知榮辱。」禮生於有而廢於無。故君子富，好行其德；小人富，以適其力。淵深而魚生之，山深而獸往之，人富而仁義附焉。[13]

There is no talk of morality before a gentleman's belly is full. Economic subsistence is a precondition for the possibility of ritual training and moral development, and by extension, all other activities that we do as human beings. This is an important point for Sima Qian. Satisfaction of our material needs is the most fundamental factor driving all our behaviors. Even when we are not actively chasing after

---

[12]　Ibid., 129.3254.

[13]　Ibid., 129.3255. The first line is a quotation from the *Guanzi*. Li Xiangfeng, *Guanzi jiaozhu*, 1.2.

profits, like when we indulge in lofty discussion about rituals and morality, it is still an essential thing that looms in the background:

The wealthy men, when yielding power, become ever more eminent. But when he loses his power, his retainers will all desert him and do not take pleasure in his company. This is even more the case among barbarians. The proverb says, "Rich young men do not die in the marketplace." These are no empty words indeed. So, it is said, "Jostling and joyous, the whole world comes after profit! Racing and rioting, after profit the whole world goes!" If even the great rulers must worry about poverty, how much more so the common peasant whose name is enrolled in the tax collector's list?

富者得埶益彰，失埶則客無所之，以而不樂。夷狄益甚。諺曰：「千金之子，不死於市。」此非空言也。故曰：「天下熙熙，皆為利來；天下壤壤皆為利往。」夫千乘之王，萬家之侯，百室之君，尚猶患貧，而況匹夫編戶之民乎！[14]

Towards the end of the text, he reiterated this point, even more emphatically:

Judging from all that has been said above, when wise men lay their profound plans in palace chambers or deliberate in audience halls, guard their honor and die for their principles, or when gentlemen retire to dwell in mountain caves and establish a reputation for purity of conduct, what is their ultimate objective? Their objective is simply wealth. So the honest official after years of service attains riches, and the honest merchant in the end becomes wealthy. The desire for wealth does not need to be taught; it is an integral part of all human nature.

由此觀之，賢人深謀於廊廟，論議朝廷，守信死節隱居岩穴之士設為名高者安歸乎？歸於富厚也。是以廉吏久，久更富，廉賈歸富。富者，人之情性，所不學而俱欲者也。[15]

In the very last part of the chapter, Sima Qian illustrates this with a series of historical figures – soldiers who braved death, wicked murderers, wandering gangsters, legendary beauties, young princes, ruthless hunters, pathological gamblers, medical doctors, occult magicians, government officials, farmers, merchants, and so on. They did what they did, in the last analysis, only to chase after material gain. They were all just "seeking wealth and trying to enlarge their possession of goods" (固求富益貨也).[16] And there is nothing wrong with

[14] Sima Qian, *Shiji*, 129.3255–3256.   [15] Ibid., 129.3271.
[16] Ibid., 129.3271.

160   *Sima Qian's Critical Past*

their motivation. They were, and we all are, economic animals after all, chasing after profits.

In the "Huozhi liezhuan," therefore, our desire for material pleasure and economic well-being is the motivating and determinative factor behind all our actions. And it is all part of the natural economy, in the sense that all these economic activities, the desire for wealth, and the activities that they inspired, all arose naturally, simply from us being in the world. In short, what the "Huozhi liezhuan" gives us is a history of the natural economy of mankind.

* * *

What is missing, strikingly, in this account of the "Huozhi liezhuan" is the idea of a government. Early on in the chapter, after Sima Qian's declaration on the inborn acquisitive spirit of men and the different local goods across key regions of the world, he asked the readers to consider the futility of government work:

All of them are commodities coveted by the people of China, who according to their customs use them for bedding, clothing, food, drink, and to supply the needs of the living and the dead. Thus, society obviously must have farmers before it can eat; foresters, fishermen, miners, etc., before it can make use of natural resources; craftsmen before it can have manufactured goods; and merchants before they can be distributed. But once these exist, what need is there for government directives, mobilizations of labor, or periodic assemblies?

皆中國人民所喜好，謠俗被服飲食奉生送死之具也。故待農而食之，虞而出之，工而成之，商而通之。此寧有政教發徵期會哉？[17]

And this passage is followed immediately by the passage that we read earlier, on the "naturalness" of the economic activities of men. Let me repeat it here:

Each man relies on his ability, uses his strength in order to obtain what he desires. So, things that are cheap would tend to have their price increased, and the expensive ones would incur price reductions. Each man applies himself in his occupation, and takes delight in his works. Like water flowing downward, this flows forth ceaselessly all day and night without being summoned, and the people engage in the production without ever being asked. Does this not tally with the Way (*Dao*), and is this not a testament to what is natural?

[17] Ibid., 129.3254.

"Huozhi Liezhuan" 161

人各任其能，竭其力，以得所欲。故物賤之徵貴，貴之徵賤，各勸其業，樂其事，若水之趨下，日夜無休時，不召而自來，不求而民出之。豈非道之所符，而自然之驗邪？[18]

Men satisfy their material needs, engage in economic activities, and accumulate wealth as a matter of the course of nature. This is a process that governs itself from beginning to end, and requires no external agents, supervision, or regulation.

This was a radical argument in the context of the early Han discussion of the economic lives of men. It had long been a commonplace to say that people were naturally inclined to seek profits, or *li* 利, beginning in the Warring States, but few would suggest that it is a fact of nature that we should just accept.[19] This desire for profits was often understood to be a moral deviance or deficiency that required correction. See, for example, this passage from a memorial to Emperor Wu by Dong Zhongshu (179–104 BCE), a contemporary of Sima Qian:

The fact that people seek after profits (*li* 利) is as natural as water flowing downward. If it is not pre-empted by instructions and transformations, it cannot be thwarted. Thus, when the proper instructions are established and all deviances are thwarted, the pre-emptive measure is said to be completed. When the proper instructions are abandoned and deviances come forth, so much so that even legal punishments cannot keep up with them, the pre-emptive measure is said to be in disrepair.

夫萬民之從利也，如水之走下，不以教化隄防之，不能止也。是故教化立而姦邪皆止者，其隄防完也；教化廢而姦邪並出，刑罰不能勝者，其隄防壞也。[20]

"Water flowing downward" was a phrase that Sima Qian also used, as we saw earlier, in reference to the self-sufficient logic of the natural economy of men. Here, however, it is used to describe men's natural desire for profit that must be dammed with "instructions and transformations" (*jiaohua* 教化). This difference between these two passages by Sima Qian and Dong Zhongshu typifies a larger pattern in the rhetoric of the "Huozhi liezhuan" that deliberately minimizes or eliminates the role of government in economic matters. For instance, it was

[18] Ibid., 129.3254.
[19] Carine Defoort, "The Profit That Does Not Profit: Paradoxes with 'Li' in Early Chinese Texts," *Asia Major*, 21.1 (2008), 153–181.
[20] Ban Gu, *Hanshu*, 56.2503. Translations from the *Hanshu* are my own.

a commonplace idea in early Han texts that the government, namely the Han imperial regime, must ensure the material well-being of its people. As Jia Yi once said,

The *Guanzi* said, "Only when the granaries are full would people bear on their minds rites and obligations; and only after they have enough food and clothing would they know glory and shame." As for people who were not sufficiently provided for but still can be properly governed, such a case has not been heard at all since the time of antiquity.

管子曰：「倉廩實，知禮節；衣食足，知榮辱。」民非足也，而可治之者，自古及今，未之嘗聞。[21]

Sima Qian, in the "Huozhi liezhuan," also quoted the same passage from the *Guanzi*, as we saw earlier, but for him, it only meant that material well-being is the precondition for all other activities, including ritual training and moral cultivation, with no implication whatsoever for the role or necessity of the work of government.[22]

In our discussion of Lu Jia's "Daoji" in the *Xinyu*, we saw how he ascribed different civilizing inventions to various sages in antiquity. Shennong, in particular, was responsible for the invention of the idea of agriculture in our civilizing progress.[23] Lu Jia, of course, was not the only one who subscribed to this idea of the civilizing effects of the work of the sages. Such narratives were popular in the late Warring States through to the early Han empire.[24] In the "Huozhi liezhuan," however, agriculture arose just spontaneously without any sagely intervention. People were hungry, they needed food, and at that point in time in the deep past, agriculture happened. Sages were not needed, and government was also not needed, in this imagination of the self-sufficient natural economy of men.

[21] Yan Zhenyi and Xia Zhong, *Xinshu jiaozhu*, 4.4.
[22] Sima Qian, *Shiji*, 129.3255. It is, of course, possible that neither Sima Qian nor Jia Yi were quoting from the *Guanzi* but were simply quoting a common saying familiar to both.
[23] Wang Liqqi, *Xinyu*, 1.10.
[24] To cite just a few famous examples, there are the "Huace" chapter of the *Shangjun shu*, the "Wudu" chapter of the *Han Feizi*, and, of course, the "Daoji" chapter of the *Xinyu* by Lu Jia. Even in the *Shiji* itself, Sima Qian included similar accounts; see the "Wu di benji" 五帝本紀 (*Shiji* 1.3–6). On these and other similar texts, see Mark Lewis's *Sanctioned Violence in Early China* (Albany: State University of New York Press, 1990), 167–174; and Michael Puett's *The Ambivalence of Creation*, 92–140.

"Huozhi Liezhuan" 163

About halfway through the narrative of the "Huozhi liezhuan," Sima Qian introduced the notion of the "untitled nobility" (*sufeng* 素封):

> Now there are men who receive no ranks or emoluments from the government and who have no revenue from titles or fiefs, and yet they enjoy just as much ease as those who have all these; they may be called the "untitled nobility."

今有無秩祿之奉，爵邑之入，而樂與之比者。命曰「素封」。[25]

He then proceeded to demonstrate this numerically. A lord who was granted 1,000 households by the government would receive, say, an annual income of 200,000 cash in taxation. Someone with no ties to the government, say a farmer, craftsman, trader, or merchant, who invested 10,000 cash in their business or industry can likewise expect an annual income of 200,000 cash. Then, he concluded, "These people are the equal of a marquis enfeoffed with a 1,000 households" (此其人皆與千戶侯等), and "they may live with all the dignity of a retired gentleman and still enjoy an income" (有處士之義而取給焉).[26] Once again, the main point is that government is not a necessary thing in the world.

The "Huozhi liezhuan" chapter concludes with a series of biographical vignettes of various moneymakers in history.[27] Consistent with the rest of the chapter, government played a minimal or no role at all in their successes. In cases where these moneymakers got mixed up with a meddling state, their wealth was always diminished and they had to work hard to regain their fortune.[28] All in all, this one key point of the "Huozhi liezhuan" is clear: government institutions are basically useless. Human beings are born with desires for material goods, and those desires can be fully met by the economy that naturally arose in the interactions between men and their environment. Sagely intervention and government institutions have never been necessary. Governance, in the sense of any deliberate attempt to transform or order the world of men, has always and necessarily been futile.

---

[25] Sima Qian, *Shiji*, 129.3272. [26] Ibid., 129.3272.
[27] Ibid., 129.3277–3281.
[28] See the case of the Zhuo family of the Zhao state: Sima Qian, *Shiji*, 129.3277.

164   *Sima Qian's Critical Past*

"Pingzhun Shu": Imperial Expansion, Magical Currencies, and Original Disorder

The "Pingzhun shu" is one of the few chapters in the *Shiji* that deal exclusively with Han times. More specifically, most of it is about the military affairs and economic policies of the empire from the 130s to the 110s BCE, which, of course, falls under the long reign of Emperor Wu. Before that, however, at the very start of the chapter, there is a short prefatory section on the first decades of the Han. It begins with the following announcement: "The Han arose, and it was left with the many failings of the Qin" (漢興，接秦之弊).[29] What follows is an account of how the central court of the early Han, from Emperor Gaozu (r. 202–195 BCE) to Emperor Jin (Han Jingdi 漢景帝, r. 156–141), struggled to maintain the fiscal health of the state, with experiments in taxation, coinage, sales of official ranks, and so on, while attempting to finance the costly territorial expansion into regions inhabited by various neighboring groups, most importantly the Xiongnu 匈奴 in the steppes north of the frontier.[30] These were all pressing and vexing issues that Emperor Wu inherited when he ascended the throne in the year 141 BCE. His approaches to these various economic and military matters are the subject of this chapter of the *Shiji*. It is a richly detailed account, full of valuable historical information for the study of the early Han empire, but more importantly for this study, Sima Qian's narrative in this chapter is also invested with a withering critique of early Han imperialism in the form that it took under Emperor Wu.

To see this critique, and then to see Sima Qian's mobilization of the past to stage his critical interventions, I will offer a reading of two narrative strands in the "Pingzhun shu," one on the imperial expansion and the other on monetary policies. And then, at the very end of the chapter, I will put the two chapters "Huozhi liezhuan" and "Pingzhun shu" together and see how Sima Qian's critical effort stands in this history of the politics of the past.

* * *

---

[29] Sima Qian, *Shiji*, 30.1417.

[30] For Han–Xiongnu relations, see Nicola Di Cosmo, *Ancient China and Its Enemies: The Rise of Nomadic Power in East Asian History* (Cambridge and New York: Cambridge University Press, 2002).

"Pingzhun Shu" 165

In modern historiography of the Han empire, one of the most popular topics is the history of the imperial expansion under the reign of Emperor Wu. Over his five decades of rule, as he worked to centralize the old territories that he inherited from his predecessors, he also directed numerous campaigns to expand the border of the Han empire in almost every direction.[31] It was indeed a momentous event in the history of early China – or even the world, one may say, with striking parallels to the contemporary expansion of the Roman Republic in the Mediterranean world. In accounts of this great expansion of the Han empire, however, one important question rarely gets asked. That is, why did it want to expand at all? What motivated the Han to expand its territory in the first place? It is quite striking how so much of the scholarship has elided this question. And it is not because the answer is so well known or so commonly accepted that it no longer needs to be mentioned. Rather, the sense seems to be that, as the early Han empire consolidated its political control in the old territories, with great new wealth being generated for the state, it was only a natural expression of its power that it would have wanted to extend its frontier, claim more territories for itself, and colonize those outside the Han order.

The "Pingzhun shu" is one of the key transmitted sources for our knowledge of this imperial expansion under Emperor Wu. How did Sima Qian account for this drive for expansion and colonial ambition of the Han court? The answer, I will argue, relates directly to his understanding and critique of the nature of early Han imperialism. To begin unpacking his view on this matter, let me start with the following passage from the "Pingzhun shu." It is prefaced by a note on how the central court had accumulated great wealth over the course of the 140s BCE, and then it describes the first expansionist initiative under Emperor Wu:

Shortly after this time, Zhuang Zhu, Zhu Maichen, and others invited the people of the region of Eastern Ou to move to China, intervening in the war between the two kingdoms of Yue, and the area between the Huai and Yangzi rivers, to which they were transferred, was put to great trouble and expense. Tang Meng and Sima Xiangru opened up a road to the land of the barbarians in the southwest, cutting a passage over a thousand *li* long through the mountains in order to broaden the provinces of Ba and Shu,

---

[31] Leung, "The Former Han Empire," 168–174.

166   *Sima Qian's Critical Past*

but the undertaking exhausted the people of these regions. Peng Wu established relations with the peoples of Weimo and Zhaoxian and set up the province of Canghai on the Korean peninsula, but the move caused great unrest among the inhabitants of the neighboring states of Yen and Qi. After Wang Hui made his unsuccessful attempt to ambush the Xiongnu at Mayi, peaceful relations with the Xiongnu came to an end and they began to invade and plunder the northern border. Armies had to be dispatched time and again and could not be disbanded, causing extreme hardship to the empire. As the conflicts became fiercer day by day, men set off to war carrying their packs of provisions, while those left behind at home had to send more and more goods to keep them supplied. Those at home and those on the frontier were kept busy guarding the empire and supplying rations until the common people were exhausted and began to look for some clever way to evade the laws. The funds of the government were soon used up and, in order to supply the deficiencies, it was agreed that men who presented goods would be appointed to official positions, and those who made appropriate contributions would be pardoned for their crimes. The old system of selecting officials on the basis of merit fell into disuse, and modesty and a sense of shame became rare qualities. Military achievement was now the key to advancement. The laws were made stricter and more detailed, and officials whose main job was to make a profit for the government for the first time appeared in office.

自是之後，嚴助、硃買臣等招來東甌，事兩越，江淮之間蕭然煩費矣。
唐蒙、司馬相如開路西南夷，鑿山通道千餘裏，以廣巴蜀，巴蜀之民
罷焉。彭吳賈滅朝鮮，置滄海之郡，則燕齊之間靡然發動。及王恢設謀
馬邑，匈奴絕和親，侵擾北邊，兵連而不解，天下苦其勞，而干戈日滋。
行者齎，居者送，中外騷擾而相奉，百姓抏弊以巧法，財賂衰秏而
不贍。入物者補官，出貨者除罪，選舉陵遲，廉恥相冒，武力進用，
法嚴令具。興利之臣自此始也。[32]

This account did not answer the question of why the Han empire wished to expand into these territories; if anything, this description made it an even more puzzling enterprise. With the exception of the Xiongnu in the north, the rest of the campaigns did not appear to be defensive. Material benefits that may result from extending into these various regions are not immediately clear. In addition to the great financial cost of these campaigns, they also exact a social cost: a great number of men were drafted to the border, leaving behind their families, who now have to persist with diminished household income. The financially depressed state began to sell more and more official

[32] Sima Qian, *Shiji*, 30.1420–1421.

"*Pingzhun Shu*" 167

ranks to those who may or may not be qualified to serve in their posts, which in turn spoiled the overall quality of officialdom.

Following this first account, Sima Qian continued to describe one expansionist campaign after another into different regions, including Henan 河南, Hu 胡, Xinanyi 西南夷, Nanyi 南夷, and Qiong 邛. The dynamics that we saw in that first account continued and escalated. The material gains from these colonialization efforts were low, while they became more and more costly for the state. They had to provide provisions for the soldiers and war captives far away from the center and established local government offices in the newly conquered territories; the state treasury was so depleted at one point that they would accept mere sheep as payment for the purchase of official rank.[33] Relief from these financial burdens would only come when there were mass casualties of the Han troops.[34]

These problems persisted and their scale became even more fantastical in the next two decades, as the Han continued its expansionist effort from the late 140s well into the 110s. And the question remains: why did the Han empire campaign to expand, even when the costs were so fantastically high? One may refer to Joseph Schumpeter's thesis that imperialism is an objectless disposition towards forcible territorial expansion originating in the militaristic institutions of the state. And that early Han China, like ancient Rome, was simply another instance of these "atavistic war machines" which simply persist in territorial conquest with an apparent lack of an objective.[35] In the "Pingzhun shu" itself, Sima Qian never expounds on this question, but he does include this speech by Emperor Wu that gives us an interesting insight on the matter. It was in the year 123 BCE, a year after an especially massive campaign against the Hu people. It was a success but ministers had reported to the emperor that the cash reserves at the ministries of both agriculture and taxation were now completely depleted. There were simply not enough funds to continue to support the troops there. To that, the emperor gave the following response:

I have been told that the Five Thearchs of antiquity did not necessarily follow the same policies, and yet they all achieved good order; that the rulers of Yu

[33] Ibid., 30.1422. [34] Ibid., 1422.

[35] Joseph Alois Schumpeter, *Imperialism and Social Classes: Two Essays* (New York: Meridian Books, 1955), 88–89. I also refer to Doyle, *Empires*, 22–24.

168   *Sima Qian's Critical Past*

and Tang did not necessarily use the same kind of laws, though they were both worthy kings. The roads they followed were different, but all led to the same ultimate virtue. Now the northern frontier is not yet at peace, a fact which grieves me deeply. Recently the general in chief attacked the Xiongnu and beheaded or captured nineteen thousand of the enemy, and yet the rewards and supplies due him and his men are held back and they have not yet received them. Let deliberations begin on a law to allow the people to purchase honorary ranks and to buy mitigations of punishments or freedom from prohibitions against holding office.

朕聞五帝之教不相復而治，禹湯之法不同道而王，所由殊路，而建德一也。北邊未安，朕甚悼之。日者，大將軍攻匈奴，斬首虜萬九千級，留蹛無所食。議令民得買爵及贖禁錮免減罪。[36]

The last remark is a familiar one; the treasuries were depleted, and therefore more sales of honorary rank were in order. But the rest of this response by Emperor Wu is rather extraordinary upon close reading. "The northern frontier is not yet at peace" (北邊未安), Emperor Wu said. But what constituted "peace"? It hardly seems to mean peaceful coexistence with the northern nomads. By this point, the goals of a typical Han expansionist campaign were clear; it was never just about fending off threatening people beyond the border, but a colonizing effort to annex new territory and establish local governance according to Han imperial administration. In fact, this was one reason why the campaigns were so expensive; the costs of establishing and then maintaining new local offices in newly conquered territories were extremely high. In this sense, we can assume that when Emperor Wu said that the "northern frontier was not yet at peace," he meant that it had yet to be integrated into the Han imperial order and remade by the empire's administration.

Furthermore, this suggests that the Han empire, under Emperor Wu, saw itself as a singular source of political order. What lies within is peaceful and orderly, and what lies without must necessarily be chaos and strife. It is a vision of the world in a state of original disorder, that requires active intervention for it to achieve a semblance of order. Like many empires before and since, the Han empire saw itself as a civilizing force, spreading its good order to the rest of the world, even if that required violent means.[37]

---

[36] Sima Qian, *Shiji*, 30.1422–1423.

[37] Cf. Alice Yao, *The Ancient Highlands of Southwest China: From the Bronze Age to the Han Empire* (Oxford: Oxford University Press, 2016), for a recent study

"*Pingzhun Shu*"   169

We can find antecedents of this presumption of disorder in the imperial ideology of the Qin empire, like so many aspects of the Han empire under Emperor Wu. In the Qin tomb at Shuihudi 睡虎地, Hubei Province, there is the "Yu shu" 語書 ("Speech Record"), a record of a speech by a local Qin official dated to the year 227 BCE. Addressing the recently conquered population in the old kingdom of Chu 楚, this official said:

> In the past, each people had its own local custom, so what they considered beneficial, and their likes and dislikes, were all different from one another. It may have been the case that these local customs were inexpedient for the people or even harmful to the states. Therefore, the sageking instituted laws and standards in order to rectify the minds of the people, to drive away their wickedness and deviances, and to do away with their harmful customs. When the laws were not yet fully sufficient, the people were often deceitful and sly, so there were those who deliberately interfered with the commands. Laws and commands are meant to instruct and guide the people; they purge the licentiousness and deviance of the people and do away with the bad customs, directing them towards what is good.

廿年四月丙戌朔丁亥。。。古者，民各有鄉俗，其所利及好惡不同，或不便于民，害于邦。是以聖王作為法度，以矯端民心，去其邪僻，除其惡俗。法律未足，民多詐巧，故後有間令下者。凡法律令者，以教導民，去其淫僻，除其惡俗，而使之之于為善也。[38]

The text continues on for about another 500 characters, first lamenting the refusal of the ignorant masses to follow these new laws and standards, and then it asks the local Qin officials to apprehend anyone who fails to observe them.

In this document, the Qin empire presented itself as the harbinger of a unified, proper order to humanity, who had long been ensnared by their own customs, inexpedient or even harmful to themselves. People were originally corrupt in nature, and they simply did not know any better; they had to wait until the arrival of a sage-king, like the First Emperor of Qin, to rectify the nature of their being and usher them into

---

of Han imperialism in the southwestern region. See also Tamara T. Chin, *Savage Exchange: Han Imperialism, Chinese Literary Style, and the Economic Imagination*, Harvard-Yenching Institute Monograph Series, 94 (Cambridge, MA: Harvard University Asia Center, 2014).

[38] *Shuihudi Qin mu zhujian*, 14–22. My own translation.

170   *Sima Qian's Critical Past*

a proper order.[39] And we saw this before too, when we discussed the Legalists and the Qin empire in the last chapter. In one of the stele inscriptions of the Qin, for instance, we are told that the First Emperor "wiped out unruly powers, rescued the peoples, and pacified the entire world to its outermost edges; and he endowed them with enlightened laws, so as to give the world order and pattern, to serve as the proper model for time unending" (烹滅彊暴，振救黔首，周定四極。普施明法，經緯天下，永為儀則).[40] The world, left to its own devices, always lapses into a state of disorder, which can only be fixed by sagely intervention.

Almost a hundred years after the demise of the Qin empire, Emperor Wu revived this claim, that the world would be mired in a state of disorder if not for the interventions of an enlightened ruler and his state. In such a world, the imperial expansion of the Han empire would require no justification. It was just what the Han empire was supposed to do for the benefit of all humanity. To put this in even stronger terms, the Han empire had a moral obligation to propagate its good order, even at great cost to itself. It was a burden that the sole civilizing force must shoulder.

* * *

Besides the history of imperial expansion, another major narrative strand in the "Pingzhun shu" is concerned with the changing monetary policies of the early Han empire. It was an area of great contention among the policy makers of the empire from the very start. One of Emperor Gaozu's first policies, as noted in the "Pingzhun shu," was to abolish the state monopoly on currency production, which was a Qin policy, and allow the use of local coinage. Two decades later, under Emperor Wen's reign (180–175 BCE), the *banliang* 半兩 coins were introduced, and great debate ensued at court on whether the state should allow private minting.[41] Over the long reign of Emperor Wu, with his pursuit of various expensive state projects, including the expansionist campaigns, monetary policy of the empire became an

---

[39] Li Ping 李平, "Qin 'fazhi' de Lilun Kunjin Touxi: Yi Shuihudi Qin Jian 'Yushu' 'Wei Li Zhi Dao' Wei Zhongxin" 秦"法治"的理論困境透析——以睡虎地秦简《語書》、《為吏之道》為中心, *Xueshu tanshuo* 學術探索 11 (2012), 28–31; and Xu Fuchang 徐富昌, *Shuihudi Qin jian yanjiu* 睡虎地秦簡研 (Taipei: Wen shi zhe chubanshe, 1993), 39–55.

[40] Sima Qian, *Shiji*, 6.249.

[41] Ibid., 30.1419; and Ban Gu, *Hanshu*, 24.1152–1157.

"*Pingzhun Shu*"   171

even more pressing issue as the empire struggled to maintain its fiscal health in a quickly expanding economy. Sima Qian, in the "Pingzhun shu," detailed the many dramatic shifts in the monetary measures of the empire under Emperor Wu. Largely and ostensibly about the history of coinage, it was in many ways an account of the contestation over the values of things and the relationship between the state and the economy under Emperor Wu.[42]

In Sima Qian's account in the "Pingzhun shu," the first major monetary measure that Emperor Wu undertook was in the year 120 BCE, about two decades after he ascended to the throne. In the year before, the Han had just concluded yet another major campaign against the Xiongnu, which, while successful, cost the empire a "total expenditure of more than ten billion cash" (費凡百餘巨萬).[43] Other state expenditures also began to mount, as Sima Qian was quick to point out. The contemporaneous construction of the great canals "necessitated expenditures ranging into billions of cash" (費亦各巨萬十數).[44] Major flooding in the Shandong area in the year 120 BCE forced the government to relocate about 700,000 people to the northwest, with a cost "estimated in the billions, the final sum reaching incalculable proportions" (其費以億計，不可勝數).[45] Emperor Wu, seemingly heedless of the dire fiscal shape of the state, also took to rearing 30,000 horses at the capital, Chang'an, for future battles with the Xiongnu. The state treasury was depleting at an alarming rate. And what compounded the problem even further, according to Sima Qian, was the indifference of the merchants throughout the country, who, despite their great wealth, offered little to relieve the hundreds of thousands of poor peasants who were affected by the floods.

In response to this escalating fiscal crisis, Emperor Wu proposed a monetary solution. "The emperor consulted his high ministers on plans to change the coinage and issue a new currency in order to provide for the expenses of the state and to suppress the idle and unscrupulous gangs who acquired huge assets" (於是天子與公卿議，更錢造幣以贍用，而摧浮淫并兼之徒).[46] The idea, in other words, was to introduce

---

[42] For this section, I have gained much insight from the discussion of Han money in Chin, *Savage Exchange*, 228–294. See also the history of money in the dated, but still accurate, Peng Xinwei 彭信威, *Zhongguo huobi shi* 中國貨幣史 (Shanghai: Shanghai renmin chubanshe, 1958).

[43] Sima Qian, *Shiji*, 30.1412.   [44] Ibid., 30.1425.   [45] Ibid., 30.1425.

[46] Ibid., 30.1425.

172   *Sima Qian's Critical Past*

a new currency, by fiat, in order to inflate the wealth of the state. In Sima Qian's narrative, it was akin to a conjuring trick whereby wealth would materialize *ex nihilo*. For the abundance of white deer at the imperial park at Chang'an, Emperor Wu decreed that the state would begin to issue a new currency, the *pibi* 皮幣 ("hide currency"). He had the white deer in the park slaughtered, and their hides made into one-foot squares embroidered with silk threads. Each would be valued at 400,000 cash, and he stipulated that members of the imperial household and other nobility must use this fiat currency when paying tribute to the central court. Like magic, an object that had no monetary value a moment ago was now state-sanctioned currency, a physical bearer of wealth that the state had not had before.[47]

In addition to the new "hide currency," Emperor Wu ordered the production of another new currency, the so-called "white-metal" coins (*baijin* 白金). It would be made with an alloy of silver and tin, two types of metal that the state possessed in great abundance, as Emperor Wu had discovered. They were to be coined in three different denominations, from the heaviest to the lightest in weight at 3,000, 500, and 300 cash each. These *baijin* coins were intended for circulation throughout the entire empire. Local officials were ordered to smelt the existing *banliang* coins and mint these new *baijin* coins according to state guidelines; moreover, counterfeiting was considered a capital offense.[48] Converting previously idle objects into bearers of monetary value, Emperor Wu was literally manufacturing wealth.

The creation of these new currencies, with raw materials that the state already had in its possession, had the magical effect of suddenly replenishing the state treasury, at least in nominal terms. The replacement of old coinage with the new also had the effect of reining in merchants throughout the country. The part of their wealth held in old coinage was now rendered worthless, unless they converted them to the new currency, whose valuations were determined by the state. Moreover, with counterfeiters now punishable by death, the Han empire now made itself the only monetary source for the entire empire, with complete control over the flow and valuation of all tokens of economic exchange.

These monetary measures, from the perspective of the central court, were all enacted for the collective good of the empire, according to Sima Qian. Most importantly, they were intended to counter the rising

[47] Ibid., 30.1425–1426.   [48] Ibid., 30.1425–1427.

"*Pingzhun Shu*" 173

power of the merchants and industrialists whose fortunes had grown exponentially in the last few decades. They had been able to exert influence over local government officials, and at the same time cared little about the public good and contributed little to the welfare of the people.[49] The central court, therefore, instituted new coinage and manipulated the currency to integrate and concentrate monetary control in its own hands, in order to "suppress the idle and unscrupulous entrepreneurs who were acquiring such huge estates" (摧浮淫并兼之徒).[50] All economic transactions would be conducted with only the pecuniary means that the state had sanctioned; the valuation of things and all economic exchange within the empire would now be inscribed with the authority of the Han empire.

The effectiveness of these monetary measures of Emperor Wu was mixed at best, according to the narratives of the "Pingzhun shu." The threat of execution did not deter the many counterfeiters of the new white-metal coins. Merchants' activities and wealth were hardly diminished; seeing that their monetary holdings were frequently devalued due to these policies, they turned to hoarding goods to store their wealth. The state treasury of the Han empire continued to teeter on the brink of bankruptcy, often unable to make payments to the troops who were fighting the expansionist campaigns of Emperor Wu.[51]

Their effectiveness aside, these monetary measures, as told to us by Sima Qian in the "Pingzhun shu," are indicative of aspects of the ideology of early Han imperialism. Earlier, in our discussion of the expansionist campaign, we saw this presumption of original disorder in humanity. These monetary episodes under Emperor Wu, I would argue, tell a very similar story. Economic exchange that lay outside the purview and control of an enlightened state was considered to be intrinsically disorderly. People, like the wealthy merchants of the empire, simply act out of their own self-interest to

---

[49] Ibid., 30.1425. E.g. as Sima Qian wrote, they were "busy accumulating wealth and forcing the poor into hire, transporting goods back and forth in hundreds of carts, buying up surplus commodities and hoarding them in the villages; even the feudal lords were forced to go to them with bowed heads and beg for what they needed" (而富商大賈或蹛財役貧，轉轂百數，廢居居邑，封君皆低首仰給), and "they did nothing to help the distress of the nation, and the common people were plunged deeper and deeper into misery" (不佐國家之急，黎民重困).

[50] Ibid., 30.1425. [51] Ibid., 30.1427–1430.

174   *Sima Qian's Critical Past*

the detriment of the collective good, and, therefore, deliberate
governance was necessary to achieve an orderly, thriving economic
world.

The Han empire took it upon itself to give order to this unruly
natural economy. Things untouched by the empire were presumed to
be disorderly – whether it was the frontier region beyond the border or
unregulated economic exchange within the state. The Han empire
under Emperor Wu, therefore, saw itself as a civilizing force that
must extend and expand its orbit of control in order to spare the
world from its immanent savagery.

Violence, Civilization, and Critical History

The landscape of the past invoked in the *Shiji* is truly vast. In just these
two chapters – out of the 130 – we have followed Sima Qian on this
complex journey from the first economic activities of men to the
aggressive act of ordering the world under Emperor Wu in the early
Han. What do the narratives in these two chapters add up to, if anything? What was the argument and how was the past mobilized to serve
its end? Let me offer a few suggestions here on the politics of the past
that emerged from these texts.

The contrast between these two chapters, the "Huozhi liezhuan"
and the "Pingzhun shu," is striking. In the former, Sima Qian
suggested a natural origin for the economic activities of men.
Furthermore, he argued that such a natural economy is entirely
self-sufficient, without any need for deliberate governance that
imposes upon its inherent logic. In the "Pingzhun shu," on the
other hand, between the two narratives on the expansionist campaign and monetary policies under Emperor Wu, we see an articulation of an imperial ideology that assumes the world is naturally
mired in a state of disorder, which can only be corrected by an
external governing power. Pitting the two texts against one
another, we begin to see the emergence of an argument in the
Shiji: while the Han empire may have seen itself as a fashioner of
order from original chaos, it may in fact have been a destroyer of
natural order.

The vision of a self-sufficient order, a world without government,
is hardly a blueprint for an alternative order, however. It serves,
above all, to defamiliarize the Han imperial vision by entertaining

Violence, Civilization, and Critical History　　175

its exact opposite. To entertain the notion that the world was at any level naturally orderly is to begin to critique the fundamental premise of the form of imperial ideology that took shape under Emperor Wu, namely a radical presumption of original disorder in humanity. Was the Han empire a humane civilizing force that tried to give the world a proper order, or was its work an act of violence that, wittingly or unwittingly, transgressed against the natural order as it foolishly tried to remake nature? Should we reappreciate the empire's act of "pacification" (*an* 安), like the northern-frontier campaign against the Xiongnu, as a horrific act of state violence? Here, we can see Sima Qian's troubling suggestion that underneath its philanthropic civilizing cloak, the Han empire may very well have been a violent, transgressive force that sought to turn awry and ultimately do away with the very natural condition under which humanity was supposed to thrive.

What is significant for us, in the context of this study, is the fact that this critique by Sima Qian of the Han imperial ideology was related through complex historical narratives. The work, in representing and then defamiliarizing the Han imperial ideology, was done through extended narratives about past practices, both historical (as in the "Pingzhun shu") and hypothetical (as in parts of the "Huozhi liezhaun"). It was an engagement of the past less to construct or support a new political order or ethical program, than to defamiliarize and relativize the increasingly menacing status quo in the present. In short, it is not a constructive but a critical use of the past that we see in these portions of the *Shiji*.

One may point out that the distinction between being constructive and being critical is not so stark in truth or in practice. After all, aren't the *Analects* or the *Mozi* critical in their spirits too? What about the *Laozi* and the *Mengzi*? Yes, these earlier texts were all critical; it was obviously their discontent with other competing models of political order or ethical program that they turned to the past to construct their own. But there is a radical quality about what the *Shiji* is doing here. These two chapters – and the rest of the *Shiji* – were entirely devoted to the past. The gaze was absolutely backwards. Against the universalizing order of Emperor Wu, Sima Qian mobilized the entire weight of the past to bear upon this new order of the present. Moreover, the narratives in these two chapters – and elsewhere in the *Shiji* – were all critiques without any recommendation for a specific course forward by

176   *Sima Qian's Critical Past*

design.[52] It was a project for a ruthless criticism of everything existing.[53] It was a critique all the way down.

[52] Cf. Michael Puett, "Listening to Sages: Divination, Omens, and the Rhetoric of Antiquity in Wang Chong's Lunheng," *Oriens Extremus* 45 (2005), 271–282. In this way, Sima Qian and Wang Chong are similar in their understanding of the purpose of criticism.

[53] I borrow and adapt this well-known phrase from Karl Marx. Robert C. Tucker, *The Marx–Engels Reader*, 2nd edn (New York: Norton, 1978), 12.

Epilogue

At the moment when the past is transformed into capital, it is no longer a thing but a relation. It is endowed with a value that gives it a function external to itself, and as such, its very being and significance now exist only in relation to another object. This study is an account of this transformation of the past into capital, and the different functions that it was made to serve, in the dialogues and debates that attended the transition from the late Bronze Age aristocratic order of the Western Zhou to the rise of the Qin and Han bureaucratic empires over the course of the first millennium BCE. It is not a comprehensive, exhaustive account, but only a delineation of key sites of this vast landscape of the past in early China.

In the first chapter, we began with an account of the Western Zhou's investment in the authority of a genealogical past, with its emphasis on moments of origins, founding exemplary paradigms, and historical continuity. Subsequent to the fall of the Western Zhou, we saw a decline in the predominance of this genealogical model of organizing the past, as was the case in both the *Analects* and the *Mozi* from the fifth and fourth centuries BCE. Despite this common point of departure between these two texts, they ultimately ended up arguing for two distinct types of politics related through two very different views of the past. The *Analects* presents the past as a repertoire of cultural practices which, through the mediation of our deliberative selves, can be selectively and creatively adapted for a new order in the present. The *Mozi*, on the other hand, saw our deliberative selves as precisely the origin of disorder in history, and its account of the past was designed to demonstrate the veracity of this claim. Moreover, it also refers to the past as a casebook of instructions, both positive and negative, on how to suppress and submit our unruly selves to a universal and supra-human set of objective principles for the establishment of a new order in the present. In this transition from Western Zhou to the early Warring

178   *Epilogue*

States, we observe a loss of authority in the genealogical past, an emergence of the figure of deliberative individuals as historical and political agents, and the idea of historical discontinuity as a new problematic.

Then, in the next chapter, we studied the peculiar historical visions articulated in the cosmogonic and ethical writings of the late Warring States. Unlike the earlier Warring States texts, which turned to the historical field as a positive ideological resource, these later Warring States writings evinced a great sense of unease and wariness regarding the presumed utility and authority of the past amongst the contemporary political elite. In response, they constructed political and ethical ideals that were deliberately situated outside history; in the case of the *Laozi*, it is the cosmogonic entity that it calls the "Way," which can be apprehended by way of a deep historical investigation of the entire world. In the case of the *Mengzi*, it is our moral potentiality, informed by a bioethical logic that is entirely independent of historical conditions. In these texts, we see not an indifference to the idea of history but a profound skepticism towards the positive valorization of the past.

Chapter Three studied the Legalist intellectual current in the late Warring States and the Qin empire from the mid-fourth century to the end of the third century BCE. The sense of historical discontinuity that earlier Warring States texts tried to overcome was simply accepted in the Legalist corpus. They appealed to a new political order that was based purely on laws and punishments, measures that would restrain and ultimately eradicate the deliberative capacity of men in submission to an internally coherent system of rules and standards dictated by the ruler and his government. The Qin empire inherited much of this ideological edifice from the Legalists, but eventually radicalized it towards a vision of itself as the end of history, the cessation of all material changes in time.

Chapter Four studied two early Han responses to the fall of the Qin empire, namely the *Xinshu* by Jia Yi and the *Xinyu* by Lu Jia. In both cases, we saw an anxious attempt to restore the idea of a meaningful past which had been categorically denied under the Qin. More specifically, we saw that Jia Yi had largely appealed to the model of understanding the past as a vast repertoire of exemplary cultural practices that was first articulated in the *Analects*. For Lu Jia, the restoration of

Epilogue 179

a meaningful past was made by an elevation of the classics as the end of a teleological past. His argument for the classics as an encapsulation of the entire past, with universal efficacy, betrays a sympathy towards the authoritarian ideal of the Qin empire and a subtle attempt at repurposing its bureaucratic institutions as historically legitimate. And finally, in Chapter Five, we studied Sima Qian's investment in historical writing as a mode of critical intervention against precisely this type of moral mystification of the state at the height of the early Han imperial consolidation effort.

In this millennium-long narrative, we have seen diverse mobilizations of the past as political capital in this tumultuous transition from the Western Zhou to the Qin and Han empires. It was deployed in wide-ranging dialogues and debates towards the construction and deconstruction of notions such as genealogical inheritance, historical (dis)continuity, deliberative individuals, moral exemplarity, cosmogonic origin, bioethical constitution, historicity of laws, classical authority, and authoritarian imperialism. This demonstration of diverse uses of the past should lay to rest the old assumption that attention to the past in early China was predominated by a didactic impulse as a matter of cultural attitude. That was only one small piece of it at most. The emergence of this vast landscape of the past over the first millennium BCE had very little to do with any supposed cultural predilection; rather, it was constructed as a ground for articulating competing models of relations of power during this long transition from aristocratic order to bureaucratic empires in early China. In this sense, the title of this study, "the politics of the past," is doubly redundant; the very notion of the past emerged and became meaningful within relations of power, and politics had invariably implicated different conceptions of the past. The past had always been political.

Political debates – contention over proper relations of power – always take place in the gap between the ideal and the real, in the space of discontent between what should be and what actually is. Political imagination, therefore, is always ineluctably oriented towards the future. And yet, as we have seen in this study, while the political elite of early China debated fiercely with one another on alternative understandings of the often deplorable present and utopic visions of the future, they found themselves time and again diverting their gazes backward onto the landscape of the past. It was mined, over and over, for ideological capital of all sorts. To envision a better future,

180   *Epilogue*

the past was endlessly exploited and remade. The future is uncertain, for it has yet to come; the past, however, is no less uncertain. Docile and capacious, the field of the past has always been eminently susceptible to capitalization, towards multitudinous ends, according to the order of the present.

Bibliography

Primary Sources

Ban Gu 班固, *Hanshu* 漢書 (Beijing: Zhonghua shuju, 1962)

Chen Qiyou 陳奇猷, *Han Feizi jishi* 韓非子集釋 (Hong Kong: Zhonghua shuju, 1974)

Lüshi Chunqiu jiaoshi 呂氏春秋校釋 (Shanghai: Xue lin chu ban she, 1984)

Cook, Scott, *The Bamboo Texts of Guodian: A Study & Complete Translation*, Cornell East Asia Series, 164–165 (Ithaca, NY: Cornell University, East Asia Program, 2012)

Fei Zhen'gang 費振剛, Hu Shuangbao 胡雙寶, and Zong Minghua 宗明華, eds., *Quan Han fu* 全漢賦 (Beijing: Beijing daxue chubanshe, 1993)

Li Xiangfeng 黎翔鳳, *Guanzi jiaozhu* 管子校注 (Beijing: Zhonghua shuju, 2004)

Qu Wanli 屈萬里, *Shangshu jishi* 尚書集釋 (Taipei: Lianjing chuban shiye gongsi, 1983)

Shijing quanshi 詩經詮釋 (Taipei: Lianjing chuban shiye gongsi, 1983)

Shizuka Shirakawa 白川靜, *Kinbun tsūshaku* 金文通釋, 7 vols. (Kōbe-shi: Hakutsuru Bijutsukan, 1964–1984)

Shuihudi Qin mu zhujian 睡虎地秦墓竹簡, ed. Shuihudi Qin mu zhujian zhengli xiaozu 睡虎地秦墓竹簡整理小組 (Beijing: Wenwu chubanshe, 1990)

Sima Qian 司馬遷, *Shiji* 史記 (Beijing: Zhonghua shuju, 1956)

Sun Yirang 孫詒讓, *Mozi jian gu* 墨子閒詁 (Beijing: Zhonghua shuju, 2001)

Wang Hui 王輝, *Shang Zhou jinwen* 商周金文 (Beijing: Wenwu chubanshe, 2006)

Wang Liqi 王利器, *Xinyu jiaozhu* 新語校注 (Beijing: Zhonghua shuju, 1986)

Wang Xianqian 王先謙, *Zhuangzi ji jie* 莊子集解 (Beijing: Zhonghua shu ju, 1987)

Yan Zhenyi 閻振益 and Xia Zhong 鍾夏, *Xinshu jiaozhu* 新書校注 (Beijing: Zhonghua shuju, 2000)

Yang Bojun 楊伯峻, *Lunyu yizhu* 論語譯注, 2nd edn (Beijing: Zhonghua shuju, 1980)

Mengzi yizhu 孟子譯註 (Beijing: Zhonghua shuju, 1981)

Yin Zhou jinwen jicheng: xiuding zengbu ben 殷周金文集成：修訂增補本, 8 vols. (Beijing: Zhonghua shuju, 2007)

Zhu Shiche 朱師轍, *Shangjunshu jiegu dingben* 商君書解詁定本 (Beijing: Guji chubanshe, 1956)

Zhu Qianzhi 朱謙之, *Laozi jiaoshi* 老子校釋 (Beijing: Zhonghua shuju, 1984)

Secondary Scholarship

Ahern, Dennis M., "Is Mo Tzu a Utilitarian?", *Journal of Chinese Philosophy*, 3 (1976), 185–193

Ames, Roger T., *The Art of Rulership: A Study in Ancient Chinese Political Thought* (Honolulu: University of Hawaii Press, 1983)

"Recovering a Confucian Conception of Human Nature: A Challenge to the Ideology of Individualism," *Acta Koreana*, 20.1 (2017), 9–27

Bakhtin, M. M. (Mikhail Mikhaïlovich), *The Dialogic Imagination: Four Essays*, University of Texas Press Slavic Series, No. 1 (Austin: University of Texas Press, 2004)

Balazs, Etienne, *Chinese Civilization and Bureaucracy: Variations on a Theme* (New Haven: Yale University Press, 1964)

Banroku Ōtsuka 大塚伴鹿, *Hōka shisō no genryū* 法家思想の源流 (Tokyo: Sanshin Tosho, 1980)

Beasley, William G., and Edwin G. Pulleyblank, *Historians of China and Japan*, Historical Writing on the Peoples of Asia (London: Oxford University Press, 1961)

Behuniak, James, *Mencius on Becoming Human* (Albany: State University of New York Press, 2005)

Bloom, Irene, "Biology and Culture in the Mencian View of Human Nature," in *Mencius: Contexts and Interpretations*, ed. Alan K. L. Chan (Honolulu: University of Hawaii Press, 2002), 91–102

"Human Nature and Biological Nature in Mencius," *Philosophy East and West*, 47.1 (1997), 21–32

Mencius (New York: Columbia University Press, 2009)

Bodde, Derk, *China's First Unifier: A Study of the Ch'in Dynasty as Seen in the Life of Li Ssŭ (280?–208 B.C.)* (Leiden: Brill, 1938)

Bossenbrook, William John, and Hayden V. White, eds., *The Uses of History: Essays in Intellectual and Social History, Presented to William J. Bossenbrook* (Detroit: Wayne State University Press, 1968)

Bourdieu, Pierre, "The Forms of Capital," in *Readings in Economic Sociology*, ed. Nicole Woolsey Biggart (Oxford: Blackwell Publishers Ltd, 2002), 280–91

Bibliography

Brashier, K. E., *Ancestral Memory in Early China* (Cambridge, MA: Harvard University Asia Center, 2011)

Public Memory in Early China (Cambridge, MA: Harvard University Asia Center, 2014)

Brindley, Erica, "Human Agency and the Ideal of *Shang Tong* (Upward Conformity) in Early Mohist Writings," *Journal of Chinese Philosophy*, 34.3 (2007), 409–425

Individualism in Early China: Human Agency and the Self in Thought and Politics (Honolulu: University of Hawaii Press, 2010)

"Moral Autonomy and Individual Sources of Authority in the *Analects*," *Journal of Chinese Philosophy*, 38.2 (2011), 257–273

Brooks, E. Bruce, and A. Taeko Brooks, *The Original Analects: Sayings of Confucius and His Successors* (New York: Columbia University Press, 1998)

Brown, Miranda, "Mozi's Remaking of Ancient Authority," in *The Mozi as an Evolving Text: Different Voices in Early Chinese Thought*, ed. Carine Defoort and Nicolas Standaert (Leiden: Brill, 2013), 143–174

Bu Xianqun 卜憲群, *Qin Han guanliao zhidu* 秦漢官僚制度 (Beijing: Shehui kexue wenxian chubanshe, 2002)

Burbank, Jane, and Frederick Cooper, *Empires in World History: Power and the Politics of Difference* (Princeton: Princeton University Press, 2010)

Butterfield, Herbert, *History and Man's Attitude to the Past: Their Role in the Story of Civilisation* (London: School of Oriental and African Studies, University of London, 1961)

Chan, Shirley, "Oneness: Reading the 'All Things Are Flowing in Form (Fan Wu Liu Xing) 凡物流形' (with a Translation)," *International Communication of Chinese Culture*, 2.3 (2015), 285–299

Certeau, Michel de, *The Writing of History*, trans. Tom Conley, European Perspectives (New York: Columbia University Press, 1988)

Chen, Chao-ying, "Text and Context: Mencius' View on Understanding the Poems of the Ancients," in *Interpretation and Intellectual Change: Chinese Hermeneutics in Historical Perspective*, ed. Jingyi Tu (New Brunswick, NJ: Transaction Publishers, 2005), 33–45

Chen Mengjia 陳夢家, *Xi Zhou niandai kao* 西周年代考 (Taipei: Shangwu yinshuguan, 1945)

Xi Zhou tongqi duandai 西周銅器斷代, 2 vols. (Beijing: Zhonghua shuju, 2004)

Chen, Ming, "The Difference between Confucian and Mencian Benevolence," *Journal of Chinese Humanities*, 2.2 (2016), 217–235

184 Bibliography

Chin, Tamara T., *Savage Exchange: Han Imperialism, Chinese Literary Style, and the Economic Imagination* (Cambridge, MA: Harvard University Asia Center, 2014)

Clark, Anthony E., "Praise and Blame: Ruist Historiography in Ban Gu's *Hanshu*," *Chinese Historical Review*, 18 (2011), 1–24

Collingwood, R. G., *The Idea of History* (Oxford: Clarendon Press, 1962)

Cook, Constance A., "Wealth and the Western Zhou," *Bulletin of the School of Oriental & African Studies, University of London*, 1997, 253–294

Cook, Constance A., and Paul R. Goldin, eds., *A Source Book of Ancient Chinese Bronze Inscriptions*, Early China Special Monograph Series, no. 7 (Berkeley: The Society for the Study of Early China, 2016)

Cook, Scott, *The Bamboo Texts of Guodian: A Study & Complete Translation*, Cornell East Asia Series, 164–165 (Ithaca: East Asia Program, Cornell University, 2012)

"The Use and Abuse of History in Early China from *Xun Zi* to *Lüshi Chunqiu*," *Asia Major*, 18.1 (2005), 45–78

Creel, Herrlee G., "The Fa-Chia: 'Legalists' or 'Administrators'?", in *What Is Taoism? And Other Studies in Chinese Cultural History* (Chicago: The University of Chicago Press, 1970), 92–120

Shen Pu-Hai: A Chinese Political Philosopher of the Fourth Century B.C. (Chicago: The University of Chicago Press, 1974)

Csikszentmihalyi, Mark, *Material Virtue: Ethics and the Body in Early China* (Leiden: Brill, 2004)

"Thematic Analyses of the Laozi," in *Dao Companion to Daoist Philosophy*, ed. Xiaogan Liu (Dordrecht: Springer Netherlands, 2015), 47–70

Dale, Eric Michael, *Hegel, the End of History, and the Future* (New York: Cambridge University Press, 2014)

Defoort, Carine, "The Profit That Does Not Profit: Paradoxes with 'Li' in Early Chinese Texts," *Asia Major*, 21.1 (2008), 153–181

Defoort, Carine, and N. Standaert, eds., *The Mozi as an Evolving Text: Different Voices in Early Chinese Thought* (Leiden: Brill, 2013)

Denecke, Wiebke, *The Dynamics of Masters Literature: Early Chinese Thought from Confucius to Han Feizi* (Cambridge, MA: Harvard University Asia Center, 2010)

Derrida, Jacques, *Specters of Marx: The State of the Debt, the Work of Mourning and the New International* (New York and London: Routledge, 1994)

Di Cosmo, Nicola, *Ancient China and Its Enemies: The Rise of Nomadic Power in East Asian History* (Cambridge and New York: Cambridge University Press, 2002)

Bibliography

Döring, Ole, "Exploring the Meaning of 'Good' in Chinese Bioethics through Mengzi's Concept of 'Shan'," in *The Book of Mencius and Its Reception in China and Beyond*, ed. Junjie Huang, Gregor Paul, and Heiner Roetz, Veröffentlichungen des Ostasien-Instituts der Ruhr-Universität Bochum, Bd. 52 (Wiesbaden: Harrassowitz, 2008), 189–201

Doyle, Michael W., *Empires* (Ithaca: Cornell University Press, 1986)

Du Weiyun 杜維運, *Zhongguo shi xue shi* 中國史學史 (Taipei: Sanmin shuju, 1993)

Zhongguo shi xue yu shi jie shi xue 中國史學與世界史學 (Taipei: Sanmin shuju, 2008)

Dubs, Homer H., "The Reliability of Chinese Histories," *Far Eastern Quarterly*, 6.1 (1946), 23–43

Durrant, Stephen W., *The Cloudy Mirror: Tension and Conflict in the Writings of Sima Qian* (Albany: State University of New York Press, 1995)

"Histories (Shi 史)," in *The Oxford Handbook of Classical Chinese Literature (1000 BCE–900 CE)*, ed. Wiebke Denecke, Wai-yee Li, and Xiaofei Tian (New York: Oxford University Press, 2017), 184–200

Durrant, Stephen W., Wai-yee Li, and David Schaberg, *Zuo Traditions = Zuozhuan: Commentary on the "Spring and Autumn Annals"*, Classics of Chinese Thought, 3 vols. (Seattle: University of Washington Press, 2016)

Dutton, Michael, "The Trick of Words: Asian Studies, Translation, and the Problems of Knowledge," in *The Politics of Method in the Human Sciences: Positivism and Its Epistemological Others*, ed. George Steinmetz (Durham, NC: Duke University Press, 2005), 89–125

Duyvendak, J. J. L., *The Book of Lord Shang: A Classic of the Chinese School of Law, Translated from the Chinese with Introduction and Notes*, Probsthain's Oriental Series, vol. XVII (London: A. Probsthain, 1928)

Elstein, David, "Beyond the Five Relationships: Teachers and Worthies in Early Chinese Thought," *Philosophy East and West*, 62.3 (2012), 375–391

Falkenhausen, Lothar von, *Chinese Society in the Age of Confucius (1000–250 BC): The Archaeological Evidence* (Los Angeles: Cotsen Institute of Archaeology, University of California, 2006)

Feeney, Denis, *Caesar's Calendar: Ancient Time and the Beginnings of History* (Berkeley: University of California Press, 2007)

Felski, Rita, "Context Stinks!", *New Literary History*, 42.4 (2011), 573–591

Feng, Youlan, *A Short History of Chinese Philosophy* (New York: Macmillan & Co., 1948)

Fraser, Chris, *The Philosophy of the Mòzǐ: The First Consequentialists* (New York: Columbia University Press, 2016)

Fukuyama, Francis, *The End of History and the Last Man*, Power and Morality Collection at Harvard Business School (New York: Free Press, 1992)

Galvany, Albert, "Beyond the Rule of Rules: The Foundations of Sovereign Power in the *Han Feizi*," in *Dao Companion to the Philosophy of Han Fei*, ed. Paul R. Goldin (Dordrecht: Springer Netherlands, 2013), 87–106

Gardner, Charles S., *Chinese Traditional Historiography* (Cambridge, MA: Harvard University Press, 1938)

Gentz, Joachim, "Historiography," in *Keywords Re-oriented*, InterKULTUR, European-Chinese Intercultural Studies, IV (Göttingen: Universitätsverlag Göttingen, 2009), 57–66

Goldin, Paul R., "Appeals to History in Early Chinese Philosophy and Rhetoric," *Journal of Chinese Philosophy*, 35.1 (2008), 79–96

"Li Si, Chancellor of the Universe," in *After Confucius, Studies in Early Chinese Philosophy* (Honolulu: University of Hawai'i Press, 2005), 66–75

"The Myth That China Has No Creation Myth," *Monumenta Serica*, 56 (2008), 1–22

"Non-deductive Argumentation in Early Chinese Philosophy," in *Between History and Philosophy: Anecdotes in Early China*, ed. Sarah A. Queen and Paul van Els (Albany: State University of New York Press, 2017), 54–77

"Persistent Misconceptions about Chinese 'Legalism'," *Journal of Chinese Philosophy*, 38.1 (2011), 88–104

Graham, A. C., *Disputers of the Tao: Philosophical Argument in Ancient China* (La Salle, IL: Open Court, 1989)

Divisions in Early Mohism Reflected in the Core Chapters of Mo-Tzu (Singapore: Institute of East Asian Philosophies, 1985)

"How Much of 'Chuang Tzu' Did Chuang Tzu Write?", in *Studies in Chinese Philosophy and Philosophical Literature* (Singapore: Institute of East Asian Philosophies, 1990), 283–321

Gu Jiegang 顧頡剛, "Lun Yao Shun Boyi Shu" 論堯舜伯夷書, in *Gushibian* 古史辨, 7 vols. (Shanghai: Guji chubanshe, 1982), Volume 1, 43–44

"Yu Qian Xuantong Xiangsheng Lun Gu Shi Shu" 與錢玄同先生論古史書, in *Gushibian* 古史辨, 7 vols. (Shanghai: Guji chubanshe, 1982), Volume 1, 63–64

Hall, David L., and Roger T. Ames, *Thinking through Confucius* (Albany: State University of New York Press, 1987)

Han, Yu-shan, *Elements of Chinese Historiography* (Hollywood, CA: W. M. Hawley, 1955)

Bibliography

Hardt, Michael, and Antonio Negri, *Empire* (Cambridge, MA: Harvard University Press, 2000)

Hardy, Grant, *Worlds of Bronze and Bamboo* (New York: Columbia University Press, 1999)

Harris, Eirik Lang, *The Shenzi Fragments: A Philosophical Analysis and Translation* (New York: Columbia University Press, 2016)

He Lingxu 賀凌虛, *Xi Han zhengzhi sixiang lunji* 西漢政治思想論集 (Taipei: Wu nan tu shu chu ban gong si, 1988)

He, Yuanguo, "Confucius and Aristotle on Friendship: A Comparative Study," *Frontiers of Philosophy in China*, 2 (2007), 291–307

Hegel, Georg Wilhelm Friedrich, *Hegel's Philosophy of Right*, trans. T. M. Knox (London and New York: Oxford University Press, 1967)

Henricks, Robert G., *Lao Tzu's Tao Te Ching: A Translation of the Startling New Documents Found at Guodian* (New York: Columbia University Press, 2000)

Herzfeld, Michael, *Anthropology: Theoretical Practice in Culture and Society* (Malden, MA: Blackwell Publishers, 2001)

Hobsbawm, Eric J., "Inventing Traditions," in *The Invention of Tradition*, ed. Terence O. Ranger and Eric J. Hobsbawm (Cambridge: Cambridge University Press, 1983), 1–14

"The Social Function of the Past: Some Questions," *Past & Present*, 55 (1972), 3–17

Huang Peirong 黃沛榮, "Zhoushu yanjiu" 周書研究, PhD dissertation (Guoli Taiwan daxue zhongwen yanjiusuo 國立台灣大學中文研究所, 1976)

Hucker, Charles O., *China's Imperial Past: An Introduction to Chinese History and Culture* (Stanford: Stanford University Press, 1975)

Hunter, Michael, *Confucius beyond the Analects* (Leiden: Brill, 2017)

"Did Mencius Know the Analects?", *T'oung Pao*, 100.1–3 (2014), 33–79

Ing, Michael D. K., *The Vulnerability of Integrity in Early Confucian Thought* (New York: Oxford University Press, 2017)

Ivanhoe, Philip J., *Ethics in the Confucian Tradition: The Thought of Mencius and Wang Yang-ming*, 2nd edn (Indianapolis: Hackett, 2002)

Jiang Runxun 江潤勳, Chen Weiliang 陳煒良, and Chen Bingliang 陳炳良, *Jia Yi yanjiu* 賈誼研究 (Kowloon: Qiujing yinwu gongsi, 1958)

Johnson, Daniel M., "Mozi's Moral Theory: Breaking the Hermeneutical Stalemate," *Philosophy East and West*, 61.2 (2011), 347–364

Johnston, Ian, *The Mozi: A Complete Translation* (New York: Columbia University Press, 2010)

Keightley, David N., *The Ancestral Landscape: Time, Space, and Community in Late Shang* China, *ca. 1200–1045 B.C.* (Berkeley: University of California, Berkeley, 2000)

Kern, Martin, *The Stele Inscriptions of Ch'in Shih-Huang: Text and Ritual in Early Chinese Imperial Representation* (New Haven: American Oriental Society, 2000)

Kern, Martin, and Dirk Meyer, eds., *Origins of Chinese Political Philosophy: Studies in the Composition and Thought of the* Shangshu *(Classic of Documents)* (Leiden: Brill, 2017)

Kim, Tae Hyun, and Mark Csikszentmihalyi, "History and Formation of the Analects," in *Dao Companion to the* Analects, ed. Amy Olberding (Dordrecht: Springer Netherlands, 2014), 21–36

Klein, Esther Sunkyung, *Reading Sima Qian from Han to Song: The Father of History in Pre-modern China* (Leiden: Brill, 2018)

Knoblock, John, and Jeffrey K. Riegel, *The Annals of Lü Buwei* (Stanford: Stanford University Press, 2000)

Mozi: *A Study and Translation of the Ethical and Political Writings* (Berkeley: Institute of East Asian Studies, University of California, Berkeley, 2013)

Kojève, Alexandre, *Introduction to the Reading of Hegel* (Ithaca: Cornell University Press, 1980)

Krijgsman, Rens, "Cultural Memory and Excavated Anecdotes in 'Documentary' Narrative: Mediating Generic Tensions in the Baoxun Manuscript," in *Between History and Philosophy: Anecdotes in Early China*, ed. Sarah A. Queen and Paul van Els (Albany: State University of New York Press, 2017), 347–379

Ku, Mei-kao, *A Chinese Mirror for Magistrates: The Hsin-Yü of Lu Chia* (Canberra: Faculty of Asian Studies, Australian National University, 1988)

Kutcher, Norman, "The Fifth Relationship: Dangerous Friendships in the Confucian Context," *American Historical Review*, 105.5 (2000), 1615–1629

Lai, Guolong, "Genealogical Statements on Ritual Bronzes of the Spring and Autumn Period," in *Imprints of Kinship: Studies of Recently Discovered Bronze Inscriptions from Ancient China*, ed. Edward L. Shaughnessy (Hong Kong: The Chinese University Press, 2017), 235–260

Lai, Karyn, "Ren: An Exemplary Life," in *Dao Companion to the* Analects, ed. Amy Olberding (Dordrecht: Springer Netherlands, 2014), 83–94

Lambert, Peter, and Björn K. U. Weiler, eds., *How the Past Was Used: Historical Cultures, c.750–2000* (Oxford: The British Academy by Oxford University Press, 2017)

Bibliography

Latour, Bruno, *Reassembling the Social: An Introduction to Actor-Network Theory* (Oxford and New York: Oxford University Press, 2005)

Lau, D. C., *Mencius* (London: Penguin Books, 1970)

Tao Te Ching (London: Penguin Books, 2003)

Leung, Vincent S., "The Former Han Empire," in *Routledge Handbook of Early Chinese History*, ed. Paul R. Goldin (London: Routledge, 2018), 160–179

Lewis, Mark Edward, *The Early Chinese Empires: Qin and Han* (Cambridge, MA: Belknap Press of Harvard University Press, 2007)

"Historiography and Empire," in *The Oxford History of Historical Writing*, ed. D. R. Woolf, Andrew Feldherr, and Grant Hardy (Oxford: Oxford University Press, 2011), 440–462

Sanctioned Violence in Early China (Albany: State University of New York Press, 1990)

"Warring States Political History," in *The Cambridge History of Ancient China: From the Origins of Civilization to 221 B.C.*, ed. Michael Loewe and Edward L. Shaughnessy (Cambridge: Cambridge University Press, 1999), 587–650

Writing and Authority in Early China (Albany: State University of New York Press, 1999)

Li Changzhi 李長之, *Sima Qian zhi renge yu fengge* 司馬遷之人格與風格 (Hong Kong: Taiping shuju, 1963)

Li, Feng, *Bureaucracy and the State in Early China: Governing the Western Zhou* (Cambridge: Cambridge University Press, 2008)

Landscape and Power in Early China: The Crisis and Fall of the Western Zhou, 1045–771 BC (Cambridge: Cambridge University Press, 2006)

Li Ping 李平, "Qin 'fazhi' de Lilun Kunjin Touxi: Yi Shuihudi Qin Jian 'Yushu' 'Wei Li Zhi Dao' Wei Zhongxin" 秦"法治"的理論困境透析——以睡虎地秦简《語書》、《為吏之道》為中心, *Xueshu tanshuo* 學術探索 11 (2012), 28–31

Li, Wai-yee, *The Readability of the Past in Early Chinese Historiography* (Cambridge, MA: Harvard University Asia Center, 2008)

Liang Qichao 梁啟超, "Shiji huozhi liezhuan jin yi" 史記貨殖列傳今義, in *Yinbingshi heji* 飲冰室合集 (Beijing: Zhonghua shuju, 1996), Volume 1, 35–45

"Zhongguo zhi jiushi" 中國之舊史, in *Zhongguo lishi wenxuan* 中國歷史文選, ed. Zhou Yutong, 2 vols. (Beijing: Zhonghua shuju, 1962), Volume 2, 352–365

Liang Rongmao 梁榮茂, "Han-chu rusheng Lu Jia de shengping ji qi zhushu" 漢初儒生陸賈的生平及其著述, *Kong–Meng Yuekan* 孔孟月刊, 7.7 (1969), 21–23

Lloyd, G. E. R., *Adversaries and Authorities: Investigations into Ancient Greek and Chinese Science*, Ideas in Context (Cambridge: Cambridge University Press, 1996)

Loewe, Michael, ed., *Early Chinese Texts: A Bibliographical Guide* (Berkeley, CA: Society for the Study of Early China, Institute of East Asian Studies, University of California, Berkeley, 1993)

The Government of the Qin and Han Empires: 221 BCE–220 CE (Indianapolis: Hackett, 2006)

"The Operation of the Government," in *China's Early Empires: A Reappraisal*, ed. Michael Nylan and Michael Loewe (Cambridge: Cambridge University Press, 2010), 308–319

Maier, Charles S., *Among Empires: American Ascendancy and Its Predecessors* (Cambridge, MA: Harvard University Press, 2006)

Major, John, Sarah Queen, Andrew Seth Meyer, and Harold D. Roth, *The Huainanzi: A Guide to the Theory and Practice of Government in Early Han China, by Liu An, King of Huainan* (New York: Columbia University Press, 2010)

Marx, Karl, *Capital: A Critique of Political Economy, Volume Three*, trans. David Fernbach (London: Penguin Books, 1981)

Meyer, Dirk, *Philosophy on Bamboo: Text and the Production of Meaning in Early China* (Leiden: Brill, 2012)

Miyazaki Ichisada 宮崎市定, "Riku Ka Shingo dōki hen no kenkyū" 陸賈新語道基編の研究, *Tōhō gaku*, 25 (1963), 1–10

Riku Ka "Shingo" no kenkyû 陸賈新語の研究 (Kyoto: Kyoto University, 1965)

Miyoshi Masao and Harry Harootunian, eds., *Learning Places: The Afterlives of Area Studies* (Durham, NC: Duke University Press, 2002)

Needham, Joseph, *Time and Eastern Man*, The Henry Myers Lecture, 1964 (London: Royal Anthropological Institute of Great Britain & Ireland, 1965)

Nemoto Nakoto 根本誠, *Chūgoku rekishi rinen no kongen* 中國歷史理念の根源 (Tokyo: Seikatsusha, 1943)

Ng, On-Cho, and Q. Edward Wang, *Mirroring the Past: The Writing and Use of History in Imperial China* (Honolulu: University of Hawaii Press, 2005)

Nivison, David S., "The Dates of Western Chou," *Harvard Journal of Asiatic Studies*, 43.2 (1983), 481–580

"Mengzi as Philosopher of History," in *Mencius: Contexts and Interpretations*, ed. by Alan K. L. Chan (Honolulu: University of Hawaii Press, 2002), 282–304

Bibliography

Nora, Pierre, "Between Memory and History: Les Lieux de Mémoire," *Representations*, 1989, 7–24

Nylan, Michael, "Assets Accumulating: Sima Qian's Perspective on Moneymaking, Virtue, and History," in *Views from Within, Views from Beyond: Approaches to the Shiji as an Early Work of Historiography*, ed. Hans van Ess, Olga Lomová, and Dorothee Schaab-Hanke (Wiesbaden: Harrassowitz, 2015), 131–170

"Mapping Time in the *Shiji* and *Hanshu* Tables 表," *East Asian Science, Technology, and Medicine*, 43 (2016), 61–122

"On the Antique Rhetoric of Friendship," *Asiatische Studien–Études asiatiques*, 68.4 (2014), 1225–1265

"Sima Qian: A True Historian?", *Early China*, 23–24 (1998), 203–246

Ōba Osamu 大庭脩, *Qin Han fazhishi yanjiu* 秦漢法制史研究, trans. Xu Shihong 徐世虹 (Shanghai: Zhongxi shuju, 2017)

Shin Kan hōseishi no kenkyū 秦漢法制史の研究 (Tokyo: Sōbunsha, 1982)

Ogle, Vanessa, *The Global Transformation of Time: 1870–1950* (Cambridge, MA: Harvard University Press, 2015)

Olberding, Amy, "Dreaming of the Duke of Zhou: Exemplarism and the *Analects*," *Journal of Chinese Philosophy*, 35.4 (2008), 625–639

Moral Exemplars in the Analects: *The Good Person Is That* (New York: Routledge, 2013)

Olberding, Garret P. S., *Dubious Facts: The Evidence of Early Chinese Historiography*, SUNY Series in Chinese Philosophy and Culture (Albany: State University of New York Press, 2012)

Owen, Stephen, *An Anthology of Chinese Literature: Beginnings to 1911* (New York: W. W. Norton, 1996)

"Reproduction in the *Shijing* (*Classic of Poetry*)," *Harvard Journal of Asiatic Studies*, 61.2 (December 2001), 287–315

Pan Mingji 潘銘基, *Jia Yi ji qi Xinshu yanjiu* 賈誼及其新書研究 (Shanghai: Shanghai guji chubanshe, 2017)

Peerenboom, R. P., *Law and Morality in Ancient China: The Silk Manuscripts of Huang-Lao* (Albany: State University of New York Press, 1993)

Peng Xinwei 彭信威, *Zhongguo huobi shi* 中國貨幣史 (Shanghai: Shanghai renmin chubanshe, 1958)

Perkins, Franklin, "Fanwu Liuxing ('All Things Flow into Form') and the 'One' in the Laozi," *Early China*, 38 (2015), 195–232

"The Laozi and the Cosmogonic Turn in Classical Chinese Philosophy," *Frontiers of Philosophy in China*, 11.2 (2016), 185–205

"No Need for Hemlock: Mencius's Defense of Tradition," in *Ethics in Early China: An Anthology*, ed. Chris Fraser, Dan Robins, and

Timothy O'Leary (Hong Kong: Hong Kong University Press, 2011), 65–81

Petersen, Jens Østergård, "Which Books Did the First Emperor of Ch'in Burn? On the Meaning of *Pai Chia* in Early Chinese Sources," *Monumenta Serica*, 63 (1995), 1–52

Peterson, Willard, "Reading *Sheng Min*," in *Ways with Words: Writing about Reading Texts from Early China*, ed. Pauline Yu, Peter Bol, Stephen Owen, and Willard Peterson (Berkeley, Los Angeles, and London: University of California Press, 2000), 31–33

Pines, Yuri, "Biases and Their Sources: Qin History in the *Shiji*," *Oriens Extremus*, 45 (2005–2006), 10–34

The Book of Lord Shang: Apologetics of State Power in Early China (New York: Columbia University Press, 2017)

Foundations of Confucian Thought: Intellectual Life in the Chunqiu Period, 722–453 BCE (Honolulu: University of Hawaii Press, 2002)

"From Historical Evolution to the End of History: Past, Present and Future from Shang Yang to the First Emperor," in *Dao Companion to the Philosophy of Han Fei*, ed. Paul R. Goldin (Dordrecht: Springer Netherlands, 2013), 25–46

"Legalism in Chinese Philosophy," *The Stanford Encyclopedia of Philosophy*, 2017 https://plato.stanford.edu/archives/spr2017/entries/c hinese-legalism, accessed May 31, 2018

"The Messianic Emperor: A New Look at Qin's Place in China's History," in *Birth of an Empire: The State of Qin Revisited*, ed. Yuri Pines, Lothar von Falkenhausen, Gideon Shelach, and Robin D. S. Yates (Berkeley: University of California Press, 2014), 258–279

"Submerged by Absolute Power: The Ruler's Predicament in the *Han Feizi*," in *Dao Companion to the Philosophy of Han Fei*, ed. Paul R. Goldin (Dordrecht: Springer Netherlands, 2013), 67–86

Poo, Mu-chou, "The Formation of the Concept of Antiquity in Early China," in *Perceptions of Antiquity in Chinese Civilization*, ed. Dieter Kuhn and Helga Stahl, Würzburger Sinologische Schriften (Heidelberg: Edition Forum, 2008), 85–102

Popkin, Jeremy D., *From Herodotus to H-Net: The Story of Historiography* (New York and Oxford: Oxford University Press, 2015)

Puett, Michael, *The Ambivalence of Creation: Debates Concerning Innovation and Artifice in Early China* (Stanford: Stanford University Press, 2001)

"Listening to Sages: Divination, Omens, and the Rhetoric of Antiquity in Wang Chong's Lunheng," *Oriens Extremus*, 45 (2005), 271–282

Bibliography

"Sages, Creation, and the End of History in the *Huainanzi*," in *The Huainanzi and Textual Production in Early China*, ed. Sarah A. Queen and Michael Puett (Leiden: Brill, 2014), 267–290

"Violent Misreadings: The Hermeneutics of Cosmology in the *Huainanzi*," *Bulletin of the Museum of Far Eastern Antiquities*, 72 (2000), 29–47

Pulleyblank, Edwin G., "Chinese Historical Criticism: Liu Chih-Chi and Ssu-Ma Kuang," in *Historians of China and Japan*, ed. William G. Beasley and Edwin G. Pulleyblank (London: Oxford University Press, 1961), 135–166

Qi Yuzhang 祁玉章, *Jiazi tanwei* 賈子探微 (Taipei: Sanmin shuju, 1969)

Qiang, Yu, "The Philosophies of Laozi and Zhuangzi and the Bamboo-Slip Essay *Hengxian*," *Frontiers of Philosophy in China*, 4.1 (2009), 88–115

Queen, Sarah A., and Paul van Els, eds., *Between History and Philosophy: Anecdotes in Early China* (Albany: State University of New York Press, 2017)

Richey, Jeffrey L., "Lost and Found Theories of Law in Early China," *Journal of the Economic and Social History of the Orient*, 49.3 (2006), 329–343.

Robinet, Isabelle, "The Diverse Interpretations of the Laozi," in *Religious and Philosophical Aspects of the* Laozi, ed. Mark Csikszentmihalyi and P. J. Ivanhoe (Albany: State University of New York Press, 1999), 127–159.

Roetz, Heiner, *Confucian Ethics of the Axial Age: A Reconstruction under the Aspect of the Breakthrough toward Postconventional Thinking* (Albany: State University of New York Press, 1993)

"Normativity and History in Warring States Thought: The Shift towards the Anthropological Paradigm," in *Historical Truth, Historical Criticism, and Ideology: Chinese Historiography and Historical Culture from a New Comparative Perspective*, ed. Helwig Schmidt-Glintzer, Achim Mittag, and Jörn Rüsen (Leiden: Brill, 2005), 80–91

Roth, Harold David, *Original Tao: Inward Training (Nei-Yeh) and the Foundations of Taoist Mysticism* (New York: Columbia University Press, 1999)

Sabattini, Elisa Levi, "How to Surpass the Qin," *Monumenta Serica*, 65.2 (2017), 263–284

Sanft, Charles, "Rituals That Don't Reach, Punishments That Don't Impugn: Jia Yi on the Exclusions from Punishment and Ritual," *Journal of the American Oriental Society*, 125.1 (2005), 31–44

Saussy, Haun, "Outside the Parenthesis (Those People Were a Kind of Solution)," *MLN*, 115.5 (2000), 849–891

Savage, William E., "Archetypes, Model Emulation, and the Confucian Gentleman," *Early China*, 17 (1992), 1–25

Schaberg, David, "Chinese History and Philosophy," in *The Oxford History of Historical Writing, Volume 1: Beginnings to AD 600*, ed. by Andrew Feldherr and Grant Hardy (Oxford: Oxford University Press, 2011), 392–414

  A Patterned Past: Form and Thought in Early Chinese Historiography (Cambridge, MA: Harvard University Asia Center, 2001)

  "Remonstrance in Eastern Zhou Historiography," *Early China*, 22 (1997), 133–179

  "Song and the Historical Imagination in Early China," *Harvard Journal of Asiatic Studies*, 59.2 (December 1999), 305–361

Schipper, Kristofer, "The Wholeness of Chaos: Laozi on the Beginning," in *China's Creation and Origin Myths: Cross-cultural Explorations in Oral and Written Traditions*, ed. Mineke Schipper, Shuxian Ye, and Hubin Yin (Boston: Brill, 2011), 135–152

Schmidt-Glintzer, Helwig, Achim Mittag, and Jörn Rüsen, eds., *Historical Truth, Historical Criticism, and Ideology: Chinese Historiography and Historical Culture from a New Comparative Perspective* (Leiden and Boston: Brill, 2005)

Schumpeter, Joseph Alois, *Imperialism and Social Classes: Two Essays* (New York: Meridian Books, 1955)

Schüssler, Axel, *A Dictionary of Early Zhou Chinese* (Honolulu: University of Hawaii Press, 1987)

Schwartz, Benjamin Isadore, *The World of Thought in Ancient China* (Cambridge, MA: The Belknap Press of Harvard University Press, 1985)

Sena, David M., "Arraying the Ancestors in Ancient China: Narratives of Lineage History in the 'Scribe Qiang' and 'Qiu' Bronzes," *Asia Major*, 25.1 (2012), 63–81

Shaughnessy, Edward L., *Sources of Western Zhou History: Inscribed Bronze Vessels* (Berkeley: University of California Press, 1991)

  "Unearthed Documents and the Question of the Oral versus Written Nature of the Classic of Poetry," *Harvard Journal of Asiatic Studies*, 75.2 (2015), 331–375

Shryock, Andrew, and Daniel Lord Smail, eds., *Deep History: The Architecture of Past and Present* (Berkeley: University of California Press, 2011)

Shun, Kwong-loi, "Conception of the Person in Early Confucian Thought," in *Confucian Ethics: A Comparative Study of Self, Autonomy, and Community*, ed. Kwong-Loi Shun and David B. Wong (New York: Cambridge University Press, 2004), 183–202

Bibliography

Mencius and Early Chinese Thought (Stanford: Stanford University Press, 1997)

"*Ren* and *Li* in the Analects," in *Confucius and the* Analects: *New Essays*, ed. Bryan W. van Norden (New York: Oxford University Press, 2002), 53–72

Slingerland, Edward, review of Michael Hunter, *Confucius beyond the Analects* (Brill, 2017), *Early China*, 41 (2018), 465–475

Soles, David E., "Mo Tzu and the Foundations of Morality," *Journal of Chinese Philosophy*, 26.1 (1999), 37–48

Strassberg, Richard E., *A Chinese Bestiary: Strange Creatures from the Guideways through Mountains and Seas* = *[Shan Hai Jing]* (Berkeley: University of California Press, 2002)

Takigawa Kametarō 瀧川龜太郎, *Shiki kaichū kōshō* 史記會注考證 ([Japan]: Shiki Kaichū Kōshō Kōho Kankōkai, 1958)

Taylor, Rodney L., "Religion and Utilitarianism: Mo Tzu on Spirits and Funerals," *Philosophy East and West*, 29.3 (1979), 337–346

Thompson, E. P., "Time, Work-Discipline, and Industrial Capitalism," *Past & Present*, 38 (1967), 56–97

Thompson, P. M., *The Shen Tzu Fragments* (Oxford and New York: Oxford University Press, 1979)

Tucker, Robert C., ed., *The Marx–Engels Reader*, 2nd edn (New York: Norton, 1978)

Twitchett, Denis C., and Michael Loewe, eds., *The Cambridge History of China, Volume 1: The Ch'in and Han Empires, 221 BC–AD 220* (Cambridge and New York: Cambridge University Press, 1986)

Van Norden, Bryan W., ed., *Confucius and the* Analects: *New Essays* (New York: Oxford University Press, 2002)

Virtue Ethics and Consequentialism in Early Chinese Philosophy (New York: Cambridge University Press, 2007)

"The Virtue of Righteousness in Mencius," in *Confucian Ethics: A Comparative Study of Self, Autonomy, and Community*, ed. Kwong-Loi Shun and David B. Wong (Cambridge and New York: Cambridge University Press, 2004), 148–182

Vandermeersch, Léon, *La formation du légisme: Recherche sur la constitution d'une philosophie politique caractéristique de la Chine ancienne*, Publications de l'École française d'Extrême-Orient, vol. 56 (Paris: École française d'Extrême-Orient: Dépositaire, Adrien-Maisonneuve, 1965)

Vervoorn, Aat, "Boyi and Shuqi: Worthy Men of Old?", *Papers on Far Eastern History*, 28 (September 1983), 1–22

"Friendship in Ancient China," *East Asian history*, 27 (2004), 1–32

Men of the Cliffs and Caves: The Development of the Chinese Eremitic Tradition to the End of the Han Dynasty (Hong Kong: Chinese University Press, 1990)

Vogelsang, Kai, *Geschichte als Problem: Entstehung, Formen und Funktionen von Geschichtsschreibung im alten China* (Wiesbaden: Harrassowitz, 2007)

"Getting the Terms Right: Political Realism, Politics, and the State in Ancient China," *Oriens Extremus*, 55 (2016), 39–71

"The Scribes' Genealogy," *Oriens Extremus*, 44 (2003), 3–10

"The Shape of History: On Reading Li Wai-yee," *Early China*, 37 (2014), 579–599

Waley, Arthur, *The Book of Songs: The Ancient Chinese Classic of Poetry*, ed. Joseph Roe Allen, 1st edn (New York: Grove Press, 1996)

Wang, Ming-ke, "Western Zhou Remembering and Forgetting," *Journal of East Asian Archaeology*, 1 (1999), 231–250

Wang, Q. Edward, and Georg G. Iggers, *Turning Points in Historiography: A Cross-cultural Perspective* (Rochester, NY: University of Rochester Press, 2001)

Wang Shumin 王樹民, *Zhongguo shixue shi gangyao* 中國史學史綱要 (Beijing: Zhonghua shuju, 1997)

Wang Xiaobo 王曉波, *Xian Qin fajia sixiang shilun* 先秦法家思想史論 (Taipei: Lianjing chuban shiye gongsi, 1991)

Watanabe Takashi 渡邊卓, *Kodai Chūgoku shisō no kenkyū: Kōshi den no keisei to Ju Boku shūdan no shisō to kōdō* 古代中國思想の研究: 孔子傳の形成と儒墨集團の思想と行動東洋, 學叢書 (Tokyo: Sōbunsha, 1973)

Watson, Burton, *The Analects of Confucius* (New York: Columbia University Press, 2007)

Han Feizi: Basic Writings (New York: Columbia University Press, 2003)

Records of the Grand Historian: Han Dynasty (Hong Kong and New York: Chinese University of Hong Kong and Columbia University Press, 1993)

Records of the Grand Historian: Qin Dynasty (Hong Kong and New York: Chinese University of Hong Kong and Columbia University Press, 1993)

Ssu-Ma Ch'ien, Grand Historian of China (New York: Columbia University Press, 1958)

Wei Wei 韋葦, *Sima Qian jing ji si xiang yan jiu* 司馬遷經濟思想研究 (Xi'an: Shanxi renmin jiaoyu chubanshe, 1995)

Wilson, Stephen A., "Conformity, Individuality, and the Nature of Virtue: A Classical Confucian Contribution to Contemporary Ethical

Reflection," in *Confucius and the* Analects: *New Essays*, ed. by Bryan W. van Norden (New York: Oxford University Press, 2002), 94–118

Woolf, D. R., *A Global History of History* (Cambridge and New York: Cambridge University Press, 2011)

Xu Fuchang 徐富昌, *Shuihudi Qin jian yanjiu* 睡虎地秦簡研究 (Taipei: Wen shi zhe chubanshe, 1993)

Xu Fuguang 徐復觀, *Liang Han sixiang shi* 兩漢思想史 (Hong Kong: Chinese University of Hong Kong Press, 1975)

Yao, Alice, *The Ancient Highlands of Southwest China: From the Bronze Age to the Han Empire* (Oxford: Oxford University Press, 2016)

Yates, Robin D. S., *Five Lost Classics: Tao, Huanglao, and Yin–Yang in Han China*, Classics of Ancient China (New York: Ballantine Books, 1997)

Yin Shengping 尹盛平, ed., *Xi Zhou Wei Shi Jia Zu Qing Tong Qi Qun Yan Jiu* 西周微氏家族青銅器群研究 (Beijing: Wenwu chubanshe, 1992)

Yuan Ke 袁珂, *Zhongguo gudai shenhua* 中國古代神話, rev. edn (Beijing: Zhonghua shuju, 1960)

Yuan Weichun 袁維春, *Qin Han bei shu* 秦漢碑述 (Beijing: Beijing gongyi meishu chubanshe, 1990)

Zhang Chun 張純, and Wang Xiaobo 王曉波, *Han Fei sixiang de lishi yanjiu* 韓非思想的歷史研究 (Beijing: Zhonghua shuju, 1986)

Zhang Dake 張大可, *Shiji yanjiu* 史記研究 (Beijing: Shangwu yinshuguan, 2011)

Zhang Qiusheng 張秋升, "Lu Jia de lishi yishi ji qi wenhua yiyi" 陸賈的歷史意識及其文化意義, *Qilu xuekan* 齊魯學刊, 5 (1997), 67–73

Index

Ames, Roger, 9
amnesia, historical, 127–128
Analects
  comparison with Western Zhou
    materials, 42–43, 49–50
  concept of antiquity, 43–44
  concept of friendship in, 52
  deliberative capacity of individuals,
    45–48
  evaluation of past practices, 44–45
  historical continuity in, 73–74
  individual cultivation, 47–48
  textual history of, 41
anecdotes, historical, 2, 76–77
antiquity, rhetoric of, 75–76, 100, 101

baijin (white-metal coins), 172
Bakhtin, Mikhail M., 14
Ban *gui* (bronze inscription), 32–33
bibliocaust (Qin empire), 104–107, 127
bioethics, definition of, 92
Boyi, 20, 49, 70
Brashier, K. E., 19
Brindley, Erica, 65
Brown, Miranda, 57
Butterfield, Herbert, 4

capital (ideological), 13, 177
Chang'an (capital of the Han), 130,
    132, 153, 171, 172
Chunqiu. See Spring-and-Autumn
    (*Chunqiu*)
Classic of Changes (*Yijing*), 21, 138,
    144
Classic of Documents (*Shangshu*),
    31–33, 138, 140, 144
  "Jiu gao," 31
  "Li zheng," 31
  in the *Mengzi*, 98
Classic of Music (*Yue*), 138, 144

Classic of Poetry (*Shijing*), 29–31, 138,
    140, 144
  dating of, 30
  "Liangsi," 30
  "Shengmin," 29–30
  "Zaishan," 30
Classic of Rituals (*Li*), 138, 144
classics (*jing*), 132, 138, *See also* Five
    Classics
Collingwood, R. G., 19
Confucius, 5, 20, 54, 93, 111, *See also*
    Analects
conservativism, political, 38
Cook, Scott, 10
cosmogony
  in the Guodian *Laozi*, 82–83

Da Yu *ding* (bronze inscription), 24–28
dao (the Way)
  in the Guodian *Laozi*, 82
  in the *Han Feizi*, 117
  in Lu Jia's *Xinyu*, 146
de Certeau, Michel, 18
deep history, 82
Derrida, Jacques, 115
dialogism, 14
didacticism
  departure from in the study of early
    Chinese historiography, 9–12
  in the study of early Chinese
    historiography, 5–9
disorder, original
  in Han imperial ideology under
    Emperor Wu, 170, 173
  in the *Mozi*, 60
  in the "Yu shu" from Shuihudi tomb,
    170
Dong Zhongshu, 152, 161
Duke of Zhou (Zhou gong), 31, 47
Duke Xiao of Qin (Qin Xiao gong), 121

198

Index

economics (in the *Shiji*)
  of the Han imperial expansion, 167
  monetary policies of the early Han, 172
  natural foundation of economic activities, 158
  origin of division of labor, 156–157
  origin of economic activities, 155–156
  origin of wealth, 157
empires
  as spatial entities, 107–108
  temporality of, 108
emulation, of historical precedents, 29
  in bronze inscriptions, 34
  in the *Classic of Documents*, 31–33
  in the *Classic of Poetry*, 29–31
  in the Western Zhou, 37
end of history
  in critical theory, 128
  under the Qin empire, 127–128
exemplarity
  in the *Classics of Documents*, 31–33
  in the *Classic of Poetry (Shijing)*, 29–31
  relation to originary acts in history in bronze inscriptions, 29, 33
  in the Western Zhou, 37

fajia. *See* Legalism
Fan wu liu xing (Shanghai Museum manuscript), 91
Fenshu. *See* bibliocaust (Qin empire)
Fingarette, Herbert, 46
First Emperor of Qin (Qin shi huangdi)
  bibliocaust, 104–107
  end of history, 127–128
  stele inscriptions, 121, 122–125
Five Classics (*Wu jing*), 144, 145
  relation to the Six Arts, 144
friendship, concept of, 50–52
Fukuyama, Francis, 128

Gaozu, Emperor of Han, 130, 140, 164
  monetary policy of, 170
Gardener, Charles, 5
genealogical history
  feminized form in the Guodian *Laozi*, 90
  in Western Zhou materials, 37–39

Gu Jiegang, 21
Guan Zhong, 98
Guanzi, 162
Guliang zhuan, 146
Guodian *Laozi*. *See Laozi*
Guoyu, 75
Gushibian. *See* Gu Jiegang

Han Feizi, 109, 111, 116, 119
  cosmogonic foundation for *fa*, 117
  "Er bing" ("Two Handles"), 118–119
Hardy, Grant, 16
Heaven
  in Lu Jia's *Xinyu*, 141
  Mandate of, 28, 36
  in the *Mozi*, 66–68
Hegel, G. W. F., 52
Hengxian (Shanghai Museum manuscript), 91
historical continuity
  in the *Analects*, 73–74
  in early Han writings, 151
  in the early Warring States, 72–74
  in Jia Yi's *Xinshu*, 137
  in Lu Jia's *Xinyu*, 148
  in the *Mozi*, 73
historical discontinuity
  in the early Warring States, 72–74
  in Jia Yi's *Xinshu*, 137
  in Legalism, 109–111
  in the Qin stele inscriptions, 123
historiography, early Chinese
  conflation with ideas of the past, 3–4
  didacticism in, 5–9
history. *See also* Past
  definition of, 18
  as political critique, 175
  relation to the concept of the past. *See* past, relation to the concept of history
Hobsbawn, Eric J., 14–15, 16
Hou Ji (of Zhou clan), 29, 142
Huainanzi, 10, 131
Huangdi (Yellow Emperor), 142
Hunter, Michael, 40, 99

imperial expansion (under Emperor Wu of the Han), 165–168

Index

innovation, 38
  in Legalism, 112–113
  in Lu Jia's *Xinyu*, 142–143

Jia Yi. *See also Xinshu*
  career of, 132–133
  "Funiao fu," 136–137
  on the material precondition for life,
    162
Jing, Emperor of Han, 164
Junzi (in the *Zuozhuan*), 77

Kern, Martin, 15
Klein, Esther, 153
Kongzi. *See* Confucius
Krijgsman, Rens, 12

Laozi
  absences of sages from antiquity in,
    80
  cosmogonic history, 82–83
  deep history, 88
  feminine genealogical history in,
    88–90
  and the *Hanfeizi*, 116
  as a historical text, 82
  sages in, 85
Legalism
  concept of *fa*, 112
  definition and usage of the term,
    102–103
  epistemological issues of, 115–117
  historical causation, 111–112
  historicity of laws and bureaucracy,
    117–119
  inevitability of historical
    discontinuity, 109–111
  role of the ruler, 119–120
  specter of history, 114–115
Lewis, Mark Edward, 15, 57
li (ritual), 29–30, 47, 95, 158. *See also*
    Classic of Rituals (Li)
  in the *Analects*, 44
  in Lu Jia's *Xinyu*, 143
  reform during mid-Western Zhou, 33
Li Si, 105–106
Li, Feng, 28
Li, Wai-yee, 11
Liang Qichao, 5
Lu Jia. *See also Xinyu*

career of, 139–140
Lunyu. See Analects
Lüshi chunqiu, 76

Mandate of Heaven. *See* Heaven
memory, relation to history and the
  past, 19
Mengzi
  common moral potential among
    individuals, 96–97
  concept of *xin* (mind), 94–95, 97
  dates of, 93
  moral potentiality in, 94–95
  sages of antiquity in, 94
monetary policies (of early Han),
    170–172
Mozi
  comparison with the *Analects*, 64–66
  comparison with Western Zhou
    materials, 63–64
  concept of Heaven in, 66–68
  etiology of disorder, 60–63
  historical continuity in, 73
  method of analysis, 55–56
  sages in antiquity, 57–59, 70–71
  textual history of, 54
  utilitarianism in, 65
Mu, King of Zhou, 32
music
  in the *Mengzi*, 98
  in the *Mozi*, 54, 55

Needham, Joseph, 6
Neiye, 101
Nivison, David, 97
Nora, Pierre, 19
Nylan, Michael, 12

Olberding, Amy, 46
oracle-bone inscriptions, 1

past
  classical encapsulation of, 147–148
  cosmogonic, 82–83
  critical use of, 176
  cultural, 43–44
  definition of, 18
  destruction of, under the Qin empire,
    127–128
  etiological, 70

Index

genealogical, 37–38
parenthetical, 101
rehabilitation of, in the early Han, 150–152
relation to the concept of history, 18
spectral, 114–115
Perkins, Franklin, 91
pibi (hide-currency), 172
Pines, Yuri, 103
politics, 179
  definition of, 18–19
Poo, Mu-Chou, 10
Puett, Michael, 12

Qin shi huangdi. *See* First Emperor of Qin (Qin shi huangdi)

ren (humaneness), 20, 47, 48, 95, 114, 145
ritual. See *li*
Roetz, Heiner, 10, 99
ru (Confucians), 54

sages from antiquity
  absences in the *Laozi*, 80
  in the *Analects*, 49
  in Lu Jia's *Xinyu*, 142–144
  in the *Mengzi*, 93–94, 97
  in the *Mozi*, 57–59
Schaberg, David, 11, 21, 76
Schumpeter, Joseph, 167
Shang dynasty, 1
Shang Yang, 102, 121
Shangjunshu, 102, 109
Shangshu. See *Classic of Documents* (*Shangshu*)
Shanhaijing (Classic of Mountains and Seas), 22
Shennong (the sage), 110, 142, 162
Shenzi fragments, 119
Shi Qiang *pan* (bronze inscription), 33–35
Shi Xun *gui* (bronze inscription), 35–37
Shiji
  on the material precondition for life, 158–160
  natural foundation of economic activities, 158
  origin of division of labor, 157

origin of economic activities, 155–156
origin of wealth, 157
scholarship on, 153–154
Shijing. See *Classic of Poetry* (*Shijing*)
Shuihudi (Qin tomb), 1, 169
  "Yu shu," 169
Shun (the sage), 21, 59, 93, 96
Shuqi, 20, 49, 70
Sima Qian. *See Shiji*
Six Arts. *See* Five Classics (*Wu jing*)
Spring and Autumn Annals (*Chunqiu*), 5, 138, 144, 146

Taiyi sheng shui (Guodian manuscript), 90
Tang (the sage), 59, 69, 93, 135
Tang, Lan, 27

Vogelsang, Kai, 11

Wang Chong, 176
Watson, Burton, 6
Wen, Emperor of Han, 132
  monetary policy of, 170
Wen, King of Zhou, 26, 28, 31, 33, 36, 38, 42, 49, 59, 63, 69, 93, 114
Wu, Emperor of Han, 161, 164, 165, 167, 170, 173
  imperial expansion under, 165–168
  monetary policy of, 171–172
Wu, King of Zhou, 26, 27, 28, 35, 36, 38, 59, 63, 69
Wuxing (Guodian manuscript), 101

Xici zhuan, 146
xin (heart). *See Mengzi*
Xinshu, 132
  "Bao fu," 138
  critique of the Qin empire, 137–138
  "Dao de shuo," 138
  "Fan jiang," 135
  "Fu zhi," 138
  "Guo Qin lun," 134–135, 137–138
  "Jieji," 135
  relation to the *Analects*, 137–139
  "Shu yuan," 135
  "Wu xu," 135

Index

Xinyu
  classical canon in, 144–145
  classical encapsulation of the past in, 147–148
  "Dao ji," 141–146, 162
  Five Classics and Six Arts, 144–145
  historical continuity in, 148
  relation to Qin imperial ideology, 148–150
  sages in, 142–144
Xiongnu, 164, 171, 175
Xizhong (the sage), 142
Xunzi, 76, 146

Yanzi, 98
Yao (the sage), 21, 49, 59, 93, 96

yi (righteousness), 95, 114, 145
Yijing. See Classic of Changes (Yijing)
Yizhoushu (Lost Documents of the Zhou), 21
Yu (the sage), 21, 49, 59, 69, 135, 142
Yuan Ke, 22
yue (music). *See Classic of Music (Yue)*

Zhanguo ce, 75
zhi (wisdom), 95
Zhuangzi, 75
ziran, 84
Zuozhuan, 76–77
  junzi in, 77
  scholarship, 11–12